During the Middle Ages, the popes of Rom[e] ... authority and worldly powers, vying with ... ruling over the Papal States, and legislating the norms of Christian society. They also faced profound challenges to their proclaimed primacy over Christendom.

The Medieval Papacy explores the unique role that the Roman Church and its papal leadership played in the historical development of medieval Europe. Brett Edward Whalen pays special attention to the religious, intellectual, and political significance of the papacy from the first century through to the Reformation in the sixteenth century.

Ideal for students, scholars, and general readers alike, this approachable survey helps us to understand the origins of an idea and institution that continues to shape our modern world.

Brett Edward Whalen is Associate Professor of Medieval History at the University of North Carolina at Chapel Hill. His previous publications include *Dominion of God: Christendom and Apocalypse in the Middle Ages* (2009) and *Pilgrimage in the Middle Ages: A Reader* (2011).

European History in Perspective

General Editor: Jeremy Black

The Medieval Papacy

BRETT EDWARD WHALEN

palgrave
macmillan

First published 2014 by
PALGRAVE MACMILLAN

Palgrave Macmillan in the UK is an imprint of Macmillan Publishers Limited, registered in England, company number 785998, of 4 Crinan Street, London N1 9XW.

Palgrave® and Macmillan® are registered trademarks in the United States, the United Kingdom, Europe and other countries.

ISBN: 978–0–230–27282–8 hardback
ISBN: 978–0–230–27283–5 paperback

This book is printed on paper suitable for recycling and made from fully managed and sustained forest sources. Logging, pulping and manufacturing processes are expected to conform to the environmental regulations of the country of origin.

A catalogue record for this book is available from the British Library.

A catalog record for this book is available from the Library of Congress.

To my wife, Malissa,
with love, friendship, and gratitude

Contents

Acknowledgments

Habemus librum! Writing this book, I incurred debts of gratitude to friends and colleagues. First, I would like to thank Jehangir Malegam, who encouraged me to tackle this project and assisted with my earliest plans for its execution. Since our days together at Stanford, he has never failed to show me such collegiality. As I often seem to do, I also turned to Jay Rubenstein and Matthew Gabriele for their feedback and general reassurance. Both reviewed and improved several chapters of this manuscript. Marcus Bull helpfully commented upon several other chapters, illustrating how lucky I am to have him as a colleague at UNC-Chapel Hill. Another departmental colleague, Melissa Bullard, provided me with valuable insights into the circumstances of the fifteenth-century papacy. In addition, I would like to thank Thomas F. X. Noble, one of the "anonymous" readers solicited by the publisher, who reminded me – among many other insights – to give the cardinals their due, along with the other, truly anonymous reader, who rightly pointed out the lack of attention to the Papal States throughout the draft of this book. The mistakes and oversights that persist are entirely my own.

My further thanks go to Sonya Barker, my editor at Palgrave Macmillan, and my copy-editor, Caroline Richards. I should also like to express my overall gratitude to my undergraduate students at UNC-Chapel Hill. While composing this work in the years 2011–13, I benefited from their dynamic energy in the classroom while we explored the European Middle Ages. In some ways, I wrote this volume for them, or at least, for future students of medieval history at Carolina and elsewhere. I dedicate this book to my wife Malissa, who has shown constant support, in profound and quotidian ways, for my scholarly life, sharing my time with medieval popes, pilgrims, monks, and other unusual companions. I cannot thank you enough, Moski.

Maps

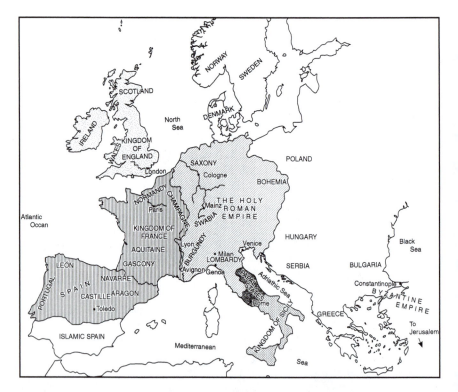

Map 1   Europe in the High Middle Ages

Map 2   The Papal States in the High Middle Ages

Introduction

Around the year 317, the Roman Emperor Constantine fell ill with leprosy. Desperate for a cure, the stricken ruler turned to pagan priests, who instructed him to bathe in the blood of slaughtered infants. Constantine refused this abhorrent act. That night, the Christian apostles Peter and Paul appeared to the emperor in a dream. The two saints told him to find Sylvester, bishop of the Christian community in Rome, who had taken refuge outside the city due to the persecution of his people by Roman authorities. Constantine summoned Sylvester, who baptized the emperor after he had rejected Satan and confessed his faith in God the Father and the Son, Jesus Christ, born of the Holy Spirit and the Virgin Mary. Immersed three times in baptismal waters, Constantine emerged free of his leprosy. Out of gratitude, the now Christian emperor exalted the Roman Church above his "empire and earthly throne," giving to it "imperial power, the dignity of glory, vigor, and honor." Constantine also decreed that the bishop of Rome should enjoy primacy over the other principal churches of the world. In addition, he granted Rome's chief priest the use of imperial vestments, the diadem, tiara, and purple robe, surrendering control over the western regions of the Roman Empire to the "universal pope," Sylvester, along with his successors. Finally, recognizing that the city of Rome belonged to the heavenly authority of the Church rather than a worldly ruler, Constantine transferred the capital of his empire to a new location at Constantinople.

This story of Constantine's leprosy, baptism and cure, and gifts to the bishops of Rome is famous – and absolutely untrue. The events described here are found in the *Donation of Constantine*, a forgery dating from the eighth century. The anonymous clerical author who composed this piece of historical fiction did so largely to defend the

authority, property, and prestige of the Roman papacy centuries after
the disintegration of the Western Roman Empire, when the growing
power of the Frankish Carolingian dynasty had extended its reach over
a good portion of Europe, including Rome. Starting in the eleventh
century, when the popes of Rome began to enjoy an unprecedented
level of influence and direct control over not just religious life and
institutions but also politics in Christian Europe, the Roman Church
pointed to Constantine's donation – believed to be authentic – as
one justification for its assertion of earthly supremacy and political
power. The papacy would continue to invoke this spurious document
until the fifteenth century, when the Italian humanist Lorenzo Valla
exposed the text as a fake, adding one more source of criticism to the
many others leveled against the popes of Rome as corrupt and abusive
of their spiritual position.[1]

The *Donation of Constantine* reveals the inherent tensions at play
in the subject of this book, the history of the Roman papacy and
its claim to universal authority across the European Middle Ages.
During the earliest centuries of Christianity, the title of pope, from
the Latin *papa* meaning "father," could be applied to any bishop,
the overseer of a Christian community. In time, however, Rome's
bishops successfully claimed unique status as *the* popes, *the* leaders
of the catholic or universal Church.[2] In this regard, the true source
of their power came not from Constantine or any other secular ruler
but rather from Jesus Christ, transmitted to them through his chief
apostle, Peter, possessor of the keys to the kingdom of Heaven, who
had founded the Apostolic See of Rome. The pope's primacy thereby
derived from a divine mandate, a pastoral mission to care for the
souls of all believers and act as shepherd for their eternal salvation.
In certain instances, however, popes tried equally to command
emperors, kings and queens, princes and others in the here-and-now,
demanding the obedience of everyone in Christian society. For much
of the Middle Ages, the bishops of Rome acted as landlords and rulers in their own right over territories in central Italy and beyond.
Popes set armies in motion not just for holy wars, but also to protect
their possessions, sometimes personally leading troops into battle.
Indeed, one can argue that the papacy's assertion of sacred authority
and worldly dominion – combining, as it were, the legacies of Saint
Peter and Constantine – formed the distinguishing characteristic of
the medieval papacy.

For generations of modern historians, the history of the Roman
Church formed a central strand in the very making, maturity, and
undoing of medieval Europe itself. After the collapse of the Western

Roman Empire, we are told, during the tumultuous Early Middle Ages from the sixth to the tenth centuries, shared Christian values, ideas, and institutions created the only kind of higher unity known by Europeans. Contributing to this conversion or Christianization of Europe, Rome fostered the creation of a new Christian European civilization: Christendom, the community of right-believing, right-practicing believers who looked to the popes of Rome as their head. During the High Middle Ages, running from about the tenth to the thirteenth centuries, Christendom entered into an era of relative political stability, economic growth, and geographical expansion. In religious life, too, Christian Europe underwent profound changes. Through their powers of persuasion and innovative forms of ecclesiastical governance, the popes of Rome enjoyed their greatest authority over the inhabitants of Christendom. With the coming of the Late Middle Ages in the fourteenth and fifteenth centuries, an era associated with famine and plague, war and economic contraction, the Roman papacy entered into a period of decline and retrenchment. While the Apostolic See still claimed its universal privileges, its right to define what Christians believed and how they lived – always contested by some – increasingly fell into doubt. By the beginning of the modern era, even the theoretical unity of Christendom came to an end with the sixteenth-century Protestant Reformation, as some European churches and nations openly rejected Rome's leadership.[3]

Like all such historical narratives, this presentation of Christendom's creation, expansion, and disintegration under papal auspices captures something authentic about the past, but relies upon sweeping generalizations and over-simplifications. For every historian who has described the medieval papacy as an agent of unity over discord, others have questioned or downplayed the role that Rome played in the formation of medieval civilization. For earlier generations of Catholic scholars, the rise of Christendom under papal leadership represented Europe's best hope for order in a chaotic world; for Protestants, the papal vision of Christendom encapsulated everything wrong with Christianity during the Middle Ages, when the Church became mired in worldly things. Popes emerge as sinners or saints, a source of inspiration or a cautionary tale of decadence and corruption. In more recent times, historians have debated what really mattered in shaping papal history, whether the Roman papacy is best understood as a continuous ideology stretching across the centuries, an enduring set of ideas and principles, or an institution of improvised governance, reacting to immediate goals and needs. Still others have pointed to the darker side of the papacy in forging medieval European attitudes and institutions, calling for holy wars against non-believers, summoning inquisitors to suppress heresy, and monitoring the lives of men and women to ensure their conformity to the faith taught by the Roman Church.

In that regard, this relatively short book surveys a vast and complicated terrain. Rather than settling old scores or advancing radically new arguments, it seeks – as even-handedly as possible – to present the history of the medieval papacy to general readers unfamiliar with the course of events that spanned the European Middle Ages. The pages below do not abandon, but qualify the premise that the papacy contributed to the project of Christendom as a meaningful source of identity for those who recognized the authority of the Apostolic See. After all, papal leadership over Europe's Christian society represented something of a paradox, located between the exalted ideal of Saint Peter's heirs, the local circumstances of Rome's bishops, and the realities of ecclesiastical governance. One should never forget that even the greatest of popes, whose influence stretched across Western Europe and beyond, were sometimes forced from their own city by angry mobs, anti-popes, or political foes. For much of the Middle Ages, popes simultaneously inhabited multiple roles, sometimes complementing each other, sometimes standing in contradiction: the head of the universal Church, bishop of Rome, and ruler of the Papal States among them. Under these circumstances, the edifice of Christendom could not help but remain a work in progress, following a general blueprint, but subject to endless contingencies of design.

To reconcile the medieval papacy's majesty and mundanity, its aspirations and limitations, we might consider the Roman Church's constant act of historical self-invention, underwritten by Christian believers close to and far from the city of Rome. As one scholar of the period recently reminded us, "The Middle Ages placed little emphasis on the objective reconstruction of past events. Instead, recollection was an interpretive act, a selective process that chose what was thought to be valuable and worthy of remembrance."[4] In the realm of remembrance if not fact, the medieval papacy created and recreated a continuous tradition that connected present-day popes with their predecessors all the way back to Saint Peter. Remembering Constantine's pious act of devotion toward Peter's heirs, popes and their supporters laid claim to the dignity of empire and lands that accompanied it. Papal reformers harked back to better times, when the Church and clergy stood in a state of pristine freedom, enjoying the devotion and obedience of earthly rulers. Popes who called for crusades did so in the name of restoring Jerusalem to Christian hands, recalling the biblical events that sanctified the holy places. Viewed from this perspective, the success of Rome's bishops at translating the theoretical principles of papal primacy into actionable forms of power effectively depended upon their ability to convince Christians – enough of them, anyway – about a certain interpretation of history.

This book begins before the medieval era, in the ancient world that gave birth to Christianity and the Roman Empire that ruled over it. Chapter 1, "The Memory of Saint Peter," explores the origins of the Christian tradition at Rome and the earliest elaboration of papal claims to possess a unique authority over the Church, concluding with the transformative conversion of the Roman Empire to Christianity starting in the fourth century. Chapter 2, "Empire and Christendom," covers the development of the papacy from the fifth to the eighth centuries, commonly associated with the disintegration of Roman imperial might in Western Europe and the spread of Christianity among the "barbarian" peoples that inherited what remained of the political order. In addition, this chapter considers the ongoing vitality of Rome's relationship with the Eastern Roman (or Byzantine) Empire. Chapter 3, "The Reordering of the West," explores the state of the Roman Church during the emergence, dominance, and eventual collapse of the Carolingian Empire during the late eighth through the tenth centuries.

Chapter 4, "Reform and Crusade," looks at a dramatic transformation in the status of the eleventh-century papacy, when a cadre of self-declared reformers assumed control of the papal office. Among other consequences, this reform of the Roman Church led to an open struggle between popes and secular rulers for a place of supreme leadership over Christian society, and also contributed to the declaration of the First Crusade, a holy war waged under papal authority for the "liberation" of Jerusalem from Islamic hands. Chapters 5 and 6, "Papal Monarchy" and "The Whole World to Govern," cover the era of the papacy's greatest prestige, religious clout, and political influence during the twelfth and thirteenth centuries. At this time, one might say that Christendom as imagined came into its closest proximity with the realities of clerical governance, although that fabrication of Christian unity produced its own stresses and strains in European life. Even at its maximum extent, Christendom existed in a coiled state of tension rather than equilibrium.

The final two chapters cover a series of challenges and transformations faced by the Roman papacy during the fourteenth and fifteenth centuries, some unlooked for and others of its own making. Chapter 7, "The Papacy in Crisis," deals with a slow shift in the gradient of power between Rome and Europe's emerging national powers, along with the related phenomenon of the so-called Avignon papacy, the installation of the Roman popes in southern France rather than Rome. This chapter also examines the Great Schism, a far-reaching division in the papal office, as well as the responses to that disastrous split. Chapter 8, "Rome at the Close of the Middle Ages," addresses the state of the Roman Church from the aftermath of the Great Schism through the end of the medieval period. As European politics, religious life, and culture continued to experience rapid changes, including the Italian Renaissance and the "discovery" of the Americas, popes responded in ways that preserved the integrity of their immediate position, but exhausted their universal reach. At the edge of modernity, the papacy endured, but the project of Christendom as an earthly society of believers united under Rome's leadership did not survive the end of the Middle Ages.

In keeping with the purpose of this book to offer an accessible tour of papal history for non-specialists, citations have been kept to a minimum, typically given to indicate a study of particular importance for the subject at hand or for direct quotations. Whenever possible, references to medieval texts direct the reader to widely available English translations rather than original versions in Latin or other languages. This way, anyone can locate the documents in question and evaluate them for themselves. At the close of this volume, the reader will find a bibliography of major works consulted, offered as selective suggestions for further reading. Needless to say, there is an almost endless amount of information on the history of the Roman papacy. The vast output of academic scholarship and popular histories on the popes of Rome, admittedly of varying quality, testifies to our continued fascination with the self-proclaimed heirs of Saint Peter, even in our supposedly secularized world. In that regard, this present book will hopefully be the start rather than conclusion of an intellectual journey for those who want to know more about the history of the Roman Church in the Middle Ages.

Chapter 1: The Memory of Saint Peter

The story of the Roman papacy begins in blood – the blood of Christian martyrs, above all the apostles Peter and Paul. The modern historian searching for reassuring facts about the first-century preaching and martyrdom of those two saints at Rome faces inevitable disappointment. Almost everything we know about their presence in the capital of the Roman Empire derives from later traditions and traces, ranging from learned ecclesiastical histories to graffiti scrawled on the walls of the apostles' shrines. Through such remembrance of the past, the first generations of Christians firmly fixed the historical foundations of their Church in the imperial city: Saints Peter and Paul had established the Christian community in Rome before dying there, victims of pagan persecution. Their holy remains stayed in the city, forming a focal point of Christian devotion. Before his death, Peter had delegated his office as the first bishop of Rome to his successor, initiating a chain of apostolic succession from bishop to bishop down through the generations. Peter, moreover, was no ordinary apostle or bishop. According to the Gospels, Christ himself had given Peter the "keys of the kingdom of Heaven," saying to him, "whatsoever you shall bind upon earth, it shall be bound also in Heaven, and whatsoever you shall loose upon earth, it shall be loosed also in Heaven" (Mt. 16: 18–19). As Peter's heirs, enjoying his power to "loosen and bind," Rome's bishops held a place of preeminence over believers everywhere, making their city into the head of the Christian faith.

As we will see, this story of "Roman exceptionalism" formed the basis for the papacy's claim to represent the one, true catholic Church. In many ways, however, the church at Rome remained rather unexceptional during its first few centuries, similar to other churches around

7

the Mediterranean world, sharing with them similar ambitions and anxieties, successes and setbacks. As a marginal and sometimes persecuted group within Roman society, first-century Christians possessed relatively few resources and no legal recognition as such. The earliest churches consisted of humble, informally organized communities centered on private homes, "cells" of believers scattered through urban areas. The very notion that each church in a city should have a single bishop to oversee its affairs emerged only slowly, several generations after the time of the apostles. Even then, much like his peers, the bishop of Rome typically acted as a local rather than universal leader, dealing with daily matters in his immediate orbit, managing the clergy under him and guiding the liturgical life of his own congregation.

Nevertheless, through the memory of their apostolic origins, their claim to Peter and Paul's physical remains, and their city's symbolic status as the heart of Roman civilization, Rome's bishops possessed a special reservoir of support for their assertion of far-reaching authority over the Church. When it suited their purposes, Christians from other parts of the Roman world just as eagerly celebrated Rome's special qualities and characteristics – not that they always agreed about the nature of the Church and the structures of authority that should govern it. On the contrary, disagreement among Christians about their own religious beliefs, practices, and the organization of their lives often fueled their strident insistence upon unity and order. Many of the most persuasive arguments for Rome's superiority emerged precisely from bitter struggles among the faithful over the boundaries that delimited the orthodox or "right believing" community from the threat of heterodoxy and schism, "wrong belief" and "division" among the faithful. Searching for a way to determine right from wrong, Christians sometimes looked to Saint Peter and the apostolic authority granted to his successors for answers and arbitration, even if they did not always get the results that they wanted.

Starting in the fourth century, when the Roman imperial state legally recognized and then adopted Christianity as its official religion, the bishops of Rome faced a substantially altered political and social landscape from the one navigated by their predecessors, sometimes persecuted, more often ignored by the ruling powers of the ancient world. Bishops had become mediators and powerbrokers of empire; proper Christian faith and discipline turned into a matter of imperial order. Under these circumstances, controversies among Christians about their faith hardly disappeared. Rather, the stakes grew higher in determining and defending orthodoxy, creating new challenges and opportunities for Rome's bishops to assert their position. Filled with monuments to pagan gods and ancient triumphs, Rome fitfully began to display a new and public identity as a Christian city, while its bishops claimed special privileges based on their status as the heirs to Saint Peter. From being the leaders of a marginal if fiercely determined community of local Christians, loosely connected to their fellow believers around the Roman Empire, the bishops of Rome had become prominent – although certainly not preeminent, whatever they claimed otherwise – players in the Christian Roman Empire.

Origins of Christianity and the Church of Rome

The first Christians in Rome stood only one step removed from the beginning of their faith with the message of Jesus Christ and the mission of his apostles. Over the following generations, believers told and retold the story of Christianity's origins and arrival at the imperial capital, where Paul and Peter had preached, died for their beliefs, and left their holy remains. In this way, the earliest Christians endowed Rome with a sacred claim to number among the principal centers of their Church.

Jesus of Nazareth and the kingdom of God

The canonical Gospels of the Christian Bible celebrate the words and deeds of Joshua or Jesus of Nazareth, a prophet and miracle worker, who preferred the company of the poor and humble to wealthy and supposedly righteous men. A Jew born in the region of Galilee, immersed in the Hebrew religious tradition, Jesus preached about the power of Almighty God, the sinful nature of humankind, the need for love, charity, and repentance, and the wonder of divine compassion to crowds of listeners, some eager and others skeptical. "Blessed are the meek, for they shall possess the land," Jesus declared to one such gathering. "Blessed are they that mourn, for they shall be comforted. Blessed are they that hunger and thirst after justice, for they shall have their fill. Blessed are the merciful, for they shall obtain mercy" (Mt. 5: 4–10). According to Jesus, that time of consolation for the meek, the mournful, and others in their company did not lie that far away – the end of the world, he implied, fast approached, when everyone would face divine judgment, followed by eternal life or damnation. Helping him to spread this message, he gathered a band of twelve devoted followers or apostles, including Simon Peter, a former fisherman.

This "Jesus movement" appealed to some, but alienated others, including members of the Jewish priesthood whom Jesus implicitly and explicitly rebuked with his criticisms of those who followed the letter of the Hebrew Law, but failed to observe its true spirit. Although he emphasized that the coming kingdom of God would not be realized in this world, but rather in the next, his words carried a subversive edge. From the perspective of Roman civil authorities, ruling over Palestine as part of the far-flung Roman Empire, Jesus of Nazareth looked like one more dangerous rabble-rouser, resentful of imperial rule. After a faction of the Jewish leadership in Jerusalem denounced Jesus, the Romans arrested and crucified him in AD 30 (that is, *anno domini*, "in the year of the Lord," a system of dating that starts with Christ's birth). Three days later, according to the Gospels, he rose from the dead, visiting his disciples before he ascended bodily into Heaven. Jesus Christ, the "messiah" or "anointed one," had fulfilled the prophecies of the Hebrew Bible, later called by his followers the Old Testament. As revealed by their holy scriptures, the New Testament, Christ was in fact the Son of God, who had assumed the flesh and sacrificed himself for the redemption of humankind. The Church, the "assembly" of the faithful known as Christians, would observe and spread his message of salvation before the end of time.

The earliest disciples of Jesus were, naturally, Jews. Obeying the Lord's instructions to go forth and share the Good News, Christ's apostles fanned out around the Roman Empire and beyond, establishing small Christian churches in mostly urban areas. The *Acts of the Apostles*, part of the New Testament, captures the action and tensions involved in the initial growth of the new faith. It pays particular attention to the activities of Paul, a Jew and Roman citizen who initially persecuted Christians, but eventually embraced Christ's message and became its most outspoken advocate. Paul insisted, against the opinion of other apostles – including Christ's disciple Peter – that Jesus's promises were intended for both Jews and Gentiles (non-Jews), who could become Christians without first observing Jewish customs and religious practices such as circumcision. Over time, Paul's position carried the day. Christianity became a universal religion open to all humankind through the act of conversion.

Due to a lack of clear evidence, it remains difficult to discern the forms of organization that characterized the first Christian churches. They seem to have been a largely communal affair, built around consensus, involving both men and women. Certain charismatic figures, starting with the apostles themselves, emerged as leaders of Christian communities, basing their authority on their personal merits and spiritual appeal rather than any sort of official position. Over time, however, Christians began to organize themselves along more formal lines, starting with a basic but crucial division between clergy, male religious specialists who acted as organizers and caretakers of local churches, and the laity, the remainder of the congregation. Among the clergy, one sees bishops and priests bearing special duties to care for the sick, administer charity, and perform rituals and other pastoral obligations, assisted by deacons. One early Christian instruction manual, *The Didache*, offers a glimpse into this developing organization around the early second century. Among other things, it describes the rites of baptism, the ceremonial washing away of sins that marked one's entry into the Church, and the Eucharist, a ritual meal of bread and wine commemorating Christ's Last Supper with his disciples. *The Didache* also told believers to appoint "bishops and deacons worthy of the Lord, men meek and not covetous, true and approved," showing a healthy distrust of wanderers who claimed to be prophets but were really just hucksters looking for money.[1]

At first, there seems to have been little distinction between bishops and priests, both seen as figures of stable leadership in local Christian communities. As the second century progressed, however, bishops began to emerge as the overarching source of authority in the Church, typically assuming spiritual and administrative responsibilities for an entire city and its immediate surroundings, including the priests, deacons, and other kinds of clergy under their care. Scholars sometimes describe this arrangement as "monarchical" rather than "collegial" to distinguish the top-down model of episcopal authority from earlier, consensual forms of ecclesiastical organization, although bishops hardly ruled over their flocks like monarchs. Written in Rome *c.*100–120, the *Letter of the Romans to the Corinthians*, also called *First Clement* due to its later attribution to the bishop of Rome by that name, compared the Church to the Roman army with its distinct ranks, soldiers obediently following their officers, officers relying upon their soldiers. In letters to his fellow Christians, Ignatius of Antioch, a second-century martyr, likewise reminded his correspondents to act in accordance with their clerical leadership. "Let all respect the deacons as representing Jesus Christ, the bishops as a type of a Father, and the presbyters as God's high council and as the apostolic college," he wrote on one occasion. "Apart from these, no church deserves the name."[2]

Peter and Paul at Rome

As far as we can tell from hints in the New Testament and other near contemporary sources, the creation and development of the first churches in Rome more or less followed this pattern. In its concluding chapters, the *Acts of the Apostles* describes Paul's arrest by Roman authorities at the urging of Jews who rejected his message, followed by his arrival at Rome to stand trial in AD 61. By that time, a small number of Christians already lived in the city, including men and women, Jews and Gentiles, locals and foreigners. A few years earlier, Paul had written a letter to such Christians in the imperial capital, addressed to "all at Rome, beloved of God, called to be saints" (Rom. 1: 7), offering his views on Christ, the Gospel, sin, and salvation. How the faith first reached the city is nowhere explained. Contemporary Rome possessed a sizable Jewish community. Presumably, Jewish immigrants or travelers to Rome brought the Christian faith with them. A later Roman historian, Suetonius, described a disturbance in Rome's Jewish community in the year AD 49 "at the instigation of Chrestus," leading to their temporary expulsion from the city.[3] The meaning of this passage remains unclear, but it might indicate an upheaval in Rome's Jewish community caused by newly arrived Christians, assuming that "Chrestus" represents a misspelling of "Christ." Regardless, in the New Testament narrative, a welcoming committee of Paul's brethren greeted him when he arrived at the city's outskirts. Under guard, he met with Rome's leading Jews to declare his innocence of any wrongdoing, proclaiming the news of Christ and the need to spread that message of salvation among the Gentiles. The *Acts of the Apostles* closes with the statement that Paul stayed in Rome for two years in a rented house, "preaching the kingdom of God, and teaching the things that concern the Lord Jesus Christ, with all confidence and without prohibition" (Acts 28: 30–31).

The New Testament says nothing about Peter coming to Rome. Nevertheless, near contemporary Christian sources revealed that Peter had also journeyed to the imperial capital. The *Letter of the Romans to the Corinthians*, for example, implied that both Peter and Paul had died in Rome during a recent persecution of the faithful, suggesting that the Romans and Corinthians shared a living memory of the saints' presence in the imperial city. Another letter written by Ignatius of Antioch, while en route to Rome as a prisoner facing his own execution, likewise suggested that the two saints had been active in the city. Exhorting the Romans not to intercede on his behalf with local authorities, seeing as he desired to die for his faith, Ignatius wrote to them: "Not like Peter and Paul do I issue any orders to you. They were apostles; I am a convict. They were free; I am until this moment a slave."[4] Based on suggestive passages such these, modern scholars have conjectured that Peter visited Rome as early as AD 42, perhaps leaving the city and returning on more than one occasion.

The New Testament does not describe what finally happened to Paul or Peter. As just mentioned, the *Letter of the Romans to the Corinthians* implies that two saints had suffered martyrdom during a recent persecution of the faithful. The first known persecution of Christians by Roman authorities occurred under Emperor Nero in AD 64. A non-Christian source from about fifty years later, the *Annals* of the Roman historian Tacitus, vividly describes the scene. Blamed for a fire that had ravaged the city, the Christians – labeled by Tacitus as a "group hated for their abominations" – were rounded up and convicted "not so much for the crime of arson, as of their hatred of the human race."[5] Some perished when torn apart by wild dogs, others were crucified, and still others were burned alive. The *Letter of the Romans to the Corinthians* does not explicitly state that the two apostles died at this exact time, or even whether they perished together. Regardless, Christians living in Rome and elsewhere soon associated the two apostles' demise with Nero's infamous persecution of the Church.

Peter and Paul's deaths thereby participated in the wider phenomenon of Christian martyrdom, self-sacrifice as a form testimony to one's faith. Christ, of course, offered the ultimate model of such sacrifice in the Gospels. The *Acts of the Apostles* also describes how one of Christ's apostles, Stephen, died in Jerusalem shortly after the resurrection, stoned by a group of outraged Jewish compatriots, making him the first recognized Christian martyr (Acts 7: 56–59). As Christians moved outside of Palestine into the wider Roman world, they encountered further derision and antagonism not just from Jews who rejected the Christian message, but also the wider pagan society around them, which came to view the followers of Christ as ostentatious drop-outs from Roman religious and civic life. Christians embraced this sense of alienation. As the soon-to-be martyred Ignatius of Antioch put it, "I would rather die and come to Jesus than be king over the entire earth." Or, as another early martyr declared when questioned by a Roman magistrate, "I do not recognize the empire of this world; but rather I serve that God, whom no man has seen nor can see."[6]

Perhaps not surprisingly, given the importance of Peter and Paul's presence in Rome and the centrality of martyrdom in the Christian tradition, later generations of believers vividly filled in the details of their preaching and deaths in apocryphal works of biblical literature such as the *Acts of Paul* and the *Acts of Peter*, dating from the second and third centuries. In these texts, the two apostles emerge as miracle-working superheroes. The *Acts of Paul* describes how that apostle rented a barn outside Rome, "where he and the brethren taught the word of truth. He became famous and many souls were added to the Lord, so that it was noised about in Rome, and a great many from the house of the emperor came to him and there was much joy." After Nero's cupbearer Patroclus fell to his death from a window while listening to Paul preach, the apostle raised him from the dead. When the resurrected Patroclus proclaimed his faith in "Christ Jesus, the king of the ages," the emperor ordered Paul's arrest. In the *Acts of Peter*, that disciple comes to Rome during Paul's absence to rescue the community from Simon Magus, a clueless character from the *Acts of the Apostles* who tried to purchase the Holy Spirit from Christ's disciples (Acts 8: 9–29). Simon, who performs magic tricks, deceives the Romans into believing that he is the true messiah; Peter combats him with various miracles, making a dog speak and a smoked fish return to life. Eventually when Simon flies into the air before a crowd of onlookers, Peter's prayers blast him to the ground, breaking his leg in three places. In the later, combined version of the *Acts of Peter and Paul*, the dynamic duo work in Rome together, converting members of the imperial household and defeating Simon Magus, whose plunge to the earth kills him.[7]

In these non-canonical works, similar forms of drama shape the apostles' demise. Arrested by Nero and brought before him for interrogation, Paul openly defies the emperor, who is outraged by the fact that some of his own soldiers had become Christian, serving their new king, Christ. Persecuting the Christians in Rome, Nero orders Paul's beheading. After praying, "Paul bent his neck, without speaking anymore. When the executioner cut off his head, milk splashed on the tunic of the soldier. And the soldier and all who stood nearby were astonished at this sight and glorified God who had thus honored Paul." Peter angers Nero and the prefect, Agrippa, along with a number of other Roman nobles, for converting their concubines and wives to a life of chastity. Despite protests by other Christians,

Agrippa orders Peter's crucifixion. Peter, who had started to leave Rome but returned after a vision of Christ revealed to the apostle his imminent martyrdom, asks to be crucified upside down, fulfilling Christ's words, "Unless you make the right as the left and the left as the right, and the top as the bottom and the front as the back, you shall not know the Kingdom." In the later *Acts of Peter and Paul*, Peter simply says he is not worthy to be crucified in the same way as the Lord.[8]

By the fourth century, ecclesiastical historians such as the Latin writer Lactantius or the Greek author Eusebius of Caesarea expressed no doubt about the apostles' deeds and deaths in Rome. In his influential *History of the Church*, Eusebius confidently wrote that Peter, "like a noble captain of God," had defeated Simon Magus in the city and "brought the precious merchandise of the spiritual light from the East to those in the West." Sent to Rome in chains, Paul had won his freedom and preached the word of God in the city for two years. Together, Eusebius believed, the two saints had won an inestimable prize for the Christian faith – the capital of the Roman Empire.[9] In his work *On the Death of the Persecutors*, Lactantius described the apostles' preaching and martyrdom as follows:

> When Nero was already reigning, Peter came to Rome. Through his performance of certain miracles which he worked by the power of God that was given to him, he converted many to the way to the way of justice and set up a firm and faithful temple unto God. This fact was made known to Nero. When he noticed that, not only at Rome but everywhere, a great multitude was daily turning aside from the cult of idols and passing over to the new religion in condemnation of the old ... he zealously strove to tear down the heavenly temple and destroy justice. And he was the first of all to persecute the servants of God: he crucified Peter and killed Paul.[10]

Soon after, as a consequence of these actions, Nero fell from power and died an ignoble death. In this way, the blood of the apostles watered the roots of Rome's Christian community, anticipating the Church's triumph over those who opposed it.

Saints, shrines, and catacombs

Early Christians in Rome also memorialized Peter and Paul's presence in their city by establishing places of veneration that claimed to house their sacred remains. Like so many other aspects of the

Roman Church's earliest history, the precise origins and development of these holy sites are difficult to determine. By the close of the second century at the latest, Christians had established two shrines associated with Peter and Paul's martyrdom, one for Paul on the road to Ostia and another for Peter on the Vatican Hill. One churchman at Rome, named Gaius (as later quoted by Eusebius), declared confidently: "I can point out the monuments of the victorious apostles. If you go as far as the Vatican or the Ostian Way, you will find the monuments of those who founded this church."[11] By the later third century, local worshipers had built yet another shrine on the Appian Way that was associated with the veneration of both apostles.

For Eusebius, the location of the saints' shrines in Rome confirmed the fact that they had indeed died there, precisely the sort of reaction that the city's Christians no doubt hoped for. Peter and Paul's remains possessed an incalculable worth. In a manner of speaking, the two apostles still lived in Rome. The Roman Church clearly knew that it possessed something special. The *Acts of Peter and Paul* describes an attempt by a band of Christians from Jerusalem to steal the holy remains of the apostles until an earthquake shook the city and drove them away, manifesting God's displeasure at their pious thievery. Divine providence had sent a message loud and clear that the relics of Peter and Paul were meant to stay in Rome. According to this version of events, the cautious Romans hid the relics in the catacombs on the Appian Way until they could prepare proper shrines for them at the Vatican and Ostian Way.

In this case, archeological evidence helps to confirm what texts tell us. Starting in 1939, a series of excavations at the Vatican under the Church of Saint Peter uncovered a second-century cemetery beneath the current site of Peter's tomb, including both pagan and Christian graves. Although the dig did not claim to find a particular burial place for Peter, it did reveal that second-century Christians buried their dead at the spot associated with his martyrdom, much as described by Gaius. An excavation at the catacombs on the Appian Way – where, contrary to the story told in the *Acts of Peter and Paul*, the apostles' remains might have been temporarily housed for safety during an imperial persecution – revealed Christian veneration at that location, including graffiti that invoked the power of the two saints. This memorializing of Peter and Paul did not stand in isolation from the wider Christian project to bury their dead as a community, anticipating the resurrection of the faithful after Final Judgment. The first Christian tombs stood alongside pagan ones in various catacombs that ringed Rome, beyond the traditional boundaries that prohibited the burial of the dead within the city. Over the second and third centuries, Christians at Rome established an increasing number of cemeteries exclusively for believers. Contrary to popular belief, the catacombs did not provide refuge for Christians huddled together during times of persecution. They did mark the growth of the church at Rome and its intensifying coherence in this world and the next. Buried in proximity to the saints, Christians anticipated their eternal reward.

Inventing the Apostolic See

A cosmopolitan city of roughly one million inhabitants, second-century Rome was home to a wide diversity of Christian believers and communities, refreshed by a constant stream of immigrants from around the empire. Far from a single "pope," there were a number of such popes, "fathers," or "grand old men" speaking for their congregations. By the later second century, however, this plurality of Christian leadership slowly gave way to a more unified community with a single head, the bishop of Rome, as recognized by catholic, right-believing Christians. Claiming legitimacy through unbroken apostolic succession from Paul and especially Peter, Rome's bishops insisted that their seat possessed an exceptional authority that reached beyond their immediate church – an insistence most evident when Christians agreed to disagree about their own faith, sacraments, and ecclesiastical discipline.

Schism, heresy, and apostolic succession

As described above, the *Didache* instructed believers to appoint bishops and deacons, implying that Christian communities had the right to install clergy and, under certain circumstances, remove them from their positions. Some early Christians, by contrast, asserted that the true source of a bishop's authority lay with the apostles themselves, who had appointed bishops as their successors. The true leadership of the Church could thereby trace its origins back to the apostles, guaranteeing unity and preventing division in the ranks of the faithful. The *Letter of the Romans to the Corinthians* addressed precisely this problem. For reasons not entirely clear, a group of Christians at Corinth had deposed their clergy and chosen new priests to lead them, creating a rift in their community. In the letter, the Romans counseled the Corinthians against such rash action, reminding them that Christ had appointed the apostles to spread the news of Christ "equipped with the fullness of the Holy Spirit." In turn, the apostles "appointed men whom they had tested by the Spirit to act as bishops and deacons for the future believers." Knowing that there would someday be disputes over the bishop's office, the apostles agreed that "when these men die, other approved men shall succeed to their sacred ministry."[12]

In addition to the problem of schism, early Christians faced a wide variety of religious teachings about the nature of Christ, his message, and the Church. Some groups – typically lumped together under the label of Gnostics – often claimed secret knowledge about Christ and his revelation, or denied that the Son of God had actually assumed human form. The followers of Valentinus formed one such Gnostic community, started in Rome around the mid-second century. The Marcionites, followers of the charismatic instructor Marcion, also active at Rome around this time, claimed that the God of the Old Testament represented a wicked deity who ruled over the earth as a tyrant – only Jesus Christ and the New Testament offered the hope of spiritual salvation. Still others claimed that true Christians must renounce all sexual relations and remain celibate to enter the kingdom of God. The presence of such influential figures as Valentinus and Marcion at Rome reminds us about the cosmopolitan nature of the imperial capital during this era, drawing people together from every corner of the Roman Empire.

Confronting this dazzling, seductive array of religious teachings in their very midst, rejecting them as dangerous and heretical, the self-proclaimed defenders of orthodoxy responded by creating the first formal list of Rome's bishops to provide a firm record of apostolic succession from the days of Peter and Paul down to Anicetus (c.155–66), bishop of Rome. Eusebius of Caesarea attributed the creation of this list to a figure named Hegesippus, an opponent of various heresies, who "pieced together the succession down to Anicetus." Christians outside of Rome responded to heretics in a similar manner. In his work *Against the Heresies*, written around 185, Irenaeus of Lyons insisted that the key to ensuring unity and orthodoxy lay with bishops, whose authority could be traced back in a direct chain of transmission all the way back to the apostles. "Since it would be too long to list the successions of all the churches," he wrote, "we shall here address the tradition of the greatest and most ancient church, known to all, founded and built up at Rome by the two most glorious apostles, Peter and Paul." All of the faithful, Irenaeus continued, should agree with this church "because in her the apostolic tradition has always been safeguarded by those who are everywhere."[13] To demonstrate, drawing upon the lists created at Rome, Irenaeus included his own genealogy of bishops from Peter and Paul through their immediate successors Linus, Anacletus, and Clement, all the way down to Eleutherus (c.175–89) in Irenaeus's own day.

Others pursued a similar strategy. According to the north African theologian Tertullian, when heretics claimed legitimacy by pointing to their own apostolic roots, their opponents should respond by demanding proof. "Let them exhibit the origins of their churches," Tertullian wrote around 200, "let them unroll the list of their bishops, coming down from the beginning by succession in such a way that their first bishop had for his originator and predecessor one of the apostles or apostolic men." Heretics, in Tertullian's appraisal, could only fabricate such a pedigree. Even if they managed to do so, the contradictions and inconsistencies in their teachings would still expose them for what they were – blasphemous enemies of the true Church. Orthodox Christians, by contrast, could look for guidance to "apostolic churches," including Alexandria, founded by Mark, Antioch, also founded by Peter, and above all Rome, site of Peter and Paul's martyrdom. "How fortunate is that church," Tertullian proclaimed enthusiastically about Rome, "upon which the apostles poured their whole teaching together with their blood!"[14]

The Easter controversy

A healthy respect for the Roman Church and its record of apostolic succession, however, did not translate into unquestioning obedience toward the city's bishops. As seen during a debate over the dating of Easter under Victor, bishop of Rome (189–99), even his admirers did not accord him the absolute privilege of dictating right and wrong to other believers. As related by Eusebius of Caesarea, who drew upon contemporary records of the controversy, Victor spoke out against the common Eastern Christian practice of observing Easter at the same time as the Jewish feast of Passover, held on the first full moon in the month of *Nisan* following the Hebrew lunar calendar. Instead, a council of churchmen at Rome decided that Christians should follow the Western tradition of fixing Easter on the first Sunday – the day of the Lord's resurrection – after the first full moon of that same month. Eusebius seemed to believe that Victor desired to impose this view on Christians everywhere. It seems more likely that Victor took this action against Christians in Rome, some of them immigrants from Asia who followed the Eastern practice of dating Easter.

Regardless, the reaction to Victor's initiative is striking. When some Eastern bishops heard about his position and objected, insisting upon their own tradition for the dating of Easter, Victor "endeavored to cut off by a single stroke the communities of the whole of Asia, together with the neighboring churches, from the common unity, and pilloried them in letters in which he announced the total excommunication of all his fellow Christians there." As Eusebius puts it, his move "was not to the taste of all the bishops," and some of them "very sternly rebuked Victor." Even Irenaeus of Lyons scolded Victor, advising him that "he should not cut off entire churches of God because they observed the unbroken tradition of their predecessors." Irenaeus also reminded him about an earlier debate over the dating of Easter between Anicetus of Rome and Saint Polycarp, who had failed to settle their disagreements, but "remained in communion with each other" and "parted company in peace, and the whole Church was at peace." From this perspective, Rome's apostolic authority did not trump the need for harmony and mutual respect among Christians. The Roman Church might provide a prominent, well-regarded example of apostolic succession in action, a line of defense against schism and heresy. All bishops, however, were created equal. They all represented successors to the apostles, providing orthodox leadership for their churches that collectively formed the one true Church.[15]

The rock of Saint Peter

The earliest lists of Roman bishops commonly included both Paul and Peter, suggesting that they formed equal sources of sanctification for the city's Christian community through their preaching and martyrdom. For that matter, the precise ordering of the bishops' succession after the apostles varied, sometimes starting with Clement, other times with Linus and Anacletus and then Clement. During the course of the third century, however, the bishops of Rome firmly fixed the origins of their apostolic office squarely on Saint Peter, who personally "laid hands" on Clement, making him the second bishop of Rome. They did so in part due to the widely held belief among early Christians that Jesus Christ had given Peter the keys of Heaven, effectively delegating to him leadership of the Church. Critically speaking, the very notion of Peter as the first bishop of the city, handing over his position to Clement, would have made little sense to first-century Christians. As described above, at that time, the office of bishop did not even exist as such. Nevertheless, Rome's claim to this

"Petrine" foundation would come to bear more and more weight as Christians appealed to Peter's particular authority when it provided them with a needed voice of support or judgment during times of conflict or disagreement.

Another episode of pagan persecution revealed the attraction of Rome's status as the seat of Saint Peter. As part of his effort to deal with the so-called "Crisis of the Third Century," a series of disasters that included foreign invasions, civil wars, and plague, the Roman ruler Decius insisted that all Roman citizens make sacrifices to the traditional gods as a sign of their loyalty to the imperial order. Those Christians who refused faced arrest and trial, followed by exile or execution. Bishop Fabian of Rome (236–50) suffered martyrdom under these circumstances. When the persecution tapered off the following year, the Christian community at Rome and elsewhere faced a dilemma. What should they do about fellow believers who had performed pagan sacrifices or bribed someone to receive a certificate indicating that they had done so? Members of the clergy disagreed. Some adopted a moderate position that lapsed believers could be reconciled with the Church immediately after sufficient penance. Others took a harder stance and declared that the fallen must perform extreme penance for the remainder of their lives, being readmitted to communion only on their deathbed. Confusing matters, in some cases Christians about to be martyred had distributed letters, stating their intention to intercede with God as soon as they reached Heaven, undoing any sins committed by the letter-bearers. The lapsed possessors of such letters effectively short-circuited the regular channels of penance, demanding immediate readmission to the Church.

In 251, the "lax" party at Rome elected a new bishop, Cornelius (March–June 251). The "rigorists" in the city rejected Cornelius, accusing him of cutting corners for the reconciliation of fallen believers, and elected their own bishop, Novatian. This disturbing situation, involving clergy from Rome and elsewhere who took sides in the schism, once again highlighted the importance of apostolic succession. In this case, those involved placed a particular emphasis on Peter – the "rock" upon whom Christ founded his Church – as the ultimate guarantor of orthodoxy and unity. In his work *On the Unity of the Church*, Cyprian, bishop of Carthage, stressed Peter's unique place as Christ's deputy on earth: "It is upon him," Cyprian declared, that the Lord "builds the Church, and to him He entrusts the sheep to feed. And although He assigns a like power to all the Apostles, He founded a single chair, thus establishing by His own authority the source and hallmark of the Church's oneness." Cyprian had his own reasons to support Cornelius and insist upon the unity of the Church as confirmed by the apostles, especially Peter. During the persecution under Decius, Cyprian had fled Carthage. When he returned, he faced his own problems with clergy who had freely readmitted lapsed Christians to communion after minimal penance. In addition, some of Novatian's sympathizers had created their own rival bishop in the city. Although Cyprian occupied a middle ground between the lax and rigorist factions, he had no patience for schism. "If a man does not hold fast to this oneness of Peter," Cyprian declared, "does he imagine that he still holds the faith? If he deserts the chair of Peter upon whom the Church was built, does he still have confidence that he is in the Church?"[16]

Much like Irenaeus generations earlier, however, Cyprian's admiration for the bishops of Rome only went so far. A further round of controversy soon erupted over the effectiveness of baptism administered by heretics and schismatics, including Novatian's followers. Speaking as the prelate who sat on the "chair of Peter," Stephen I (254–57) declared the effectiveness of any baptism made in the name of Christ or the Trinity, insisting that an orthodox bishop needed only to lay his hands upon an improperly baptized believer to "catholicize" them. Cyprian disagreed, declaring that those baptized by heretics should be rebaptized. The bishop of Carthage also insisted that Stephen had been too quick to readmit lapsed believers from the recent persecution, polluting his own church by communion with them. In a letter sent to a neighboring bishop, Cyprian struck a quite different tone than he did in his work *On the Unity of the Church*, referring to Peter's dispute with Paul over the need for Gentiles to be circumcised following the Jewish Law. Disagreeing with Paul, Peter "did not assert that he had the rights of seniority and therefore upstarts and latecomers ought rather to be obedient to him." Rather, Cyprian observed, Peter "welcomed any counsel that brought the truth and he readily agreed to the just reasons advanced by Paul." There are signs that the bishop of Carthage later revised *On the Unity of the Church* to downplay his earlier emphasis on Peter's special qualities. Corresponding with Cyprian during this debate, Firmilian of Caesarea likewise emphasized the need for consensus among the parties involved and blasted the current bishop of Rome:

> At this point I become filled with righteous indignation at Stephen's crass and obvious stupidity. He is a man who finds the location of his bishopric such a source of pride, who keeps insisting that he

occupies the succession to Peter, upon whom the foundations of the Church were laid; and yet, by using his authority to defend heretical baptisms, he is introducing many other "rocks" and he is laying the foundation of and building up many new churches.

Through this play on the Gospel of Matthew, Firmilian suggested that Stephen had fostered schism by falsely assuming powers that did not belong to him, based upon his erroneous understanding of Rome's apostolic origins and what they meant for the Church.[17]

After Stephen died in 257, his successor Sixtus (257–58) struck a conciliatory tone with the church in northern Africa. The following year, Cyprian went to a martyr's death during a renewed round of imperial persecution. Sixtus died during the same crackdown on the Christian clergy, when Peter and Paul's remains were apparently moved to a hiding place on the Appian Way for safekeeping. At some point during these events, the controversy over baptism settled down. That contentious episode, however, vividly displayed the elastic nature of apostolic succession as understood by contemporaries. On the one hand, Rome benefited from a common emphasis on the unity of the Church under the authority of orthodox bishops, leaders in the fight against schism and heresy. On the other, contemporaries did not hesitate to judge any given Roman bishop for falling short of that apostolic ideal, nor did Christians lose sight of the idea that Christ's commission to "feed his sheep" belonged to bishops everywhere. The bishop of Rome's special status as Peter's heir, and just what that position meant for the governance of the Church, lay in the eye of the beholder.

The Church and Constantine

By the turn of the fourth century, Christians formed a small but well-organized minority in the pagan society around them, representing about 10 percent of the population, including in their ranks rich and poor, the humble and the powerful, the illiterate and the highly educated. Judging from a letter written by Cornelius of Rome, the city's orthodox clergy consisted of forty-two priests, seven deacons, forty-two acolytes, and fifty-six readers, along with exorcists and doorkeepers – hardly an inconsequential organization.[18] Nevertheless, Christians still occupied an uneasy place in the Roman Empire, subject to periodic persecution. The Church's fraught position changed profoundly during the reigns of Constantine I and his successors, whose adoption of Christianity would profoundly reshape the political and religious life of the Roman world.

Christianity becomes legal

During the closing decades of the third century, the determined and capable ruler Diocletian restored stability to the Roman Empire after its ongoing military, economic, and political crisis. He did so by initiating an expansion of the army and a wide-ranging series of administrative reforms, including the division of imperial territories into Western and Eastern halves, each with its own emperor and deputy emperor. Much like Decius before him, he also insisted that citizens show their loyalty by making sacrifices to the traditional gods in support of the emperor. Also like Decius, Diocletian viewed Christians with growing suspicion. Starting in 302–3, along with his deputy ruler in the East, Galerius, he unleashed a persecution against Christian communities, calling for the razing of churches, the burning of Bibles, and the public performance of pagan sacrifices. Arrests, trials, and executions followed. Christian historians such as Eusebius and Lactantius, who lived through these events, viewed Diocletian's attack on the Church as the final, most horrific action taken by the Roman Empire against their faith.

Final, because of what happened next. After Diocletian retired in 305, struggles broke out between his imperial successors. On October 28, 312, one of the contenders, Constantine, defeated his rival Maxentius at the Battle of the Milvian Bridge on the outskirts of Rome, making him the sole ruler of the Western Roman Empire. According to later reports, before engaging in battle, Constantine experienced a dream or vision or some combination of the two involving a symbol similar to a labarum or a cross. Realizing that his soldiers would be fighting under that sign's protection, he instructed them to mark it on their shields and attributed his subsequent victory to the Christian God. Modern scholars have long debated Constantine's motivations for his embrace of Christianity; the exact reasons for his decision will no doubt remain a mystery. For Christian contemporaries and later generations of church historians, this moment represented a genuine, miraculous conversion for the emperor.

Whatever exactly happened in 312, Constantine's policies initiated a remarkable change in the Church's fortunes. Together with his co-emperor, Licinius, Constantine issued the so-called Edict of Milan in 313. This proclamation declared religious toleration for the worship of Christians and all others in the Roman Empire, "so that by this means whatever divinity is enthroned in heaven may be gracious to us and to all who have been placed under our authority."[19] The edict specifically revoked the previous policy of persecution against Christians, restoring the goods and property seized from them. Suddenly, the Church had become a legally recognized entity in the Roman world.

One should not exaggerate Constantine's actions as a complete turnaround for Christianity. Although Christians before Constantine suffered periodic persecution and celebrated martyrdom as an unrivaled expression of their faith, the popular image of Christians being constantly hounded and "fed to the lions" fails to capture the mixed feelings many Christians had toward the Roman order, not to mention how pagans viewed Christianity. On the one hand, Rome represented for Christians the new Babylon, the biblical symbol of wickedness that would try to destroy the Church at the end of time. On the other, since the second century, Christians did not fail to recognize that the Roman Empire created a certain peace for all of its inhabitants, thereby fostering the spread of the Gospels. Some of them even declared that Christians – although they should not fight in imperial armies – might support the empire by their prayers. Over a year before the Edict of Milan, an ailing Galerius had already issued his own edict of toleration for Christians, declaring his desire that "it will be their duty to pray to their god for our good estate, and that of the state."[20] Much like Galerius before him, Constantine's decision seems less surprising when one considers the admittedly minor but undeniably significant place occupied by well-organized churches in cities across the Roman Empire. Over the following years, Constantine openly turned toward Christian bishops as a source of support for his imperial rule, granting them tax exemptions, freeing them from various civic obligations, and establishing the Christian holy day of Sunday as one of rest from official business. Bishops began to act as legal landowners of their churches, quasi-imperial administrators, and judicial figures, hearing cases between Christians and eventually between Christians and pagans.

As the recipients of such imperial favors, accompanied by a flood of private bequests, churches began to enjoy unprecedented visibility and prosperity. At Rome, Constantine donated imperial property on the Caecilian hill, the Lateran palace, for the construction of a monumental basilica church, modeled after the structure of a Roman law court. The Church of Saint John Lateran soon became the central complex of ecclesiastical business for Rome's bishops, a high-profile sign of the emperor's support for the Christian community. Of course,

Constantine inaugurated similar Christian building projects in other cities around the Roman Empire, including Jerusalem, and, eventually, his new imperial capital, Constantinople – he did not show exclusive favor toward Rome. Likewise, there are no signs that he enjoyed especially close relations with the bishops of Rome, Miltiades (310–14) and Sylvester I (314–35), who, despite later traditions to the contrary, had no role in the emperor's conversion. In 313, Constantine referred a dispute to Miltiades over a developing schism in northern Africa involving the so-called Donatists, a group that had adopted a rigorous position against lapsed clergy during the recent persecution under Diocletian. When the council convoked by Miltiades decided against them, the unsatisfied Donatists appealed again to the emperor. At this point, Constantine transferred the case to a synod of bishops from Gaul, who likewise decided against the Donatists. Judging by this episode, in Constantine's eyes the bishop of Rome occupied a notable place among Christian authorities, but did not stand above other bishops, who possessed a collective responsibility to assist their ruler in maintaining the peace and unity of the Church for the good of the empire.

The Council of Nicaea

After crushing his former ally Licinius in 324, Constantine stood as the sole ruler of the Roman world, his fortunes linked to Christian bishops scattered around the empire. Still the business of church officials, policing the borders of orthodoxy had become a matter of consequence for the well-being of the Roman imperial order. In 325, demonstrating his concern for the unity of the Church, the emperor called the ecumenical or general Council of Nicaea, even offering to pay for the attendees' traveling expenses. Well over two hundred bishops assembled from around the Roman Empire to address a number of ecclesiastical disputes. First and foremost on the agenda, they tackled a growing controversy over the teachings of Arius, a priest from Alexandria, who claimed that the Trinity consisted of three "hypostases" or persons, placing the Son and Holy Spirit in a subordinate position to the Father. Christ, by this logic, represented a created being, not fully divine in the same way as the Father. The opponents of "Arianism," championed by Athanasius, bishop of Alexandria, argued for Christ's full and uncompromising divinity. To a modern observer, such theological disagreements might seem obscure or overly technical. For contemporary Christians, however, they struck a chord of extreme significance, determining the precise workings of the Incarnation, the central act of human salvation and the foundational moment of the Church.

Sylvester, bishop of Rome, did not attend the council, although he sent two legates, who supported the formulation of the Nicaean Creed, a statement of orthodoxy that among other things recognized the Son as "begotten not made, consubstantial with the Father." The creed condemned those who believed otherwise. As part of its deliberations, the council also issued a number of canons that dealt largely with the proper rules and regulations for members of the clergy (for example, prohibiting them from living with women other than their immediate relatives, or forbidding bishops to transfer their position from one see to another). In its sixth canon, the council declared: "Let the ancient customs hold good which are in Egypt and Libya and Pentapolis, according to which the bishop of Alexandria has authority over all these places. For this is also customary to the bishop of Rome. In like manner in Antioch and in the other provinces, the privileges are to be preserved to the churches."[21] The following canon specifically added Jerusalem, honored due to "custom and ancient tradition," to this list of privileged churches. Interpreted conservatively, this statement meant that the bishopric of Rome represented the metropolitan or primary see of the churches located in its immediate orbit, similar to the authority that the bishops of Antioch, Alexandria, and Jerusalem enjoyed over their provinces. Taken generously, this piece of legislation could be interpreted to mean that Rome enjoyed the rights of a metropolitan see over the entire Western Roman Empire. Later generations would remember Nicaea as a watershed in the history of the papacy, when the first Christian Roman emperor and the first general council had recognized Rome's place of universal primacy, based upon its apostolic succession from Saint Peter. Seen from this perspective, the Council of Nicaea placed an official stamp on a situation ordained by none other than Jesus Christ through his chief disciple. .

Rome and the Constantinian "peace"

For Christian historians such as Eusebius of Caesarea, the conversion of Constantine had marked an end to the age of martyrs, bringing peace to the world through the union of the Roman Empire and the Church. However long it took for the majority of its inhabitants to convert, the Roman world had begun its transformation into one where the teachings, rites, and symbols of Christianity shaped institutions, laws, and languages of authority. Reigning from their new capital at Constantinople, founded at the site of Byzantium by Constantine in 330, Christian emperors stood as God's deputies on earth, guaranteeing the stability of the Church and protecting the divinely ordained imperial order from its enemies. These historical developments, however, did not so much bring about peace for Christians as redirect violence into other channels when new struggles emerged over exactly what kind of faith and discipline should characterize the Christian Roman Empire.

Despite the statement of orthodoxy formulated at Nicaea in 325, clergy sympathetic to Arius had rejected the council's outcome and continued to occupy important ecclesiastical positions, eventually gaining access to Constantine's inner circle. The emperor himself apparently changed his feelings toward the Arian party. Not long before he died in 337, he met personally with Arius and briefly exiled Arius's chief opponent, the outspoken Athanasius, from Alexandria. Constantine's son and heir in the Eastern Empire, Constantius II, did not hide his sympathies for Arianism and once again exiled Athanasius, violently harassing his supporters. Some of the parties involved in the ongoing dispute appealed to the bishop of Rome, Julius I (337–52), hoping that his outside intervention might provide some resolution to the controversy. Julius convened a council to deliberate over the issues in 340. To the disappointment of Athanasius's opponents, many of whom ultimately decided not to attend the synod, the pope and assembled clergy decided that the bishop of Alexandria had been unjustly deposed from his office. The matter, however, did not end there. Three years later, Constantius and his brother Constans, co-emperor in the West, summoned a council that met in Sardica (modern Sofia) to settle the controversy. After many of the "Arian" bishops refused to participate, the majority again decided in Athanasius's favor. As part of its deliberations, the Council of Sardica also declared that the church of Rome held jurisdiction as final court of appeals for bishops accused of wrongdoing and deposed by their peers – a statement that had a long future ahead of it in Latin canon law as a basis for Rome's claims of judicial primacy over the Church.[22]

Immediately speaking, the decision reached at Sardica did little good. Those leading the opposition to Athanasius and the settlement at Nicaea rejected its outcome and excommunicated Julius for good measure. Following his brother's death in 350, Constantius reigned as sole emperor and began pushing his pro-Arian policy even more aggressively, pressuring bishops around the empire to support Athanasius's condemnation. As the emperor supposedly put it on one occasion, "What I want must be regarded as canon law."[23] When Julius I's successor Liberius (352–66) refused to renounce his support for Athanasius and his sympathizers, viewing them as new Christian martyrs, the emperor banished him. Initially, the clergy in Rome refused to accept Liberius's exile. In time, however, a group of them elected a replacement bishop, Felix. The situation grew more complicated when Liberius returned to the city in 358, finally giving in to Constantius's demands after years of pressure and abuse. After the people in Rome rejected an unworkable proposal for the two bishops to share office, the majority favoring Liberius, Felix withdrew to the city's suburbs, although a faction of the clergy remained loyal to him. After Constantius died in 361, the controversy over Arianism more or less settled down, but the problems in Rome continued. In 366, when Liberius passed away, a new dispute broke out when his followers refused to recognize the next bishop, Damasus (366–84), because he had formerly supported Felix's claim to the office during the recent schism. These dissidents chose their own bishop, Ursinus. According to one report, Damasus organized a gang of gladiators, charioteers, grave-diggers, and other clergy to assault Ursinus's followers in the Church of Santa Maria Maggiore, slaughtering well over a hundred men and women. Although the fighting continued for about a year, Damasus eventually won the day, forcing Ursinus to leave Rome. In the era of the Constantinian peace, becoming the successor of Saint Peter could be a bloody business.

Rome's Christian landscape

Despite its turbulent beginnings, Damasus's time as bishop proved significant for Rome's future as a Christian city in a number of ways. As noted above, soon after the Edict of Milan, Emperor Constantine had ordered the construction of a new church on the site of the Lateran palace, creating a public center for ecclesiastical governance in Rome. The foundation of the Lateran basilica signaled a veritable boom in church-building over the course of the fourth century, including sites on the outskirts of the city such as the Church of the Apostles on the Via Appia, the Church of Saint Paul "Beyond the Walls," and the Church of Saint Peter on the Vatican Hill. Modern historians once attributed this wave of monumental architecture to Constantine's initiative, although there is little evidence that he played a direct role in these subsequent building projects. Much of the driving force for the restoration or construction of Rome's churches lay with private individuals and aristocratic families, who also expanded, enriched, or founded smaller "titular" churches inside the city walls, so called because of their association with the names of particular donors. Eighteen titular churches claimed foundation before the era of Constantine; by the end of the fifth century, they numbered as many as twenty-five or twenty-eight.

As they had for generations, Rome's bishops took a hand in managing these churches, cemeteries, and shrines, sometimes founding titular churches themselves. Damasus, moreover, took a far more active role in organizing and financing the city's growing number of ecclesiastical sites, remolding their profile in ways that Constantine could have never imagined. In particular, Damasus elevated the cult of saints to a new prominence, officially recognizing the feast days of martyrs associated with the city, restoring and building shrines inscribed with poems about the saints' triumph. Peter stood first and foremost among the martyrs, honored on June 29, the day of his martyrdom, and on February 22, the day he became bishop of Rome. Although the Lateran remained the center of clerical business, the Church of Saint Peter began to emerge as Rome's ritual heart. As part of these plans, Damasus also pushed for the standardization of Rome's liturgical rites, written down and performed in Latin rather than Greek, coordinating feast days, processions, and other ties of religious observance between the major basilica churches and the smaller titular churches throughout the city. (As a sign of his commitment to Latin, Damasus also encouraged Saint Jerome, a leading intellectual of his day, to create a new Latin translation of the Bible, the Vulgate, which became the standard biblical text in the Western Church for the remainder of the Middle Ages.)

These changes from the pagan capital of Romulus and Remus to the spiritual capital of Peter and Paul did not happen quickly. The thorough transformation of Rome's cityscape would take hundreds of years, lasting throughout the fifth, sixth, and seventh centuries. Emperors continued to fund the construction of civic monuments, testimonies to Rome's ancient greatness and symbolic status as the imperial capital, while wealthy pagan aristocrats spent lavish amounts of money – far more than the church at Rome possessed, in fact – on traditional "pagan" ceremonies and civic structures. In one telling episode, the Roman prefect Symmachus fought a losing campaign to preserve the "Altar of Victory" in the Senate House, removed under Gratian, restored, and then abolished for good by Emperor Theodosius I, who formally outlawed pagan cults in 395. According to one of Symmachus's opponents, the Christian poet Prudentius, the third-century martyr Saint Lawrence had long ago envisioned a future when Roman rulers would outlaw pagan sacrifices, banishing the ancient gods from Rome. As described by Prudentius, Lawrence envisioned this situation before his execution: "Grant, Christ, the prayer of your Romans that the city through which you have brought all into a single religion may be Christian. All members of the empire are henceforth allied in the one creed. The conquered world is growing peaceful; peaceful too let its capital be." Looking around him, Prudentius could see the martyr's prayer coming to pass with the building of churches and shrines that marked Rome's Christian past, memorializing what it meant to be both Christian and Roman.[24]

The primacy of Peter

The first Roman bishop who regularly employed the expression "Apostolic See" to describe his position, Damasus did not hesitate to broadcast Rome's claims to primacy due to its foundations by Saint Paul and above all Saint Peter. He did so, in large part, as a response to Constantinople's growing importance as the center of Christian imperial governance. In 381, trying to settle the controversy over Arianism once and for all, Emperor Theodosius I had convened the first general Council of Constantinople, which restated and clarified the orthodox creed crafted at Nicaea. As a catholic ruler, Theodosius valued Rome's eminence and tradition of orthodoxy. In 380, for example, he had issued an edict declaring that the Christian faith of the Roman Empire was the very same faith taught by Saint Peter, observed by the churches at Rome and Alexandria. The third canon of the Council of Constantinople, however, also modified Nicaea's sixth canon, inserting Constantinople into the list of privileged sees including Rome, Alexandria, Antioch, and Jerusalem, awarding the imperial capital a position second only to Rome. From this viewpoint, it only made sense that the "New Rome" should enjoy a place of honor after the "Old Rome."[25]

Damasus refused to recognize this change in Constantinople's status, which suggested that political currency rather than apostolic tradition determined a city's ecclesiastical rank. A council held at Rome in 382 declared in response: "Though all the catholic churches diffused throughout the world are but one bridal chamber of Christ, the holy Roman Church has been set before all the rest not by the decrees of any council, but has obtained primacy by the voice of our

Lord and Savior in the Gospel." As formulated here, the position of metropolitan churches stood above debate, equivocation, or modification – Christ had made Peter his successor, and Peter along with Paul had established the church at Rome, consecrating it by their blood and setting it "above all others in the whole world by their presence and venerable triumph."[26] The matter remained unresolved. For clergy in the East, the bishop of Rome possessed a special dignity, but remained one bishop among many, all of whom shared in Christ's apostolic commission to watch over his Church. For the bishop of Rome, Christ's delegation of authority to the apostles gave priority of place to Saint Peter and by extension his successors, placing them at the apex of the hierarchy that governed the Church. Indeed, with this episode, one can discern the contours of a struggle that would resurface repeatedly over following centuries between the churches of Constantinople and Rome, based on their divergent views of ecclesiastical authority.

As for Damasus, he died in 384. About fifteen years later, the church historian Rufinus of Aquileia translated an apocryphal Greek letter into Latin that claimed to be from Clement, bishop of Rome, to the apostle James, bishop of Jerusalem. This text provided the first detailed description of a critical moment in the history of the Roman Church, when Peter placed his hands on Clement and designated him as his successor to the Apostolic See. Sensing that his martyrdom drew near, Peter had spoken to the assembled congregation of believers as follows:

> Listen to me, my brothers and fellow servants, for I was instructed by He who sent me, our Lord and teacher Jesus Christ. The day of my death draws near. I ordain for you this bishop, Clement, to whom alone I hand over the seat of my preaching and teaching, since, from the beginning up until now, he was my constant companion in every way, and in this manner recognized the truth of my preaching ... for this reason, I hand over to him the power of loosening and binding, given to me by the Lord, so that in each and every way, whatsoever that he might decree on earth might be decreed in Heaven.[27]

Had he still lived, Damasus no doubt would have read this letter with immense satisfaction. One could hardly ask for a more evocative remembrance of apostolic succession at Rome, the basis for the city's bishops to speak as the preeminent voice of Christian authority. This letter and others like it also described how Peter assigned bishops and preachers to all the peoples of the West, making him the ultimate originator of churches in Italy, Spain, Gaul, and elsewhere. By the turn of the fourth century, the recognizable contours of the medieval papacy had begun to emerge. While there might be many popes, fathers who acted as shepherds for their flocks, there was only one heir to Saint Peter and his binding authority over the Church, the pope of Rome.

Chapter 2: Empire and Christendom

In 410, the Visigothic warlord Alaric and his barbarian army plundered the city of Rome. Associated with this particular episode, the word "barbarian" might conjure images of brutish outsiders, bent on the destruction of Roman civilization, a process famously described by the eighteenth-century English historian Edward Gibbon as the "decline and fall of the Roman Empire."[1] The truth of the matter was somewhat more complicated. Like many of the barbarian peoples from the margins of the Roman world, the Goths hardly represented strangers, living along the imperial frontier of the Danube for years. They were also Christians, albeit Arians. Threatened by the marauding Huns, another barbarian people from the Asian steppes, the Visigoths first entered the empire in 376 as settlers and military allies. Famine and abuse by Roman officials soon led to their uprising, culminating in the battle of Adrianople in 378, when the defeated Roman ruler Valens lost his life. An uneasy peace followed between imperial authorities and Alaric, who served as a "master of soldiers" in the Roman army. Rather than a capricious act of savagery, his sack of Rome in 410 is perhaps best understood as a protest against the Roman Empire's broken promises, taking what he felt was rightfully owed to him.

Regardless, this dramatic turn of events shocked contemporaries. By the time that the Visigoths attacked Rome, the city's significance as a center of military and civil administration had been replaced by Constantinople and other cities closer to endangered frontiers. Yet Rome's symbolic importance endured. As Saint Jerome put it, writing from Jerusalem, "The city which had taken the whole world was itself taken." Another leading theologian of the day, Augustine, bishop of Hippo, reacted by starting to compose his masterpiece

The City of God, responding to critics who blamed the empire's turn to Christianity for the fall of the Eternal City.[2] For such contemporaries, however, the Roman Empire did not so much fall as shift its center of gravity more starkly toward the wealthier, cosmopolitan regions of the East. During the fifth through the eighth centuries, the Eastern Roman Empire – labeled the Byzantine Empire by modern historians – continued to embody the authority and majesty of Christian imperial rule. Popes remained loyal subjects to their sovereigns at Constantinople, although, from their perspective, emperors sometimes got carried away in their role as Christ's deputies on earth. Questions of faith and ecclesiastical discipline ultimately belonged to the clergy rather than secular rulers, who remained laymen despite the sacred character of their reign. When the situation called for it, popes did not hesitate to rebuke emperors who overstepped their bounds, treating bishops like lackeys rather than partners, failing to respect the dignity of priests in matters of religious doctrine and discipline. Above all during times of theological controversy among Eastern Christians, Rome's bishops tried with varying degrees of success to intervene as figures above the fray, speaking with the unique authority of Saint Peter.

In their own backyard, popes confronted a shifting political landscape, as imperial power began its slow decompression into the hands of barbarian kings, warlords, and Roman aristocrats, who theoretically remained imperial subjects, but acted without much constraint from Constantinople. In certain instances, especially in Italy, the emperors of Byzantium showed that they still possessed an effective reach – as some defiant popes would learn to their dismay. For the most part, however, Rome's bishops found themselves taking on new roles and responsibilities, not just in clerical but in civic governance, filling the gaps left by the receding tide of empire as best as they could. Similar to other bishops in Western Europe, they reacted, adapted, and took advantage of their altered circumstances, dealing among other local interests with Christian barbarian kings, admittedly less lofty than the emperors at Constantinople and prone to the heresy of Arianism. Similar to their imperial counterparts, at certain junctures, such kings likewise challenged the papacy's integrity, threatening Saint Peter's heirs.

With the emergence and rapid expansion of Islam in the seventh and eighth centuries, the beleaguered Byzantine Empire faced an even greater challenge to its political dominion, fighting for its survival when Arab forces and their allies overran vast territories in northern Africa and the Middle East. Increasingly alienated from their imperial sovereigns, popes faced in the West an ever more balkanized Christian community of prelates, monasteries, and local saints' shrines that carried out their day-to-day business without oversight or input from any outside authority. Nevertheless, as Christianity sank deeper roots into the Western regions of the defunct Roman Empire and spread beyond its ghostly borders, new opportunities arose for the papacy to offer a reassuring and sometimes cajoling voice of unity in a world that no longer seemed to possess a political center, but shared a common Latin language, religious culture, and sense of connection through Saint Peter – the world of medieval Christendom.

The Papacy and the Later Roman Empire

What we now call the medieval papacy emerged from the profound dislocation of Roman imperial power, fragmenting in the West, enduring and transforming its character in the East. During this era, the popes of Rome tried to enact their claims of primacy as an ecclesiastical reality in both the Western and Eastern Churches, addressing questions of church practice and discipline, as well as controversies of great theological significance. They also faced profound divisions among the faithful, dangerous challenges to their position, and the uncomfortable fact that Christians did not always embrace the Apostolic See's self-proclaimed primacy.

Rome's spiritual empire

During the years after Pope Damasus, Rome's bishops continued to insist that they possessed a special authority to determine the norms of the Christian faith. Among Western communities, they found a relatively sympathetic audience for this assertion. For one thing, while cities such as Milan boasted of their own rights and venerable Christian traditions, Rome possessed no ecclesiastical competitors in the West that could match its former imperial glories and apostolic tradition. Pope Damasus's successor, Siricius (384–99), highlighted this fact by issuing the first recognizable papal decretal in 385, directed to Bishop Himerius of Tarragona in Spain. Modeled after imperial decrees, decretals responded to questions or problems raised for the bishop of Rome's consideration, yielding a response meant as the final word on the subject. In the decretal to Himerius, Siricius addressed a range of issues from the excommunication of heretics to the problem of priests who violated their vows of chastity, claiming that the pope of Rome bore responsibility for all such burdens, or rather, "the blessed apostle Peter bears them though us, he who, so we believe, protects us in each and every matter of governance and safeguards his successors." As Siricius wrote in another decretal to the bishops of Italy, the "care of all churches" remained his responsibility. In still another decretal to the bishops of Gaul, he asserted, "one tradition ought to endure. If there is one tradition, one discipline ought to be kept throughout all the churches." That tradition and discipline, of course, flowed from Rome.[3]

After the brief papacy of Anastasius I (399–401), Pope Innocent I (401–17) followed Siricius's lead and pushed the declaration of Roman primacy even farther. In a decretal sent to Victricius of Rouen in 404, for example, he emphasized that the key to maintaining ecclesiastical discipline lay with "observing the same forms that the Roman Church holds." The pope also affirmed that all "major causes," that is, important legal cases, should be referred to Rome as the final court of appeals.[4] It is unclear how Innocent reacted to the Visigothic sack of his see in 410. He was not even present when Alaric assaulted Rome, visiting the imperial stronghold at Ravenna to participate in unsuccessful negotiations for peace between the menacing barbarian leader and Emperor Honorius. He only returned to Rome in 412, presumably staying away because of the damage and disruption caused by the city's plundering. The pope and his immediate successors, however, including Zosimus (417–18), Boniface I (418–22), Celestine I (422–32), and Sixtus III (432–40), plainly had to confront the uncomfortable fact that the stability of the Roman Empire in the West could no longer be taken for granted.

It remained for Pope Leo I (440–61), sometimes called Leo the Great, to turn this disturbing situation to his advantage, solidifying Rome's claims of supreme clerical leadership in ways that left a significant legacy for the papal office. As bishop, Leo remained first and foremost a shepherd for his flock, offering spiritual and moral guidance to those under his pastoral care, the leading figure of Rome's liturgical life and worship. He also found new roles thrust upon him in the absence of strong imperial and civic authorities. In 452, for example, the pope joined Roman emissaries who prevented another attack on Rome by the marauding Huns; in 455, he helped to intercede with an army of Vandals menacing the city. For Leo, such barbarian incursions threatened the political order of the Roman Empire, but they failed to destroy the higher unity of the Christian Church that remained centered on Rome. Peter and Paul, he believed, not

Romulus and Remus, represented the true founders of Rome, the creators of a "spiritual empire" under the peace of Christ that had subdued more peoples than the "labors of war" waged by the pagan Romans. Whatever happened to empire, the pope presided over an enduring Christian order.

In a series of sermons commemorating his election as pope on September 29, 440, along with other sermons that celebrated the feasts of Peter and Paul, Leo stressed Peter's living presence in his office. "Regard him as present in the lowliness of my person," Leo declared on one such occasion. "In him continues to reside the responsibility for all shepherds, along with the protection of those sheep entrusted to them. His dignity does not fade even in an unworthy heir." Regardless of who currently held the position, Peter still presided over the Apostolic See. Although Christ had granted the power to "loosen and bind" to all of the apostles, he had set Peter above the others, entrusting him with the commission to "feed his sheep" (Jn. 21:17) and watch over his Church. Using the terminology of Roman law, Leo stressed the status of the pope as Peter's heir, the legal successor to his office as the head of the Church. Harnessing the spirit of earlier decretals, he insisted upon Rome's status as the final court of appeals, the source of ultimate juridical power over other churches. Leo even began to employ the term *principatus*, an imperial term denoting "preeminence" or "dominion," to describe the papacy, although he never failed to appreciate the possibility of his own failings and the need for humility in his exalted position.[5]

Leo's involvement in the case of Hilary, bishop of Arles, displayed the practical consequences of these theoretical claims. When word reached the pope that Hilary had overstepped his bounds, appointing other prelates at will, traveling in the company of soldiers, and plundering church property (or so his critics claimed), Leo declared him cut off from the communion of the faithful, overriding the decision of a local council that had found in Hilary's favor. As the pope wrote to the bishops of Gaul in July 445, through his actions Hilary had tried to "subject you to his authority while not allowing himself to be under the jurisdiction of the blessed apostle, Peter." Anyone who denied the primacy of Saint Peter, Leo added, "buries himself in hell."[6] Hilary, under pressure from the pope's unfavorable judgment, traveled to Rome to appeal Leo's decision and later sent legates to the city as part of his ongoing and ultimately unsuccessful effort to swing Leo around to his side. After Hilary died in 449, his successor quickly patched things up with Rome, a sign of the papacy's growing clout as an arbiter and judge in the ecclesiastical business of the Western Church.

Pope Leo and controversy over Christ's nature

In his dealings with the Eastern Church, Leo found other, high-profile chances to speak as Peter's heir. Although the bitter disputes over Arianism had died down, new and equally disruptive controversies had arisen in the East over the nature of Christ. These included the teachings of Nestorius, patriarch of Constantinople, who argued for a considerable degree of separation between Christ's human and divine natures. From this perspective, the human being Jesus Christ, a man uniquely linked to God, had been born of the Virgin Mary, suffered, and died on the cross, but God himself had not. Reacting to "Nestorianism," as orthodox Christians labeled this heretical doctrine, Nestorius's opponents formulated a position known as Miaphysitism (called Monophysitism by its critics), which stressed in contrast Christ's unitary, divine nature. For still others, either position threatened the essential meaning of the Incarnation – the complete unity of man and God, manifest in Christ, fully and distinctly human and divine, bridging the gap between Heaven and Earth for human salvation.

Even before Pope Leo got involved, Rome's popes had not stood on the sidelines during this latest Christological controversy. When Celestine I had received a dossier of documents about Nestorius's teachings from one of the patriarch's foes, Cyril of Alexandria, he summoned a council at Rome to review the matter in August 430. Celestine and others were also troubled by Nestorius's rejection of the title "Mother of God" for the Virgin Mary. The council condemned his teachings as heretical and called upon him to renounce his views or suffer excommunication. During the course of this dispute, Celestine insisted that all Christians, including those in the East, formed part of his flock, giving the pope the right if not obligation to make pronouncements about the orthodox faith. His legates took part in the ecumenical council of Ephesus starting in June 431, which affirmed the Nicaean Creed and also condemned Nestorius. Celestine expressed great satisfaction when he heard the news, not realizing that the battles over Christ's divinity and humanity were just heating up.

About two decades later, the Byzantine patriarch Flavian condemned one of Nestorius's outspoken opponents, Eutyches, for going too far in the other direction and emphasizing Christ's divinity to the detriment of his humanity. In 449, Emperor Theodosius II called another council at Ephesus to hear this case. When Eutyches appealed to Rome, Pope Leo leapt into action. In a series of letters sent to the emperor and Eastern prelates, the pope denounced both Nestorius and Eutyches as two "enemies" of the Church for failing to recognize Christ's full and equal natures as human and divine. As Leo proclaimed in his so-called *Tome*, a lengthy letter sent in June 449 to Flavian: "In the whole and perfect nature of the true man, then, the true God was born, complete in His own nature, complete in ours."[7] Addressing the bishops at Ephesus, Leo explained that Emperor Theodosius had asked the Apostolic See to "effect a holy settlement" of the current dispute. Nonetheless, the assembly – later called the Robber Synod by its detractors, starting with Pope Leo – found in Eutyches' favor and rejected Leo's *Tome*.

In the council's aftermath, Theodosius continued to support its verdict, despite Leo's relentless insistence that he nullify its outcome. When the emperor died in 450, his sister Pulcheria's new husband, Marcian, assumed the throne and reversed course on many of Theodosius's policies. Showing more sympathy for Leo's views, Marcian summoned another ecumenical council at Chalcedon in 451 to revisit the unresolved disagreements over Christ's nature. This time the synod reached far more favorable conclusions from Leo's perspective, condemning Eutyches and reaffirming Christ's equal divinity and humanity. According to one report, when they heard Leo's *Tome* read aloud at the council, the assembled clergy proclaimed, "Peter has spoken through Leo!" Later generations of Western Christians would remember this moment as a triumph for papal authority. Based upon his position as the heir to Saint Peter, Leo had emerged as a decisive voice, the guarantor of orthodoxy in the face of heresy.

The fact remained, however, that a considerable number of churchmen rejected Leo's "holy settlement," and the disputes over Christ's nature continued, eventually splitting the Eastern Church into a number of rival communities. Even those who approved of the pope's intervention hardly viewed him as the final word on the matter. Leo himself dragged his feet before formally ratifying Chalcedon's outcome, angry over the council's twenty-eighth canon that restated Constantinople's position as second only to Rome in the ecclesiastical hierarchy. Like Damasus before him, Leo viewed this claim as an illicit innovation suggesting that Rome's former status as the imperial capital – a position currently held by Constantinople – formed the basis for its primacy. Under pressure from the imperial family and Eastern theologians, Leo finally acknowledged Chalcedon's ecumenical statement of the faith in 453, although he and his successors continued to reject Constantinople's elevation as the "New Rome." Peter might have spoken through Leo at Chalcedon, but the universal harmony promised by the apostle's voice remained elusive.

The two powers

Before the Council of Chalcedon, Pope Leo had praised Emperor Theodosius II for protecting God's Church. "You have the mind not only of a king, but also of a priest," the pope wrote, "since, aside from your cares for the realm and people, you have a most devoted concern for the Christian religion."[8] In this case, Leo celebrated the majesty of the Roman Empire's ruler, a partner for orthodox churchmen in the struggles against heresy. Likewise, during his dispute with Hilary of Arles, Leo had gladly acknowledged an edict issued in 445 by the Western Emperor Valentinian III, declaring that Rome held uncontested ecclesiastical primacy over the churches of the West. In other instances, however, Roman popes tried to draw an unmistakable line in the sand between the roles of bishops and temporal rulers in the life of the Church. Emperors, sometimes with powerful directness, could act in God's name in ways that popes could not, and not always in accordance with Rome's teachings.

Such proved to be the case during the Acacian Schism, so called after the patriarch of Constantinople, Acacius, who sought points of theological compromise with Miaphysite Christians after his election in 471. The current emperor, Zeno, trying to reconcile estranged Miaphysites with Constantinople, endorsed Acacius's *Henotikon* in 482, a statement of faith that did not mention Chalcedon or Pope Leo's *Tome*. Seeing this statement as an affront against orthodoxy, Pope Simplicius (468–83) objected and furthermore accused Acacius of keeping company with known heretics. His successor, Pope Felix III (483–92), formally condemned Acacius in 484, insisting that the church at Constantinople expunge his name from its diptyches, the formal list of the city's patriarchs. The next pope, Gelasius I (492–96), likewise kept up the pressure on his Eastern coreligionists. In a letter sent in 494 to Zeno's successor, Emperor Anastasius I, the pope berated him for his refusal to follow Rome's lead in matters of faith, failing to recognize the priority of priestly authority over secular rulers. Gelasius insisted:

> There are two powers, august emperor, by which this world is chiefly ruled, namely, the sacred authority of the priests and

the royal power. Of these that of the priests is the more weighty, since they have to render an account for even the kings of men in the divine judgment. You are also aware, dear son, that while you are permitted honorably to rule over human kind, yet in things divine you bow your head humbly before the leaders of the clergy and await from their hands the means of your salvation. In the reception and proper disposition of the heavenly mysteries you recognize that you should be subordinate rather than superior to the religious order, and that in these matters you depend on their judgment rather than wish to force them to follow your will.[9]

With this statement, Gelasius articulated an idea that would reappear time and again in future papal correspondence, decretals, and canon law – the notion that God ordained "two powers" to govern the world, that of priests and kings, clerical and secular figures, with a clear sense that temporal rulers must ultimately answer to those who held sacerdotal office.

The Laurentian Schism

Closer to home, Rome's bishops faced more immediate challenges to their priestly authority. Over the previous century, various barbarian groups had continued to seize direct political control over the Western Roman Empire, including the Vandals in northern Africa, the Visigoths in Spain, and the Franks in Gaul. In 476, a barbarian strongman named Odoacer had deposed the puppet emperor Romulus Augustulus, marking the end of the imperial office in the West. Seventeen years later, Theodoric, leader of the Ostrogoths – another Romanized barbarian people – assassinated Odoacer and assumed control of Italy. Similar to other barbarian kings, Theodoric continued to profess his loyalty to the rulers of Constantinople, although he effectively reigned with autonomy over the Goths and Romans, two peoples living somewhat uncomfortably in a single kingdom. Relations between the Goths and Romans suffered additional complications due to the fact that the Ostrogoths, like many of the barbarian successors to Roman power, professed Arian Christianity. As a result, although Pope Gelasius enjoyed friendly enough relations with Theodoric, his successors found themselves walking a tightrope between the Byzantine Empire and the Ostrogoths, answerable not just to emperors but to Arian Christian kings. Popes also had to struggle with Rome's senators, other civil officials, and aristocratic families, whose interests did not always align with those of their bishop.

After the death of Pope Anastasius II (496–98), a division broke out between supporters of the newly elected Pope Symmachus (498–515), who continued to take a hardline stance on the Acacian Schism, and an opposition candidate, Laurentius, favored by Roman nobles who sought reconciliation with the imperial capital. The conflict between the two factions also involved a dispute over the pope's direct administrative control of titular churches, including his right to sell their goods and properties. The resulting "Laurentian Schism" illustrated the complex tangle of loyalties and interests that characterized Rome at the turn of the sixth century. Theodoric initially supported Symmachus, who had support from the majority of the Roman clergy. The party backing Laurentius, however, appealed to Theodoric, accusing Symmachus of sexual misconduct and misusing church property, among other charges. When Symmachus refused to appear before the king for judgment at Ravenna, he lost some of Theodoric's goodwill. Although a council held at Rome in 502 upheld Symmachus's election and cleared him of all charges, Laurentius remained in contention for the papal office, installing himself in the Lateran church, while Symmachus resided in Saint Peter's basilica. Their struggle, which sometimes turned violent, persisted until 506, when Laurentius finally withdrew from Rome.

Among other consequences, the Laurentian Schism contributed to another stage in the formation of papal memory, marked by the forgery of documents and histories that legitimated the bishop of Rome's powers and privileges. One of Symmachus's supporters crafted the so-called "Symmachan forgeries," a collection of texts emphasizing Roman primacy, including the declaration that "no one can judge" the Apostolic See and its occupant, the source of justice for all, not "the emperor nor the whole clergy nor kings nor people." In addition to claiming that the pope stood above the judgment of others, these documents stressed the pope's ultimate rights over church property, thereby addressing the dispute over titular churches. The Symmachan forgeries took their place alongside genuine and false decretals, laws, and histories in the papal archives of the period. Around this time, other spurious works appeared on the scene. These included *On the Primitive Church and the Council of Nicaea*, which featured Constantine telling the bishops assembled at the council that they stood above any earthly judgment, and the *Legend of Saint Sylvester*, which first described how Pope Sylvester baptized Constantine, converting him and cleansing him of his leprosy.[10]

A similar version of events featured in the *Book of Popes*, a history of the papacy begun *c*.535–40 that traced the origins of the Roman Church from the time of Saint Peter to the present.[11] Subsequently revised and periodically updated, the *Book of Popes* represented a semi-official record of papal history that did not even pretend to be even-handed, produced as it was during the fallout from the Laurentian Schism – it presented Symmachus and not Laurentius as the true pope of Rome, likewise choosing "real" popes and "anti-popes" in former instances of schism. Rather than an outright fabrication, for those involved in its production, this one-sided history no doubt seemed like a salvage operation, a recovery of details from the hazy past, filling in the blanks in a story believed to be true. This work also offered an historical record of the papacy's donations of property, liturgical vessels, and other goods to basilica and titular churches around Rome, providing a written complement to the ongoing transformation of the city's landscape from a pagan capital into a Christian one. For the pope – a title increasingly reserved in the West for the bishop of Rome and no other – to stand above earthly judgment and exercise priestly authority over worldly rulers, the past had to speak loudly and clearly, leaving no doubt about the lofty dignity of the Apostolic See.

Eastern empire resurgent

In 518, the election of the orthodox Byzantine Emperor Justin opened the door to a rapprochement between the churches of Rome and Constantinople. In a moment of doctrinal triumph for the papacy, Justin pressured prominent Eastern bishops into accepting a formula of the faith crafted by Pope Hormisdas (514–23), condemning Acacius and ending the Acacian Schism on highly favorable terms for Rome. Once again, a theological dispute in the Eastern Church offered the pope a chance to speak as orthodoxy's defender. The Ostrogothic rulers of Italy, however, took a dim view of this reconciliation between the pope and the Byzantine emperor. Reacting to Justin's crackdown on Arian Christians, including the closure of Arian churches in Constantinople and the banning of Arians from holding civil or military offices, Theodoric dispatched Pope John I (523–26) to Constantinople to negotiate with the orthodox ruler. If he intended to treat John as his errand-boy, the plan backfired. The imperial capital rolled out the welcome mat for John, cementing his warm relations with the emperor. When John returned to Ravenna in 526, Theodoric accused him of failing to reverse Justin's anti-Arian measures. Detained at Ravenna, physically abused, John died shortly after, victim of the dangerous middle ground between the increasingly antagonistic Ostrogoths and Byzantines.

The short pontificates of Felix IV (526–30), Boniface II (530–32), and John II (533–35) followed, all of them on friendly terms with the next Ostrogothic king, Athalaric. Originally named after the pagan god Mercury, John II chose a new papal name upon election, making him the first pope known to do so, a practice that later became customary. In 536, Athalaric's successor Theodahad sent Pope Agapitus (535–36) on another diplomatic mission to Constantinople. Theodahad and everyone else could see that Justin's successor, Emperor Justinian, had set plans in motion for a military invasion of Italy. When Agapitus died in Constantinople, the papal envoy in the city, Vigilius, returned to Rome with the pope's body, hoping to secure his own election to the Apostolic See. According to later accusations, Vigilius had become overly friendly with Justinian's wife, Theodora, a committed Miaphysite Christian, taking gifts and money from her in return for pledges of future cooperation. Reaching Rome, which had been recently seized from the Ostrogoths by Byzantine forces, Vigilius discovered that the city's clergy and nobles had already chosen a new pope, Silverius (536–37). Undeterred, he managed to have Silverius banished and assumed the papal office for himself in 537.

Vigilius might have regretted his eagerness to become pope. In 543, as part of his effort to unify Eastern Christians in the Byzantine Empire, Justinian condemned the so-called Three Chapters, select writings by three deceased theologians, Theodore of Mopsuestia, Theodoret of Cyrus, and Ibas of Edessa, all despised by Miaphysite Christians for their emphasis on Christ's two natures. By doing so, the emperor hoped to appeal to Miaphysite communities without directly challenging the Council of Chalcedon. Western bishops, however, denounced his condemnation of the Three Chapters as a sneak attack on Chalcedonian orthodoxy. Despite his close connections to Empress Theodora, Vigilius refused to sign the document. In 545, Justinian ordered his arrest and had the pope hauled to Constantinople. The two briefly patched up their differences and experienced another falling out. On two occasions, Vigilius tried unsuccessfully to flee the city. They finally agreed to summon a new council at Constantinople in 553. When the council affirmed the Three Chapters' condemnation, Vigilius again balked at supporting the decision. At the emperor's prompting, the assembled clergy condemned the pope and placed him under house arrest. Exhausted,

Vigilius finally agreed to the condemnation of the Three Chapters and endorsed the council's outcome. Released in 555, he died en route back to Rome.

Whatever claims they made to the contrary, popes could in fact be judged by others, found lacking, and sometimes suffer extreme consequences. Beyond its immediate fallout, the controversy over the Three Chapters exposed a growing gap between Christians in the West and the East, a divergence in their sense of who exercised authority to determine proper doctrine, if not their ability to agree on the norms and practices of their faith. After all of his flip-flopping on the Three Chapters, moreover, Vigilius had become extremely unpopular in Rome and its surroundings. When his successor Pelagius (556–61) eventually accepted the Three Chapters' condemnation, it further eroded confidence among Western churchmen in the papacy. Some bishops in Italy refused to recognize Pelagius as pope, while others in Gaul mocked him for changing course on Rome's opposition to Justinian's theological violations.

Meanwhile, Italy had fallen into a state of exhaustion and decay. By the time that Justinian declared the official victory of his forces over the Ostrogoths in 554, the so-called Gothic Wars had devastated much of the peninsula. Coming on the heels of this conflict, a newly arrived barbarian people, the Lombards, invaded northern Italy starting in 568, violently seizing cities and territories from Byzantine officials and local powers. An outbreak of plague, first hitting Rome in 542, compounded an already desperate situation, contributing to famine, economic stagnation, and a rapid decline in the city's inhabitants. Rome's population, which had numbered around one million citizens in the era of Nero, was reduced to somewhere around one hundred thousand residents, perhaps even less than that. Pelagius I's successors, John III (561–74), Benedict I (575–79), and Pelagius II (579–90), struggled against this tide of misfortune. The bishops of Rome presided over a city – and looked outward upon a world – in crisis.

Rome and the Christian West

In the popular imagination, the early medieval centuries represent Europe's "Dark Ages," a time of pessimism, violence, and disorder after the waning of the Western Roman Empire. There are grains of truth to this outmoded but persistent image. That same era, however, also witnessed the emergence of new institutions, societies, and cultural forms, a process often associated with Europe's birth or making as a Christian civilization, a diversity of kingdoms, churches, and peoples sharing a common religion that looked toward Rome as its spiritual center. Admittedly, one should not exaggerate the papacy's role in creating medieval Christendom, which consisted of profoundly localized societies – "micro-Christendoms," as the eminent scholar Peter Brown calls them – that did not depend upon Rome for direction.[12] At the same time, as contemporaries themselves recognized and celebrated, the Apostolic See of Saint Peter occupied a special place in their religious lives that transcended such limited horizons.

Gregory the Great: servant of God's servants

Situated in these times of trauma and innovation, Pope Gregory I (590–604) stands out as a figure of remarkable importance for the historical development of the papacy, if not for medieval Europe as a whole. This evaluation would no doubt have struck Gregory himself as ironic. Much like Pope Leo the Great, Gregory the Great made his decisions based on immediate pastoral needs, pressing problems, and unexpected opportunities. When he pondered the future, he seems to have contemplated apocalyptic trials for God's people followed by Christ's return in the Final Judgment. The time to act was now, Gregory believed, before the end of all things, whether acting as the shepherd for his flock, administering church properties, caring for the poor, or spreading Christianity among the peoples of the world who had not yet embraced the Gospel.

Born around 540 into a distinguished Roman family (Pope Felix III was his great-great-grandfather), Gregory received a fine education and served in Rome's civic government, appointed prefect in 572–73. The following year, however, he founded a monastery dedicated to Saint Andrew on family property and withdrew into a life of monastic obedience. For the remainder of his days, no matter how involved he became in ecclesiastical business, Gregory continued to express himself in the language and emotional idioms of a monk, a figure devoted to the inward contemplation of God, invested in the renunciation of temporal goods and pleasures. Although he tried to leave the world behind, the world came knocking on his monastery door. Made a deacon in 579, he traveled to Constantinople to serve as Pelagius II's envoy in the city. Returning to Rome six years later, Gregory reentered the monastery of Saint Andrew, but in 590 accepted his election as pope when Pelagius died of plague.

In a letter sent to his former companion John, patriarch of Constantinople, Gregory revealed his mixed feelings about assuming the burdens and responsibilities of the papal office. As he wrote to John:

> But because, while unworthy and infirm, I have taken on an old and very broken down ship (for the waves pour in from all sides and the rotten planks, shaken by daily and powerful storms, suggest a shipwreck), I ask by our almighty Lord that in this danger of mine you stretch forth the hand of your prayer.[13]

However much he protested, Gregory clearly possessed considerable shrewdness, rising as he did to the top position of the Roman Church. One typically did not become pope by chance or accident. At the same time, it is easy to understand his reservations about assuming the duties of Rome's bishop, a position fraught with spiritual hazards, earthly responsibilities, and more than its fair share of headaches.

Although on friendly terms with the Byzantine patriarch, the new pope did not hesitate to rebuke John for using the title "universal patriarch," employed by the bishops of Constantinople since the time of Acacian Schism. For Gregory, this presumption – already decried by Pelagius II – threatened to diminish the honor of other Eastern sees such as Alexandria and Antioch, not to mention Rome. This disagreement lasted for years to come. Closer to home, the pope faced more pressing problems. After decades of war, economic stagnation, and disease, Rome effectively lacked institutions for civil government. Like other bishops in the scaled-down world after empire, Gregory assumed responsibility for urban management, drawing upon papal properties in southern Italy, Sicily, northern Africa, and elsewhere to feed Rome's inhabitants. Unlike other bishops, as pope Gregory numbered among the largest landlords in Europe, overseeing hundreds of estates attached to the Roman Church. For someone who desired the quiet contemplation of the monastery, worrying about grain prices, unjust taxation, and the abuse of farmers must have seemed like a relentless distraction from what really mattered. Confronting the Lombards with little or no help from the overstretched and ineffective Byzantine Empire, Gregory also found himself responsible for Rome's military defense. Searching for a long-term solution to this problem, he negotiated with the Arian barbarians to spare the city, cultivating a relationship with the Lombard Queen Theodelinda, who favored catholic Christianity.

Facing these and other demands, Gregory reconciled tensions between the active life of the bishop and the contemplative life of the monk through a profound sense of service to others, captured in his use of the title "Servant of God's Servants." Whatever distractions he faced, Gregory found ample time to write, leaving a legacy of influential Christian texts about the burdens of the world and how a proper prelate should care for his charges. In his *Commentary on the Book of Job*, begun during his time in Constantinople, Gregory meditated upon the nature of human existence as a condition of exile from God. This subject formed a common theme in Christian thought, yet for Gregory Job's suffering must have seemed particularly telling for those living in an age of uncertainty marked by war, famine, and plague. His *Dialogues*, a collection of stories about recent miracles and Italian saints including the monastic father Benedict of Nursia, illustrated the power of God's grace and compassion for believers surrounded by suffering, temptation, and evil. In the *Pastoral Rule*, written after his election as pope, Gregory tackled the role of bishops and other rectors in the Church, who straddled the divide between the affairs of the world and those of the spirit – a perilous position for experts in the care of souls. As Gregory well knew, a bishop needed to know how to wield practical power, but he also needed to be more than a crafty administrator. Responsible for the well-being of others, he would ultimately answer to God, measured not just for his own shortcomings but also for those of his flock.[14]

For Gregory, the coming of the Final Judgment did not seem too far off. Everywhere he looked, the pope saw signs of Antichrist at work, trying to undo the labors of the faithful and lead them astray. As he wrote on one occasion, describing the violent arrival of the Lombards:

The population of Italy, which had grown vast, like a rich harvest of grain, was cut down to wither away. Cities were sacked, fortifications overthrown, churches burned, monasteries and cloisters destroyed. Farms were abandoned, and the countryside, uncultivated, became a wilderness. The land was no longer occupied by its owners, and wild beasts roamed the fields where so many people had once made their homes. I do not know what is happening elsewhere, but in this land of ours the world is not merely announcing its end, it is pointing directly to it.[15]

At moments like this, Gregory no doubt exaggerated the apocalyptic devastation of his day for dramatic effect. He never predicted a specific time for the end of the world. Like most "respectable" Christian thinkers, he believed that only God knew the hour of the end and resisted the urge to make concrete predictions that might fail to come true. The "imminent" apocalypse could be days, weeks, or years away, perhaps even more than that. Nevertheless, the pope believed that history represented a cosmic battle between the forces of good and evil, leaving each and every Christian – including the bishop of Rome – with a choice to make about how they would comport themselves and carry out the Lord's work in the time that remained to them.

Mission to the Anglo-Saxons

Pope Gregory's conviction that the end of days lay closer than farther away did not fill him with a sense of hopelessness or despair. On the contrary, if time was running out, doing the Lord's work became all the more important, above all spreading the word of God among non-Christians, including Jews and pagans. In the case of the Jews, the pope wrote to fellow bishops in places such as Marseilles and Sicily about the need to avoid violence against them, instead "inviting them" to believe in Christ through the "sweetness of preaching and the coming terror of future judgment." In another case, Gregory addressed the problem of pagan peasants on Sardinia, people whom he described as "given over to idolatry." Addressing the nobles of the island about these rustics living on their estates, he called upon the landowners to "restrain them from the error of idolatry, so that, by leading them led back to the faith, you may make almighty God amenable towards yourselves."[16]

In 596–97, looking farther afield, Gregory directed a group of forty missionaries under the leadership of a monk named Augustine, former prior at the monastery of Saint Andrew, to establish a new church in the Anglo-Saxon kingdom of Kent. The British Isles hardly represented unknown territory for Christians, who had already spread their faith in the region during the waning days of Roman imperial power. By the sixth century, monks from Ireland were fostering their own distinctive brand of Christianity among the Anglo-Saxons. En route, Augustine and his companions passed through the neighboring kingdom of the Franks, a barbarian people that had settled in Roman Gaul, ruled by the catholic family of the Merovingians since the conversion of King Clovis around 500. Bertha, the Frankish-born wife of Kent's ruler, King Ethelbert, professed Christianity in the king's household before the first missionaries from Rome arrived with their display of books, incense-burners, and liturgical vestments. What the Romans offered to the Anglo-Saxons was the *right kind* of Christianity, as they understood it, a church that looked toward the pope of Rome for spiritual guidance, following Roman teachings, rituals, and ecclesiastical discipline.[17]

From a distance, Gregory supported the new church among the Anglo-Saxons. He dispatched letters of advice and encouragement to the nearby Frankish kingdom, seeking support for the Anglo-Saxon mission from the Merovingian Queen Brunhilde, while writing directly to Ethelbert, Bertha, and Augustine, who was later made archbishop of Canterbury and received his *pallium* – the ritual garment of a bishop's office – from Rome. As with his other duties as pope, Gregory approached the conversion of Kent with a combination of lofty ideals and pastoral attention to the daily needs of Christian life, showing a pragmatic flexibility at some points, striking a firm stance at others. In a letter sent to Bertha in June 601, he praised her for her support of Augustine and her efforts to bring her husband to acknowledge Christ. Addressing Ethelbert in an accompanying letter, he called upon him in martial terms to "extend the Christian faith among the races subject to you, redouble your righteous enthusiasm in their conversion, hunt down the worship of their idols, and overturn the building of their temples." Writing to Mellitus, another missionary who later joined Augustine, Gregory offered advice on how to deal with pagan sites in Kent. In this letter, perhaps mindful of his audience, the pope took a different tack than he did when writing to Ethelbert, stating that:

> the temples of the idols among that people ought not to be destroyed at all, but the idols themselves, which are inside them, should be destroyed. Let water be blessed and sprinkled in the same temples, and let altars be constructed and relics placed there for if those temples have been well constructed, it is necessary that they should be changed from the cult of demons to the worship of the true God.[18]

In other letters, the pope adopted an equally moderate tone, writing about the need to gather religious customs from the churches in Rome and Frankish Gaul, "blending" them together in the church of the English, as it was "still new in the faith." Paying attention to issues of pastoral care, Gregory offered guidance on a host of problems ranging from marriage practices to the theft of church property to whether a pregnant woman should be baptized. (His answer to the latter question was affirmative.) On another occasion, he praised Augustine for his own deeds, declaring that through him God had "expelled the darkness of errors" from the English people and flooded them "with the light of holy faith, as they now trample the idols with the most blameless of minds." At the same time, the pope warned him about the dangers of vanity or taking too much pride in the miracles that God had worked through him. Constant vigilance was necessary: Temptation, evil, and the wiles of Antichrist posed an ever present danger.[19]

The road from Rome to Britain

Gregory's sponsorship of the Roman mission to Kent had set in motion an historically important connection between northern reaches of Europe and Rome, understood not as the former imperial capital but as the Apostolic See. When the pope died in 604, however, neither he nor his contemporaries could have foreseen the long-term implications of the Roman Church's outreach to the Anglo-Saxons. The *Book of Popes* offered only a brief entry about Gregory and did not even mention his connection with the far-off people. To its author, no doubt, the mission to that distant island must have seemed of marginal interest, if he even knew about it.

Time demonstrated quite the opposite. For seventh-century Northumbrian churchmen such as Benedict Biscop (also known as Baducing) and Wilfrid, bishop of York, the link between the British islands and Rome played a vital role in connecting their Christian community to the wider world, transcending the limitations of their localized age. Baducing, who founded the monasteries of Jarrow and Wearmouth, made six visits to Rome, bringing back relics and books with him. Wilfrid, who accompanied Baducing on a pilgrimage to Rome around 653, belonged to the retinue of King Oswy of Northumbria. At the king's court, he pushed for the "Romanizing" of the church in Northumbria, observing the Roman practice of dating Easter, giving monks Roman-style tonsures, and following Roman rites along with other ecclesiastical practices. All of these traditions ran contrary to the teachings, habits, and rituals of Irish Christians, who had sunk deep roots in Northumbria. In 664, Oswy convened a synod at Whitby, declaring that those who served God should "observe one rule of life" and "not differ in the celebration of heavenly sacraments." During the deliberations, Wilfrid debated with a prominent Irish bishop, Coleman, each arguing for the soundness and orthodoxy of their religious rites, until Wilfrid played his trump card – the teachings of the Roman Church could be traced back to Saint Peter, who held the keys to Heaven. Referring to Peter and by extension his successors, Oswy replied: "Then, I tell you, since he is the doorkeeper I will not contradict him; but I intended to obey his commands in everything to the best of my knowledge and ability."[20]

At least, this is how the Venerable Bede, a monk writing at Wearmouth and Jarrow around 731, remembered the synod in his *Ecclesiastical History of the English People.* Bede also chronicled Theodore of Tarsus's arrival on the island, a Greek-speaking cleric of Eastern origins, sent by Pope Vitalian (657–72) after requests from King Oswy of Northumbria and King Egbert of Kent. Vitalian instructed Theodore to educate the Christians of the island in Roman – not Greek, the pope carefully added – teachings, rituals, and practices, including proper liturgical chants. Before Theodore departed, the pope consecrated him archbishop of Canterbury, chief see of the English Church. According to Bede, Theodore followed the pope's instructions eagerly and efficiently. Perhaps not surprisingly, such efforts to cultivate uniformity introduced new tensions into the region. Wilfred, for example, temporarily expelled from his see by King Oswy's successor, resisted what he saw as Theodore of Tarsus's encroachment on York's ecclesiastical rights and jurisdiction. Such disagreements, however, did nothing to alter the big picture. For Bede, the mission sent by Gregory the Great, the decision made at Whitby, and Theodore of Tarsus's pastoral activities led to an outcome that the history-writing monk already knew as an accomplished fact – the fate of the English Church lay with Rome.

Rome, the Franks, and Christian frontiers

Among other consequences, the Roman mission to the Anglo-Saxons also tightened the bonds between the Roman and Frankish churches. Since the conversion of the Frankish ruler Clovis to catholic Christianity around the year 500, the Franks had felt the attraction of Rome, making pilgrimages to the "threshold of Saint Peter," bringing sacred relics and books back with them much like Baducing and Wilfrid would do in Northumbria generations later. The story of two such pilgrims, told by the sixth-century Frankish bishop Gregory of Tours, captures a sense of Rome's special sanctity and the power of local saints, the push and pull of wider and narrower horizons that characterized the age. According to Gregory, the parents of a deaf and dumb man from Angers asked a deacon, who was traveling to Rome to acquire holy relics, if he would take their son along with him. They believed that if he could "visit the tombs of the blessed apostles he would immediately be cured." The deacon and his new companion set out for Rome, but before ever leaving Gaul encountered the holy man named Hospicius, who healed the deaf and dumb man by his prayers. The deacon was awestruck: "I was on my way to Peter, I was going to Paul and Lawrence, and all the others who have glorified Rome with their blood. I have found them all here. In this very spot I have discovered them!"[21]

Gregory does not say whether the pilgrims in question continued on their way to Rome or not. Regardless, over the following centuries, such networks of travel and exchange between the Franks and Rome intensified, with particular consequences for the spread of Christianity on the eastern borders of the Frankish kingdom. In this region, missionaries from the British Isles assumed the role of spreading God's word, supported by the papacy and the leaders of the Franks, Dukes Pippin II, his son Charles Martel, and his grandsons Pippin and Carolman – not kings, but rather the king's "mayors" and the real power behind the Merovingian throne. In 690, a monk from Northumbria named Willibrord arrived in Frisia, a coastal region on the North Sea, sent there by Duke Pippin II to convert the Frisians "from idolatry to faith in Christ." Before reaching his new missionary territory, however, Willibrord journeyed to Rome to receive the holy relics and blessings from Pope Sergius I (687–701). Years later, he visited the city a second time. In 696, with Pippin's assent, the pope ordained the English monk as the first bishop of the Frisians. Over the following years, Willibrord founded numerous churches and monasteries in the region, contributing to the creation of a new Christian landscape that bore the traces of its foundational link to the Roman Church.[22]

Another English missionary from Wessex named Winfrid, who later adopted the Roman name of Boniface, likewise channeled Rome's prestige into his mission among the "heathens" beyond the Rhine. Boniface had already begun to proselytize among the Frisians in 716. Three years later, while the English monk visited Rome, Pope Gregory II (715–31) appointed him as the "missionary to the Germans," instructing him "to teach them the service of the kingdom of God," as well as the "sacramental discipline prescribed by the official ritual formulary of our Holy Apostolic See."[23] The *Book of the Popes* proclaimed that through Boniface, Gregory had "preached the message of salvation in Germany and by teaching light to a people that sat in darkness, he converted them to Christ."

In 732, his successor Gregory III (731–41) named Boniface archbishop of the Germans during another visit to Rome by the tireless missionary. In the correspondence between Boniface and successive Roman popes, one sees the combination of local initiative and papal support, working to construct a new "micro-Christendom" that would look toward Rome for inspiration and guidance. As Pope Gregory III encouraged Boniface in his work among the Germans: "Cease not therefore, most reverend brother, to teach them the holy and apostolic tradition of the Roman see, that the natives may be enlightened and may follow in the way of salvation and so may gain eternal reward."[24]

To be clear, many of those "natives" did not consider themselves heathens or wallowing in darkness. Christianity was not exactly new to the region. Earlier generations of wandering monks from Ireland, including the famous Saint Columban, had already preached the Gospel on the eastern frontiers of the Frankish kingdom, combating false gods and demons, creating Christian outposts in the supposedly pagan wilderness. Much like Augustine of Canterbury among the Anglo-Saxons, Boniface did not so much bring Christianity to uncharted territories, as a particular kind of Christian faith, practice, and discipline to places where the line between pagan and Christian – from his perspective – remained far too blurred. In a similar spirit, Boniface equally applied himself to the reform of the Frankish Church, denoting among other things a stricter adherence to Roman rites and traditions. By such means, Latin Christians across early medieval Europe wove meaningful and lasting ties between their own religious communities and the Apostolic See, bonds that helped to condition their sense of belonging to a common society of catholic believers.

The Papacy between Worlds

For all of their initiative and interest in the barbarian kingdoms of the West, popes still considered themselves faithful subjects of the Eastern Roman or Byzantine Empire, members of the universal Church centered on the Mediterranean. During the seventh and eighth centuries, however, unexpected developments permanently reconfigured the relationship between Rome and Constantinople. Partly as a reaction to the unexpected emergence of Islam, an imperial insistence on new forms of religious conformity drove a lasting wedge between the popes of Rome and Byzantium, forcing the

Roman papacy to look in new directions for friends and allies in an era of persistent disorder.

Muhammad and Islam

During the later imperial era, while the Western Roman Empire experienced severe disruptions, the Eastern half of the Roman world – the wealthier, more urban, and cosmopolitan part – had remained comparatively undisturbed. This situation changed dramatically, however, in the seventh century. First, a devastating war broke out with Byzantium's rival along its eastern border, the Sassanid Empire in Persia. Under their aggressive leader Chosroes II, the Persians overran much of the Byzantine Empire, attacking Damascus in 613 and Jerusalem the following year. During their assault on Jerusalem, to the dismay of Christians, they seized the city's relic of the True Cross supposedly discovered by Emperor Constantine I's mother, Helena, during her fourth-century pilgrimage to the city. Eventually the Byzantine ruler Heraclius beat the Persians back, recovering the stolen relic of the True Cross through some strong-armed negotiations. By 630, the war had ended but it left in its wake weakened local economies, damaged cities, and exhausted armies.

Even as the Byzantine conflict with the Persians wound down, a new and dramatic force began to reshape the political and religious landscape of the Eastern Mediterranean and beyond – the emergence of Islam. This monotheistic tradition began in the Arabian city of Mecca in 610 when Muhammad, member of an influential local family, began to receive a series of divine revelations stressing the need for "submission" to God, known in Arabic as Allah. Although many Arabs were polytheistic, they were no strangers to Judaism and Christianity. Muhammad's revelations, eventually recorded in the Qur'an, proclaimed that Allah – the same God worshipped by Jews and Christians, albeit improperly – had directly given his final message to his prophet, Muhammad. Unpopular in Mecca, Muhammad and his earliest followers fled to nearby Medina in 622 (the start date of the Islamic calendar). In Medina he gained more followers, eventually returning to seize control of Mecca in 630. By the time that he died two years later, the vast majority of Arabic tribes had united under this new faith.

Bound together in the "ummah," the "best community" of Muslims, Arabic forces turned their energies outward, beginning a series of campaigns against the worn-out Byzantine and Sassanid Empires. As merchants and raiders, the Arabs had long experience of their neighbors. Now they arrived as conquerors, seizing lands promised to them by God. Muslim forces captured Antioch and Damascus in 635, Jerusalem in 637, and Alexandria in 642. During this same period they progressively took control of Persian territories and expanded their authority across northern Africa. Although the Muslims created a new ruling elite in these regions, Christians and some Jews remained the vast majority of the population in places captured from Byzantium, subject to a tax imposed on non-believers, but still allowed to practice their religions. Indeed, some Eastern Christians did not greet the Muslim conquests with dismay, at least not at first. For Miaphysite communities, in particular, under renewed pressure to accept orthodoxy by Constantinople, the imperial capital – not the Islamic newcomers – represented the true oppressor of their faith.

It is not clear how well Western Christians understood Muslims, called "Saracens" or "Hagarenes" in Latin sources, or the magnitude of the Islamic conquests. The Frankish pilgrim Arculf, who visited Jerusalem about the year 670, seemed remarkably unfazed by the relatively recent change of ownership over the city, worshipping undisturbed at the site of Christ's tomb in the Church of the Holy Sepulcher. Over time, however, this lack of concern began to change. In 711, a Muslim army from northern Africa crossed into Spain, destroying the kingdom of the Visigoths, catholic Christians since the conversion of their ruler Recared in 589. Over the following decades, Muslim raiding parties made incursions into Merovingian Gaul, although Charles Martel's victory over one such force at the battle of Tours in 732 discouraged further campaigns in that direction. Piracy along the Mediterranean coast continued, sometimes menacing Rome. Boniface, the intrepid missionary, cautioned one prospective visitor to the city to wait until the "threats of the Saracens who have recently appeared about Rome should have subsided." The *Book of Popes* also took note of recent conquests made by the "unspeakable race" of the Hagarenes in the West and the East, including their siege of Constantinople in 718.[25]

Indirectly, the rise of Islam had an incalculable impact on the history of the papacy and medieval Europe as a whole. The Belgian historian Henri Pirenne once suggested that the Islamic conquests of the seventh and eighth centuries truly shattered the unity of the ancient world centered on the Mediterranean, not the earlier barbarian invasions of the Western Roman Empire. Generations of scholars, above all archeologists, have poked numerous holes in his argument, providing conclusive evidence that the later Roman economy and society experienced profound dislocation well before the coming of the

Muslims. Nevertheless, the emergence of Islamic power redrew what we might now call the geopolitical map of the late antique world. Vast portions of the Byzantine Empire no longer belonged to the imperial order. Where Christians used to number five major sees, after the Muslim conquest of Jerusalem, Antioch, and Alexandria, only two remained under Christian control: Rome and Constantinople. The beleaguered rulers of Byzantium seemed at once more remote from their nominal subjects in the West and yet far more insistent about their endangered right to rule over them. The implications of these transformations for the development of the Roman papacy would become clear over the following generations, marked by new disputes between Eastern and Western Christians over the nature of Christ and the religious imagery used to represent him and other saints.[26]

Controversy over Christ's will

During the period after Gregory the Great, Byzantium had enjoyed a renewed influence over the church at Rome, when a series of Eastern-born, Greek-speaking bishops sat on the Apostolic See. This apparent state of close relations between the Byzantines and the Roman Church, however, did not prevent their continued divergence over religious dogma and practices. Despite repeated councils, theological debates, and sometimes bloody conflicts, Eastern Christians had still not settled their disputes over the human and divine nature of Christ. After war with the Persians and the rapid expansion of Islamic power, the need for ending such disruptive controversies and achieving Christian unity must have seemed more pressing than ever to imperial authorities and churchmen.

Trying to reconcile those who still refused to accept the orthodox creed from Chalcedon, theologians under Emperor Heraclius formulated the doctrine of "Monoenergism" or "Monotheletism," which taught that Christ had one unitary "energy" or "will," but allowed for a certain degree of separation between his divine and human natures. The Roman papacy faced a choice whether to support this doctrinal compromise or reject it as a violation of Chalcedonian orthodoxy. Pope Honorius I (625–38) showed his sympathies toward Monothelete teachings, perhaps not examining their implications too closely. His successors, however, Severinus (May–August 640), John IV (640–42), Theodore I (642–49), and Martin I (649–53), all opposed the doctrine of Christ's "one will" as heresy. In 649, Pope Martin held a council in Rome, attended by over one hundred

Western bishops, which condemned Monotheletism. The consequences of this action, for Martin, were quite serious. Showing the persistent reach of Byzantine power into Roman affairs, in 653 agents of the current Byzantine ruler Constans II seized the pope and dragged him to Constantinople. Accused of treason, Martin avoided execution but was sent into exile. Back at Rome, the cowed clergy elected his more compliant successor, Eugene I (654–57). Years later, campaigning against the Lombards in Italy, Constans visited Rome, the first emperor personally to set foot in the city for roughly two centuries. Pope Vitalian received him with a formal procession and celebrated mass in Saint Peter's basilica with the Byzantine ruler. Constans's cordial relations with the pope, however, did not stop him from plundering much of the city's precious metals, even stripping churches of their roofs. When assassins strangled the emperor in a bathhouse in Syracuse not long afterward, local chroniclers showed a grim delight at the demise this heretical tyrant.

Although Vitalian backed away from a direct confrontation with Constantinople over Monotheletism, his successors kept up their opposition to this latest Christological heresy, seeking support from Western clergy as far afield as the British Isles. In 680, when Pope Agatho (678–81) dispatched a papal legate to "inquire carefully into the beliefs of the English Church, and report on them on his return to Rome," Theodore of Tarsus – who originally fled his homeland as a refugee from Islamic conquests – convened a synod of English bishops at Hatfield.[27] Among its other business, the synod explicitly rejected the heresy of Monotheletism, confirming the orthodoxy of the English Church. Afterwards, the participants at the synod circulated a statement of the faith previously drafted by Pope Martin, condemning the Monotheletes. In this way, the clergy assembled at Hatfield displayed the alignment of Western Christendom with the Apostolic See, set at odds against their Eastern coreligionists.

Eventually Constans's son and successor Constantine IV turned his back on Monotheletism, condemned at the sixth general Council of Constantinople in 680. Legates sent by Pope Agatho attended the council and participated in its deliberations, not even protesting when the assembly suggested that Pope Honorius I might have been a heretic himself because of his support for the doctrine of Christ's unitary will. Even when they agreed, however, the churches of Rome and Constantinople found room to disagree. During the follow-up "Quinisext" council held in 691–92, the largely Greek attendees affirmed their own practice of allowing clerical marriage (as opposed to the Roman tradition of clerical celibacy), its fasting practices (in contrast to the ones followed by Rome), and the title of ecumenical patriarch for the bishop of Constantinople (a continued sore point for the Roman Church). In reaction, Pope Sergius I refused to sign the council's acts. Trying to follow in the footsteps of Constans II, Emperor Justinian II ordered Sergius's arrest and deportation to Constantinople to stand trial. Local militias from Ravenna and Pentapolis, however, protected the pope and nearly killed Justinian's soldiers. In contrast to Pope Martin's fate, this episode demonstrated the evident limits of Byzantine power in Italy, although not for want of trying.

Trouble with icons

In retrospect, the conflict over Christ's will foreshadowed a more consequential struggle between Rome and Constantinople over the Lord's image and that of other holy figures. During the later seventh century, reacting to the Islamic conquests and other challenges to the Byzantine order, many Eastern Christians showed an increasing devotion toward icons, religious imagery that functioned as a conduit of divine power and grace. In 691–92, the Quinisext council passed some of the first ecclesiastical legislation to regulate the proper use of icons in worship. As the shock of the initial Islamic conquests waned, learned theologians began to debate the legitimacy of such religious images, some arguing that they represented a form of idolatry. The fact that the victorious Muslims were known to prohibit depictions of the divine and human form might have encouraged some Christians to become more critical of the practice. For some, the belief that only Christ's human nature – not his divine one – could be depicted in "lifeless" matter suggested that portraits of the Lord committed the heresy of dividing his humanity and divinity. Unsettling events, such as an Islamic attack on Constantinople in 718 and the eruption of a volcano on the Greek island of Thera in 726, intensified such speculations about the propriety of icons.

In time, voices critical of religious images gained the upper hand. According to later accounts, including the *Book of Popes*, Emperor Leo III adopted a policy of iconoclasm, issuing an edict in 726 that banned the veneration of art depicting Christ and the saints. Supposedly, he decided to remove an image of the Lord from the Chalke Gate before the imperial palace at Constantinople, provoking a riot. In fact, the evidence for Leo's iconoclastic policies remains uncertain, although he showed a clear concern with the threat of idolatry and might have tightened regulations for the proper use of icons. At the council of Hiereia in 754, however, his son Constantine V formally banned icons, leaving only the Lord's Cross as a legitimate Christian symbol in the Byzantine Empire. Although reports of icon smashing and defacing might be exaggerated, episodes of violence followed between iconoclasts and iconophiles (or iconodules), those who defended icon veneration. Such Christians, especially monks, resisted or fled, hiding or removing their precious icons.[28] As imperial subjects, Rome's bishops were expected to follow these marching orders. They had other ideas. As the *Book of Popes* described the situation, during the time of Pope Gregory II, "the emperor had decreed that no church image of any saint, martyr, or angel should be kept, as he declared them all accursed." Already at odds with Leo III over new imperial taxes imposed on papal estates in southern Italy, the pope responded by "arming himself against the emperor as against an enemy, denouncing his heresy and writing that Christians everywhere must guard against the impiety that had arisen." Following this lead, Gregory III held a synod at Rome in 731 that excommunicated anyone who should "remove, destroy, profane, and blaspheme against this sacred veneration of images." In retaliation for such defiance, or so papal sources tell us, Leo transferred the provinces of southern Italy and Illyricum to the ecclesiastical jurisdiction of Constantinople's patriarch, a blow to Rome's prestige and also pocketbook.[29]

From the papacy's vantage point, the imperial meddling with icons represented yet another example of wrong-headed interference in religious doctrine by a secular ruler, a position made clear in two letters supposedly sent by Gregory II to Leo III. As just noted, Leo's own involvement in iconoclasm remains open for debate, and the letters in question might be forgeries or contain passages added decades later. Regardless, the letters attributed to Gregory played on the refrain of the two powers in terms that the pope would doubtless have recognized and appreciated. "The making of laws for the church is one thing," one of the letters proclaims, "and the governing of the empire another."[30] According to the other letter, a defiant Gregory declared to the Byzantine ruler that he would turn for aid to the newly Christianized peoples of the West, who regarded the pope as their leader:

> Many have great confidence in us, whom you have threatened to destroy along with the image of Saint Peter, whom all the royal Western Churches consider a "God on earth." If you dare to attempt this, the Westerners can certainly revenge the Easterners,

whom you have treated with such injustice ... all of the West offers the fruits of its faith to the sainted prince of apostles. If you send anyone to destroy the image of Saint Peter, we warn you in advance that we will be innocent of any bloodshed. The guilt will fall on your head.[31]

Even if the pope was exaggerating, even if these letters are a later fabrication, these boastful sentiments captured something genuine about the eighth-century Roman Church's turn away from the Byzantine world toward those "kingdoms of the West," above all, toward the Franks and the emergent power of the Carolingians, the family of Charles Martel. Sometimes assisted by those new "friends of Saint Peter," sometimes eclipsed by their ambitious rule, the popes of Rome stood on the precipice of far-reaching transformations in the political landscape of Western Europe, not to mention their status as temporal rulers in their own right.

Chapter 3: The Reordering of the West

In the winter and spring of 754, Pope Stephen II (752–7) met with the Frankish ruler, Pippin, not far from Paris, first at Ponthion and later at Quierzy. Beleaguered by the Lombards, at odds with the iconoclastic Byzantines, Stephen had come to seek Pippin's protection and assistance. During his stay, the pope anointed Pippin with holy oil, marking him as a sacral king in the style of Old Testament rulers. Pippin no doubt appreciated this ritual stamp of approval, since he had only become king of the Franks three years earlier after deposing the final Merovingian ruler and packing him off to a monastery. According to some accounts of the meeting, he promised to subdue the Lombards and restore lands that they had stolen from the papal patrimonies. Pippin took his promise seriously, putting military pressure on the Lombard kingdom to make peace with Rome. His son Charles, known as Charlemagne, finally destroyed Lombard rule in northern Italy in 774, confirming Pippin's donation of Italian territories to the popes of Rome. On Christmas day in 800, this decades-old relationship between the Carolingians and the Roman popes reached its apotheosis. When Charles attended mass at the Church of Saint Peter, Pope Leo III (795–816) placed an imperial crown upon his head while the assembled onlookers cried out three times: "To Charles, pious Augustus, crowned by God, great and pacific emperor, life and victory!" In a new guise, the power of empire had reemerged in the West, reborn in the sacred precincts of Saint Peter's basilica.[1]

From a modern perspective, this so-called "Franco-papal alliance" represented a pivotal episode in the history of the papacy and medieval Europe. First, by seeking help from the Franks, the popes of Rome completed their turn away from Byzantium, ceasing to view themselves as subjects of the Eastern emperors. Second, through the crowning of Charlemagne, the papacy contributed to the rise of a new imperial power in Europe, the greatest political success story since the disintegration of the Western Roman Empire centuries earlier. Finally, rejecting Byzantine sovereignty and benefiting from Carolingian recognition of their territorial claims, popes began to present themselves as temporal rulers in their own right, reigning over significant portions of the Italian peninsula. Although the precise borders of this "Republic of Saint Peter" were in a state of almost constant uncertainty, and the mechanisms of papal administration remained limited in scope, the origins of what historians call the Papal States – a convenient label, one used in this book – can be traced back to this era, at least as a concept, if not a practical governing reality.

There are good reasons for all of these assertions. Indeed, medieval chroniclers, not just modern scholars, identified the union between the Franks and Rome as an epoch-making event of the utmost importance for both the Carolingians and the papacy. At the same time, this affiliation created as many tensions as it resolved. Needless to say, popes did not always get what they wanted from Carolingian rulers, any more than they had from Byzantine emperors. Once he wore the imperial crown, Charlemagne did not adopt a submissive stance toward the pope who placed that symbol of empire on his head. Quite the opposite: Carolingian authority frequently weighed upon the bishops of Rome, threatening to reduce their rights and stature. Under Carolingian auspices, the assembly of Christian peoples into a single society of believers became an imperial rather than papal project, even if Frankish rulers continued to cultivate public devotion to the Apostolic See.

Yet the Carolingian reordering of Europe did not endure. In the mid- to late ninth century, a fresh round of external pressures, including Viking attacks and Muslim raids accompanied by internal political divisions among the Franks, disrupted the relative stability created by the Frankish Empire. After a brief window of opportunity to reassert their leadership in the absence of strong imperial power, the popes of Rome – much like everyone else – had to contend with the uncertainties of the age. Among other consequences, feuding aristocratic families dominated the papal office, treating it as a means to govern Rome and as a prize in their rivalries. Even allowing for exaggeration about the misdeeds of the era's "bad popes," the tenth-century Roman papacy existed in a state of contracted horizons and scaled-down aspirations.

Rome and the Carolingian Empire

By the middle of the eighth century, popes confronted a number of problems. First, they struggled with the emperors of Constantinople, who continued to insist that they enforce the imperial policy of iconoclasm. More pressing, they faced renewed aggression by the Lombards, who had seized papal holdings in Italy and menaced Rome itself. In response, the heirs of Saint Peter looked for assistance to the nascent power of the Carolingian dynasty, a decision with far-reaching consequences for both parties involved.

Forging the Franco-papal alliance

In a letter sent to Charles Martel in 739, Pope Gregory III called upon the Frankish warrior as a "son of Saint Peter" to defend the "Church of God" and Peter's "peculiar people," showing his love and devotion toward the apostle by defending Rome from the Lombards. If he did stand with Peter, Gregory declared, Charles would earn a heavenly reward and peoples everywhere would celebrate his devotion to the Apostolic See. The Frankish duke and warlord, enjoying a truce with the Lombards at the time, declined to answer the pope's appeal. His heirs did not. In 750–51, finally abandoning the pretense of service to the ineffective Merovingians, his son Pippin assumed the kingship of the Franks. According to the *Annals of the Kingdom of the Franks*, the previous year Pippin had sent envoys to Gregory III's successor, Zachary I (741–52), asking whether "it was good or not that the king of the Franks should wield no royal power." The pope replied that "it was better to call him king who had the royal power than the one who did not." The *Annals* declared that the pope "commanded by virtue of his apostolic authority that Pippin should be made king," undoubtedly stretching the truth since Zachary had no right to issue such a command. Some scholars question whether this exchange ever really happened. In any event, as presented by this chronicle, the pope sanctioned Pippin's coup d'état.[2]

Supposedly, Boniface, missionary to the Germans, anointed Pippin with holy oil as king in 751. Three years later, as described above, Pope Stephen II performed this ritual act during his visit to Francia. The *Book of Popes* reported that Pippin humbled himself before the pope during their meeting at Ponthion, acting as a groom and leading his horse on foot. One Frankish chronicle reversed this scene, making the pope the one who threw himself prostrate before the Frankish king. Regardless, they obviously decided that they needed each other. Pippin had the swords and the pope an exceptional religious status to sanctify Pippin's rule. Meeting Pippin at Quierzy, Stephen apparently received some sort of promise from him about the restoration of territories seized from papal estates by the Lombards, the so-called "Donation of Pippin," although no such actual document by this name exists. The following year, Pippin marched against the Lombard ruler, Aistulf, forcing him to sign a treaty that recognized papal holdings in the region. When Aistulf reneged and attacked Rome in 756, Pippin returned to Italy and soundly defeated the Lombard king. During his visit to Rome, according to the *Book of Popes*, the Frankish king created a record of the territories he surrendered to the papacy. "Concerning all the cities received," as the anonymous author described it, Pippin "issued a donation in writing for their possession by Saint Peter, the holy Roman Church, and all of the Apostolic See's pontiffs for ever; it is kept safe even until now in the holy church's archive."[3] Apparently, Pope Stephen's calculated journey to Francia had been worth the trouble.

Charlemagne and Rome

Securing control of those promised territories was easier said than done. Perhaps not surprisingly, the Lombards resisted the Carolingian settlement imposed upon them. During the papacy of Paul I (757–67), the next Lombard king, Desiderius, seized the duchies of Spoleto and Benevento, despite their newly recognized affiliation with the papacy. After Paul died, an aristocratic faction opposed to the Lateran clergy installed a layman named Constantine as the next pope, rapidly ordaining him and consecrating him in quick succession. The clerics opposed to Constantine and his backers managed to oust the upstart pope, relying upon the support of local militias, help from Spoleto, and troops provided by none other than King Desiderius, no doubt happy to intervene in the dispute. In August 768, the winners in this scramble over the papal office elected Pope Stephen III (768–72). Pippin died a month later, leaving his sons Charles and Carlomann as his heirs. The following year, the new pope watched with growing alarm as Charles married Desiderius's daughter, signaling a thaw in Carolingian relations with the Lombards. Feeling pushed into a corner, Stephen tried to make his own alliance with the Lombard king, a policy that only served to increase Desiderius's influence in Rome. In 771, however, Charles's brother Carlomann died, leaving Charles the sole ruler of the Franks. He soon abandoned his Lombard wife and any plans for an alliance with Desiderius. By this time, Desiderius had begun another military push against Rome, leading Stephen III's successor, Hadrian I (772–95), to call yet again for the Franks to enforce the peace, recovering the cities "stolen" from Rome and securing "all of Saint Peter's lawful rights." In 773–74, Charles defeated the Lombards in northern Italy once and for all, assuming the title "king of the Lombards."

During this campaign, Charlemagne came to Rome, a cross between a victorious liberator and a pilgrim. As described by the *Book of Popes*, Hadrian sent a procession of leading Roman citizens, members of the city militia, and children to greet him, bearing palm and olive branches, chanting and praying as they welcomed the king of the Franks. Pope Hadrian met Charles at the Church of Saint Peter. When the Frankish ruler arrived,

> he kissed every single step leading up to Saint Peter's holy church, and so came to the pontiff where he was waiting in the atrium at the top of the steps, close to the church doors. He was greeted and they embraced each other; the Christian king Charles held the pontiff's right hand, and in this way they entered the venerable hall of St Peter prince of the apostles.[4]

Together, the pope and Frankish ruler prayed before Peter's shrine and thanked God for Charles's victory over the Lombards. During his stay at Rome, Charles visited other churches, and also confirmed the earlier donation made by Pippin, depositing a written record of the lands ceded to the papacy on the altar of Saint Peter, including the duchies of Rome, Spoleto, and Benevento, along with the exarchate of Ravenna and other neighboring territories.

Over the following years, Hadrian continued to remind Charles about his promises. The Frankish ruler, governing a vast realm stretching across much of Western Europe, clearly had other priorities, although the Franks never wavered from their sense of special duty to the Apostolic See. In 799, when a faction of Roman nobles attacked and almost blinded Pope Leo III, the exiled pope sought Charles's aid and protection, meeting with the emperor at Paderborn that summer. With Frankish support behind him, Leo managed to return to Rome, although he continued to experience challenges from his aristocratic opponents in the city. In November 800, Charles himself came to Rome to settle this disreputable situation, holding a hearing of the charges against Leo. In Saint Peter's basilica, the pope swore an oath on the Gospels that he had done no wrong, clearing his name. Not long after, celebrating mass in that same church on Christmas, Leo crowned Charlemagne as emperor.

The Franks and Saint Peter

For the Carolingians, their relationship with the papacy formed one component of their Christian governance. For the Frankish elite, including bishops, abbots, and other members of the clergy that helped to manage Carolingian society, the Roman Church represented a valuable lodestone of apostolic traditions, a standard by which to measure and modulate their own churches. Since the sixth and seventh centuries, Roman forms of worship, rituals, and prayers – or at least ones that the Franks believed to be authentically Roman – had occupied an important place in the diverse liturgies of Frankish churches and monasteries. Under Pippin, Frankish clergy prepared the so-called *Gelasian Sacramentary* as a source of guidance for the kingdom's liturgical services, based on a supposedly authentic Roman model. Under Charlemagne, such processes of Romanization became more explicit. In 774, the Frankish king asked Pope Hadrian I to send him a Roman canon-law collection known as the *Dionysio-Hadriana*, an ecclesiastical code dating to the sixth century. Around a decade later, Charles requested a sacramentary from the pope known as the *Gregorianum* or *Hadrianum*, which purported to preserve uncorrupted liturgical practices dating back to the days of Gregory the Great.[5]

At the same time, the Frankish adoption of Roman customs and rules only went so far. However much respect and spiritual devotion they might have shown toward the Roman Church, Frankish rulers and clergy did not hesitate to diverge from papal exemplars and pronouncements when it suited their purposes. The *Hadrianum*, for example, came nowhere close to satisfying local Frankish communities with their own particular saints, feast days, and rites. Some highly placed members of the Carolingian court, including one of Charlemagne's closest advisors, Alcuin of York, questioned the value of replacing time-honored, native liturgical traditions with imported ones. In the ninth century, the famous monastic reformer Benedict of Aniane went one step further, heavily revising the *Hadrianum* to meet Frankish needs. In this sense, the Roman Church formed one significant but not exclusive point of reference in the constellation of Carolingian religious life.[6]

In other instances, Frankish churchmen did not hesitate to directly question or attack papal decisions. The ongoing controversy over icons provoked one such disagreement. In 787, the iconophile Byzantine empress Irene, acting as regent for her son Constantine VI, had called the Second Council of Nicaea to revisit the imperial policy of iconoclasm. Led by the patriarch of Constantinople, Tarasius, the assembled Greek theologians defended the veneration of sacred images, distinguishing it from the worship of idols. Pope Hadrian, whose legates were present at the council, endorsed its proceedings. The Franks, however, due in part to a poor translation from the Greek acts of the council, judged that the iconophile Greeks had strayed too far in the other direction, calling for the adoration of icons. At Charlemagne's request, one of his leading theologians and the future bishop of Orléans, Theodulf, composed the so-called *Work of King Charles against the Synod* (also known as the *Caroline Books*) in response. In his work, Theodulf celebrated the primacy of the Roman Church, as well as the special role of the Franks in defending Rome and spreading the authority of Saint Peter among the peoples of the West. Nevertheless, he vehemently took issue with the judgment of the current pope, who had supported the erroneous decision of the Greeks about icons. At the Council of Frankfurt in 794, the assembled Frankish clergy repudiated both the Greek and papal position on icons, creating their own formulation of orthodox faith and practice, including the proper place of religious images. Rome and the Carolingians also remained at odds over the Frankish modification of the Nicaean Creed to reflect that Latin belief that the Holy Spirit proceeds from the Father "and from the Son" (*filioque*), not just from the Father, as maintained by the Greek Church. Pope Leo III, who agreed with the theology of the Holy Spirit's "double procession," nevertheless objected to any modifications of the traditional creed. In religious life, as in the political arena, the Franco-papal alliance clearly knew its limits.

The Republic of Saint Peter

For the papacy, the rebirth of imperial power in the West also raised troublesome questions about the proper relationship between secular powers and priestly authority, another iteration of the centuries-old dilemma faced by the popes of Rome. Creating further complications, with Carolingian support, the city's bishops found themselves ruling over a patchwork of duchies, cities, and other patrimonies in central Italy. As the chief priests of Christendom and the rulers of the so-called Papal States, popes had to negotiate and manage rapidly shifting patterns of authority during the Carolingian era.

The two powers revisited

From the Carolingian perspective, Saint Peter's heirs legitimated and supported Frankish rule, not the other way around. Charlemagne himself captured these sentiments in a well-known letter to Leo III, written shortly after Leo's election in 796, when he informed the pontiff that it was the Frankish ruler's duty to defend the holy Church of Christ by arms from the "attack of pagans and devastation of infidels" and also to fortify the faith; it was the pope's duty to pray for the success of the pious king in those endeavors. Charles represented God's deputy on earth, defending the Church, while the pope played a supporting role. According to Charlemagne's biographer, Einhard, Charles reacted with surprise and displeasure to his crowning as emperor in Saint Peter's basilica – if he had known in advance about Leo's plan, he claimed, he would have never entered the church that day. This story that the pope "ambushed" Charles seems unlikely, but the circumstances of the coronation might have troubled some Frankish observers. If a pope gave the imperial crown, a pope might also claim the right to place demands on the person who wore it, including the right to take it away. Charles, the message seemed clear, did not owe his imperial dignity to the pope, the citizens of Rome, or anyone else.

For their part, since the beginning of the Franco-papal alliance, popes had celebrated the Frankish bond with Saint Peter, who had elevated them above other peoples, enabling their triumphs and expanding their realm. Christians everywhere, Pope Stephen II addressed Pippin in 755, knew that the Lord brought about justice through the "strong arm" of the Franks in their battles against the Lombards, pagans, and other foes. It was the "sword of God, not man" that fought for their victories. In return, the Franks were obliged to defend Peter's patrimony, the Roman Church and republic, along with its inhabitants. Saint Peter, of course, could protect his own if he wished; instead, he desired to test the faith of his followers. In one remarkable letter, the pope used the first-person voice of Saint Peter himself, who called the Franks his "adopted sons," who were meant "to defend this Roman city from its adversaries and the people commissioned to me by God from the hands of their enemies." The real duty of Frankish rulers, in short, lay with their obligations to protect and serve the Roman papacy.[7]

The Donation of Constantine

Under these circumstances, someone close to papal circles, perhaps in the Lateran itself, crafted one of the most famous forgeries in

European history, the so-called *Donation of Constantine*. Modern scholars debate its precise date, placing its genesis anywhere from 754 to 796 or later, some suggesting that it might have been written and revised in stages. This document claims to record events in the fourth century, offering an apocryphal account of when Pope Sylvester baptized Emperor Constantine, curing him of leprosy (much as featured in the *Book of Popes* and the *Legend of Saint Sylvester*). In return, Constantine decreed that the holy Roman Church and Apostolic See

> shall be honored with veneration; and that, more than our empire and earthly throne, the most sacred seat of Saint Peter shall be gloriously exalted; we giving to it the imperial power, and dignity of glory, and vigor and honor. And we ordain and decree that he shall have the supremacy as well over the four chief seats Antioch, Alexandria, Constantinople, and Jerusalem, as also over all the churches of God in the whole world. He who for the time being shall be pontiff of that holy Roman Church shall be more exalted than, and chief over, all the priests of the whole world. According to his judgment, everything which is to be provided for the service of God or the stability of the faith of the Christians is to be administered.

The emperor bestowed numerous estates on the papacy and conceded to Sylvester and his successors the right to wear the tiara and other imperial regalia. Constantine also relinquished his control over "the city of Rome and all the provinces, districts and cities of Italy and the western regions," conceding them as an "inviolable gift" to the bishops of Rome. Last but not least, he declared his intention to move his imperial capital from Rome to Constantinople, since it did not seem fitting for an "earthly ruler" to have jurisdiction "where the supremacy of priests and the head of the Christian religion have been established by a heavenly ruler."[8]

In these breath-taking terms, the *Donation of Constantine* proclaimed that the popes of Rome possessed rights over imperial power in the Western regions of the Roman world, a temporal dominion coupled with their spiritual primacy over all Christians. A mosaic commissioned in 798 by Leo III in the Lateran church expressed similar sentiments in visual terms. At the center of this image, Saint Peter sits enthroned with the keys to heaven lying in his lap. Pope Leo kneels on Peter's right, receiving his *pallium* from the saint. Charles kneels on his left, accepting a banner from Peter, who – the inscription below reads – is asked to give life to the pope and victory to the king. The programmatic design of this fresco, with Peter as the central figure handing over symbols of authority to Leo and Charles, not so subtly rebutted the Carolingian interpretation of the Franco-papal alliance – the emperor's duty lay in service to Peter and his successors, not the other way around. One wonders if Leo showed this image to Charles when he visited Rome the following year. An accompanying mosaic depicts a similar cluster of figures, consisting of Christ in the middle, handing the keys of heaven to Saint Peter on his right and a banner to Emperor Constantine on his left. The message of these two mosaics would have been hard to miss. Both spiritual and temporal authority ultimately derived from Christ through his successor Saint Peter, who delegated power to priests and kings alike.[9]

Governing the Papal States

Despite considerable losses over the previous centuries, the eighth-century papacy possessed vast properties on the Italian peninsula and beyond. As described in the previous chapter, the disintegration of imperial power in and around Rome meant that the city's bishops played a growing role in civil governance. Under these circumstances, members of the papal household functioned as administrators of papal properties and other sources of revenue, including the *sacellarius*, the pope's "chief financial officer," the *vestarius*, in charge of papal ceremonies, and the librarian, who maintained records and archives. Popes also employed notaries and appointed rectors to oversee and manage directly major papal estates. Others, often laymen, served the papacy in a military capacity, such as the *primicerius*, head of the guardians (*defensores*), forming a sort of papal militia. The prefect, judges, and other remnants of Roman civic offices rounded out the city's government. Although the border between clergy and the laity remained porous, members of the church hierarchy sometimes had to compete with the secular aristocratic elite for control of the city. Indeed, possession of the papal office remained the greatest prize a family could seek in an effort to rule over Rome.

During the second half of the eighth century, the papacy extended and formalized its claims to authority over the duchies of Rome, Spoleto, the exarchate of Ravenna, Benevento, and adjacent territories. For one thing, popes openly began to reject Byzantine claims of sovereignty over Rome and its surroundings. During negotiations with the Lombards, Pope Zachary suggested that he rightfully represented the "Roman people" or the "republic" of the Romans. His successors, starting with Stephen II, likewise emphasized papal rule independent of other earthly powers, forming "our republic of the

Romans" or the "Church of God of the republic of the Romans," that is, the lands of Saint Peter's "peculiar people." Pippin's so-called donation, confirmed by Charlemagne, formally recognized roughly these same territories, although their precise boundaries were never fixed. Indeed, while the *Donation of Constantine* made staggering claims for the popes of Rome, styling them the inheritors of imperial rule in the entire West, the primary concern of the document's forger no doubt remained the far more immediate need to justify papal rule over nearby regions "restored" to the popes by the Carolingians.

To be clear, the "Papal States" as such did not exist in the eighth or ninth centuries, at least not measured by modern standards of statehood. Similar to other governing bodies in Western Europe during this era, popes ruled through personal bonds of dependency and loyalty, oaths of allegiance and promises of military aid, family connections and other informal ties rather than effective bureaucracy. Even so, by the standards of the day, the Lateran church and surrounding complex represented a remarkably well-developed machine for governing the church of Rome and the territories that acknowledged papal sovereignty, receiving and paying out considerable incomes, keeping and producing records, and hearing legal disputes.

During this same period, one can also glimpse the emergence of the cardinal clergy as a distinctive and privileged group at Rome. Although the precise origins of this concept remain unclear, by the eighth century the word "cardinal" came to designate seven "leading" or "principal" bishops from churches just outside of Rome – Ostia, Albano, Palestrina, Porto, Silva Candida, Gabii, and Velletri – and priests from the twenty-eight titular churches within the city. Their special status originated from their long-standing liturgical duties: the cardinal bishops performed weekly religious ceremonies in the Lateran church, while the cardinal priests rotated through services at Rome's four major basilicas, the churches of Saint Peter, Saint Paul, Saint Lawrence, and Santa Maria Maggiore. The cardinal deacons later came to include seven such clerics attached to the pope's household, as well as other deacons responsible for day-to-day ecclesiastical administration in Rome. At a council in April 769, reacting to the recent scandal caused by the layman Constantine's hasty ordination and election, Stephen III and the assembled clergy had declared that a legitimately elected pope must have been a deacon or cardinal priest, trying to regularize papal elections and limit lay involvement in them. As we will see later in this book, the so-called "College of Cardinals" would eventually develop into an institution of central importance for the governance of the Roman Church.[10]

Anyone visiting Rome during the later decades of the eighth century would have been able to see that the city was experiencing an economic and cultural boom, enabled by the stability and prosperity of Carolingian supremacy. Successive popes, above all Hadrian I, initiated numerous building projects, great and small, including churches, chapels, hostels for pilgrims and other visitors, fountains and baths, paved walkways, and other structures. Close at hand, individual popes donated their own lands and made other bequests to the church at Rome. Farther afield, the papacy received new estates in Frankish territories, along with revenues such as Peter's pence, an annual payment supposedly promised to Rome by the Mercian king, Offa. After centuries of slow, staggered changes in its architectural landscape, Rome stood as an indisputably Christian city, a center of pilgrimage and devotion, a hub of ecclesiastical business.[11]

Rome and the Unmaking of the Carolingian Order

After the death of Charlemagne, his son Louis the Pious ruled for years with relative calm, but later in his life faced growing challenges from his three sons, including successive rebellions against him. Following Louis's demise, the Treaty of Verdun in 843 divided the Frankish empire into three kingdoms among Charlemagne's grandchildren, who wasted little time fighting each other. Meanwhile, Europe faced a renewed round of invasions by Vikings, Magyars, and – a particular concern for the city of Rome – Muslim raiders. After decades of adjustment to the return of empire, popes recalibrated their position to deal with the era's growing uncertainties and renewed fragmentation.

Popes and emperors after Charlemagne

During the early reign of Louis the Pious, the Carolingians continued to dominate local and regional politics in Italy as one part of their empire, maintaining relatively close ties with the papacy. In 813, Charles had crowned his own son as emperor, displaying the fact that his family did not need the popes of Rome to wield imperial power. Three years later, however, during a visit to Reims by Pope Stephen IV (816–17), Louis arranged for the Roman pontiff to anoint him and crown him as emperor. Issuing an agreement known as the *Ludovicianum*, the Frankish ruler confirmed many of his obligations toward the papacy, guaranteeing the autonomy of the papacy's governance over its territories, and securing the pope's rights to election by Rome's clergy and citizens without imperial interference, although the agreement required any new pope to inform the emperor about his election after consecration. Following in the footsteps of his father, Louis also reserved for himself the right to act as judge in extraordinary disputes involving the papacy.

Such an "extraordinary" situation occurred under Stephen's successor, Paschal I (817–24). In 823, when Louis's son Lothar visited Rome, Paschal crowned him as king of Italy and co-emperor in Saint Peter's basilica. Despite his father's assurances of papal autonomy, Lothar apparently threw his weight around while in the region. After he left, his recent actions provoked a backlash among some of Rome's leading families and clergy, leading to the arrest and execution of several Roman nobles serving the emperor, including the current *primicerius*, Theodore. When Louis dispatched envoys to Rome get to the bottom of this situation, Paschal took a sacred oath, swearing to his own innocence in the matter, although continuing to defend the men who had killed the emperor's servants as traitors to the patrimony of Saint Peter. Louis allowed the matter to drop, but the Carolingians began to ratchet up their efforts to impose new constraints on the papacy. After Paschal died, Lothar returned to Rome and issued the so-called *Constitutio Romana*, formalizing the imperial right to approve papal elections, and called for the Romans – including the pope – to swear an oath of fidelity to the Carolingian emperor or his representatives. Present at Rome for the election of Pope Eugene II (824–27), Lothar personally received Eugene's fidelity in Saint Peter's basilica, sworn over the Gospels, a cross of the Lord, and the body of Saint Peter.[12]

As the *Royal Frankish Annals* described these events, Lothar "ordered the affairs of the Roman people, which had for a long time been confused due to the wickedness of several popes."[13] His direct involvement in Eugene's election and reception of the new pope's oath served as a reminder that the protection afforded to the papacy by the Carolingians could involve an uncomfortable an amount of papal deference to secular rulers. Years later, when the Romans elected Pope Sergius II (844–47) without imperial approval, Lothar sent his son Louis II, along with Bishop Drogo of Metz and an unruly Frankish army, to investigate. According to the *Book of Popes*, Sergius greeted Louis on the steps of Saint Peter's basilica, perhaps meant to recall the encounter between Pope Hadrian I and Charlemagne, refusing the Frankish king permission to enter the church until he made his peaceful intentions toward the Roman Church clear.

Sergius's position, however, remained far more precarious than his papal biographer let on. Over the following weeks, the pope anointed Louis as king in Saint Peter's basilica, while Drogo investigated his election. Presumably under pressure, Sergius conceded to Drogo the status of "apostolic vicar" of all the provinces beyond the Alps, a departure from papal resistance to such infringements on Rome's universal ecclesiastical jurisdiction. Before Louis and his followers departed from the city, the pope crowned Louis emperor and swore fidelity to the young ruler, a ceremony again held in the Church of Saint Peter.[14]

Muslim raiders and the sack of Saint Peter's

For the most part, effective Carolingian power in Italy grew weaker and not stronger as the ninth century progressed. This turning of the tide became evident in August 846, when Muslim pirates from northern Africa sailed up the Tiber and attacked Rome. Disembarking, they plundered a number of religious sites including the Church of Saint Peter, located outside the city's defensive walls, stealing the holy altar above the apostle's tomb. Over the following years, such raids continued to menace Rome. In response, Lothar called for an expedition against the Saracens, blaming Christian sins for the assault on the Roman Church, the "head of Christendom."[15] The campaign never materialized. The Carolingians, beset by Viking raiders in the northern parts of the empire, had little to offer Rome in the way of concrete military aid. Most local Italian rulers, some of whom employed Muslim mercenaries for their own ends, likewise failed to respond.

Under these circumstances, the newly elected Pope Leo IV (847–55) took charge of protecting the city himself, raising fortifications around Rome and its outskirts, including the basilica churches of Saints Peter and Paul. When the walls were finished in 852, the pope staged a liturgical sanctification of the new defenses that would protect the Romans from future raids. Leo himself led a ritual procession of clergy around the entire perimeter of the walls, marked with ashes on their foreheads, chanting hymns and litanies. At three spots, the procession stopped and the pope offered a prayer to Christ to protect the newly consecrated city from the infidels. This procession of Romans and "people of other nations" ended at Saint Peter's basilica, where all gave thanks "for the salvation of all Christians." Through the pope's rebuilding of Rome's defenses and this liturgical celebration, both the physical and the spiritual bulwark of Christendom had been renewed against God's enemies.[16] Around this time, Leo also met with a large force of Neapolitans, who were preparing for battle against another Muslim fleet, administering the Eucharist to the assembled soldiers and praying for their success. During the ensuing battle, when the Christian fleet engaged the Muslim raiders, a storm scattered the enemy ships. Bound in iron, the surviving "Saracens" were forced to labor on the reconstruction of Rome's walls. Finally, the pope issued a proclamation to any Franks who came to battle the infidels that "whoever dies faithfully in a battle of this war will not be denied the heavenly kingdom," a compelling promise of spiritual rewards for those who protected God's Church.[17]

Pope Leo IV's effort to defend Rome and its surroundings from Muslim pirates illustrated the disruptions caused by the waning of the Carolingian Empire, filled with new danger and opportunities. On the one hand, Leo had acted like any territorial lord, building walls around his city for its defense when he could no longer rely on outside help. Just like any other bishop, he offered his prayers for the protection of his flock. Rome, however, was not just any other city. Leo's charge to protect the Roman Church had an impact on all the peoples of Christendom, who looked to Rome for spiritual guidance and the promise of salvation. The collapse of the Carolingian order did not alter this fundamental dynamic. If anything, this deteriorating political situation had the potential to call fresh attention to Rome's unique status among Western Christians, at least in the short term.

Nicholas I: Papal authority renewed

Under Nicholas I (858–67), Roman papacy briefly but compellingly reasserted its supremacy over Christendom. From the beginning of his pontificate, Nicholas recharged the papal language of universal primacy, insisting upon the position of Rome as the "head of all churches." The pope found help in this task from capable assistants including Anastasius the Librarian, a highly educated cleric fluent in Greek who had made his own unsuccessful bid for the papal office years earlier. Nicholas and his entourage also benefited from access to the *Pseudo-Isidorean Decretals*, a collection of church canons and papal decretals – some authentic, but most forgeries – that supported Rome's juridical claims. An unknown Frankish cleric had compiled this volume around the mid-ninth century, attributing it to the well-known seventh-century Spanish churchman Isidore of Seville. His main concern seems to have been protecting the rights of bishops to appeal to Rome when others attacked or deposed them. Taken as genuine, the *False Decretals* (as they are also known) included the letter from Pope Clement to the apostle James, *On the Primitive Church and Synod of Nicaea*, and the *Donation of Constantine*. In Nicholas's hands, the *Pseudo-Isidorean Decretals* made for welcome reading, taking their place in the papal archives as yet another historical justification for the authority of the Apostolic See.

Over the course of his papacy, Nicholas embraced situations that gave him a chance to put his convictions about the papal office into action. In 862, when Archbishop Hincmar of Reims deposed his fellow bishop Rothad of Soissons for disobedience, the disgruntled cleric took his case to Rome, citing the *Pseudo-Isidorean Decretals* as evidence for the Roman Church's status as a final court of appeals. It seems likely that he brought a copy of the legal collection to Rome with him, if so, making it the first time that anyone in papal circles would have encountered the collection. Nicholas claimed jurisdiction over the case and restored Rothad. Typically an outspoken supporter of papal claims, Hincmar unsuccessfully opposed this particular decision by the pope. The following year when a synod of bishops at Metz approved of Emperor Lothar II's decision to abandon his childless wife Theutberga for his mistress, Nicholas denounced this decision as contrary to canon law, despite the fact that his own legates had consented to the synod's outcome. This time backed by Hincmar of Reims, Nicholas deposed Archbishop Gunther of Cologne and Bishop Tietgaud of Trier, two notable clerics who supported Lothar's divorce. Despite forcible pressure from Lothar and his son, Louis II, Nicholas refused to compromise his position on the deposed bishops, although he never managed to reconcile the emperor and his wife.

Mission to the Bulgars and the Photian schism

In his dealings with the wider world, Nicholas showed equal assertiveness, as evident in his famous pastoral letter to the Bulgars in 866. In this response to a number of questions from those newly converted Christians, the pope addressed a wide range of topics, including fasting practices during Lent, whether to eat meat on feast days, correct marriage practices, and appropriate clothing habits during religious services. In addition to encouraging the Bulgars to follow Roman customs, Nicholas directly contradicted some of what Greek missionaries – also active in the region – had already told them. Nicholas assured their king that only the holy Roman Church remained untainted by heresy and fit to teach them "true and perfect Christianity" without a "blemish or a wrinkle."[18] When news of his advice reached Constantinople, it made an already tense situation even worse. In 858, the Greeks had elected a new patriarch named Photius after the deposition of his predecessor, Ignatius. Ignatius's supporters, who viewed this removal from office as unjust and irregular, had appealed to Rome. In 863, Nicholas declared that Photius should step down and that Ignatius should be restored to office. Photius refused, creating a serious breach between Rome and Constantinople. The pope fired off a number of letters to the Byzantine rulers and church, reminding them about the primacy of Rome and the need for Greeks to respect the Apostolic See's judgments. In 865, a letter reached Rome, forwarded by the king of the Bulgars, in which the Byzantine Emperor Michael III and his co-ruler Basil I denounced Latin Christian habits, fasting practices, and forms of clerical discipline. The Greeks also complained about the Latin belief that the Holy Spirit proceeds from the Father "and from the Son," contrary to the Greek doctrine that the Holy Spirit proceeds from the Father alone. In response, Nicholas called upon Hincmar of Reims and the Frankish clergy to refute this attack on "our church in particular and every church in general that uses the Latin language."[19] The Franks obliged, excoriating the Greek emperors for their wrongful meddling in the affairs of the Church.

After Nicholas died in 867, his immediate successors Hadrian II (868–72) and John VIII (872–82) attempted to maintain the assertive stance taken by their predecessor. In June 869, when he heard that Photius had anathematized Pope Nicholas I, formally condemning him, Hadrian held a council at Rome that excommunicated the Greek patriarch. Hadrian's legates attended a subsequent council held at Constantinople in 869–70, which confirmed the recently deposed Photius's excommunication by the Roman Church, but insisted that Bulgaria remained under Byzantine jurisdiction. Hadrian's legates protested and the pope continued to monitor missionary activities in the region. Seeking allies against the Muslims plaguing papal territories, John showed himself open to an accommodation with the Byzantines over the situation in Bulgaria and other disagreements. In 879, his envoys attended another council in Constantinople, presided over by Photius, who had resumed his position as patriarch. Concessions were made by all concerned: John recognized Photius, whose previous condemnation was overturned, while the Greeks listened to statements of papal primacy lead aloud. An informal compromise placed Bulgaria under Rome's jurisdiction, but allowed Greek missionaries free access to the area. After a decade of crisis, relations between the two churches began to settle down.

Rome and the new localism

For all of their attempts to follow in Pope Nicholas's footsteps, Hadrian II and John VIII faced growing problems on their watch, as the window for renewed papal leadership began to close. Under pressure, Hadrian lifted the sentence of excommunication against Lothar II for his repudiation of his wife. During John's pontificate, intensifying raids by Muslim freebooters placed growing pressure on Rome and its surroundings. The pope appealed far and wide for assistance against the infidels, calling upon the entire society of the faithful to defend Rome, the "head of all churches." Tellingly, he spent much of his energy railing against his neighbors, such as Naples, which employed Muslim mercenaries, sometimes even against Roman forces. With papal support, the Carolingian emperor Louis II waged a series of campaigns in southern Italy against Muslim strongholds, but with little lasting success.

In 875, after the death of Louis II, John VIII crowned the Western Frankish king, Charles the Bald, as emperor. Charles, beset by problems, never made any show of force in Italy. After Charles died two years later, the pope turned to his nephew, the Eastern Frankish ruler Charles the Fat. Pope John, embroiled in a dispute with nearby Spoleto and desperate for assistance, crowned him as emperor in 881, the last Carolingian ruler with a meaningful claim to the imperial title. After decades of internal turmoil and outside pressures, the Carolingian Empire had lost coherence and momentum. Looking back at these events about a century later, the monastic chronicler Benedict of Monte Soratte marked them as the end of an era. In his *Little Book on Imperial Power in the City of Rome*, showing some confusion, he traced the history of the city from the time of the apostles Peter and Paul and Emperor Constantine through the pontificate of Zachary I, who – he erroneously claimed – had traveled to France to offer Charlemagne the imperial scepter. Charlemagne and his heirs had safeguarded Rome, preserving law and order in the city until Pope Nicholas I betrayed his loyalties to Lothar II and Louis II. Not long after, Charles the Bald died leaving no one with the strength or wisdom to pick up the imperial mantle or royal power in Italy. "From this time forward," Benedict concluded his tract, "there were many battles, devastations, and rapine in the kingdom."[20]

Although he did not always have his facts straight, this monk had offered an apt description of the age. Without a strong imperial presence in Italy, Roman aristocratic families began to play a far more aggressive role in the city's politics, drawing the papal office into local feuds and rivalries. Supposedly John VIII met his demise when murdered by a greedy relative, a story reported only in a single Frankish chronicle far from Rome, but still repeated as symbolic of the papacy's imminent slide into decadence. Some modern scholars have called the following century the papacy's "Dark" or "Iron Age," also labeling it the "Pornocracy." Undeniably, popes rose and fell with unseemly quickness, while members of Rome's nobility dominated the A postolic See. In the course of factional rivalries, various popes were accused of murder, black magic, adultery, sexual perversion, and other crimes, hardly the sort of qualities that distinguished the successor of Saint Peter as the leader of Christendom.

A wider sense of historical context, however, helps to explain some of the papacy's admittedly sensational characteristics during this period. As the heyday of Carolingian rule receded, civil strife and uncertainty replaced relative peace and stability. In this regard, the bishops of Rome experienced a contraction of their horizons, involving them – much like other bishops around the former territories of the Frankish empire – in less exalted matters of local politics. For Roman families and churchmen, the universal claims of the pope as the heir of Saint Peter no doubt seemed less important than the prominence of Rome's bishop in city affairs, not to mention the considerable properties and resources attached to the papal office. One result of these reduced circumstances is a relative lack of surviving written sources for the period. The *Book of Popes* effectively ends at the close of the tenth century, with no one bothering to compose a papal biography over the following hundred years or so. If they had, we might have a very different understanding of the Roman papacy during its so-called Iron Age.

None of these caveats changes that fact that the papacy after John VIII experienced serious problems. Persistent Muslim raids in central Italy did not help matters, creating a sense of panic and draining the Lateran of its revenues. After several brief and ineffective popes, including Marinus I (882–84), Hadrian III (884–85), and Stephen V (885–91), the unsettled pontificate of Formosus (891–96) led to one of the more lurid moments in papal history. Formosus's enemies accused him of moving his see from Porto to Rome in order to take up the position of pope, violating a long-standing prohibition against a bishop making such a transfer. Formosus died, but, not to be deterred, his detractors put him on trial anyway. The question of Formosus's legitimacy had wide-reaching repercussions. If he were found guilty, any ordinations he had made as pope would be considered invalid, a boon for some clergy, but a disaster for others. During the so-called "Cadaver Synod" in 897, Pope Stephen VI (896–97) read the charges against the deceased pontiff, whose corpse sat on the papal throne in full priestly regalia while a deacon answered for him. After reaching a guilty verdict, the court tossed his body into the Tiber. Indicative of the high stakes in this drama, some of Formosus's followers soon murdered Stephen VI.

Lingering imperial politics after the death of Charles the Fat further complicated this unsettled scene. Caught between two rising powers in central Italy, Margraves Berengar of Fruili and Guido of Spoleto, Pope Stephen V had tried to convince the East Frankish King Arnulf to claim the imperial title in Rome, but without success. After Guido emerged victorious, the pope had little choice but to crown him as emperor in 891. Formosus crowned him again later that year along with his son, Lambert. After Guido died in 894, Arnulf finally arrived on the scene, driving Lambert from Rome and receiving his own coronation from the pope in 896. This political free-for-all continued after Formosus died, when Arnulf returned to Germany and Lambert resumed control of Rome. Following the outcome of the Cadaver Synod and the three-week pontificate of Theodore II, the anti-Formosus party elected Sergius III (898, 904–11). Lambert, however, drove Sergius from the city – Pope Formosus, after all, had crowned Lambert as emperor, meaning that he had little incentive to support those who denied Formosus's legitimacy. In 898, John IX (898–900) invalidated the Cadaver Synod and restored Formosus's good name. Lambert, however, did not have long to savor this outcome, dying in a hunting accident later that year.

Following the brief and unsettled pontificates of Benedict IV (900–3) and Leo V (903–4), Sergius III returned to the papal office. He did so in part by allying himself with a rising aristocratic power in the city, Count Theophylact of Tusculum, who dominated the city's militia and papal coffers. Over the following decades, with the papacy more or less under its thumb, Theophylact's family restored an appreciable level of calm to Rome. Factionalisms, rivalries, and intrigue nevertheless persisted, involving the Tusculans and other prominent families, including the Crescentii. In 928, Theophylact's daughter Marozia and her husband conspired against Pope John X (914–28), pushing him from office, imprisoning him, and supposedly murdering him. According to later accounts, John had only become pope in the first place because he was Marozia's lover. Regardless, he had proven himself to be a relatively effective leader, organizing a military coalition of regional Italian powers that drove Muslim forces from one of their remaining strongholds at Garigliano in 915. After two short-lived popes, one of Marozia's sons became Pope John XI (931–36); another, John's half-brother Alberic II, governed Rome from 932 to 955 after imprisoning their mother. A series of compliant popes held office during Alberic's reign. On his deathbed, it was later claimed, Alberic made Pope Agapitus II (946–55) swear to elect his illegitimate son as the next pontiff, who became John XII (955–64). At that moment, it must have seemed that business as usual would prevail in Rome, as it had during previous generations, for better or for worse. In fact, the papacy's restricted horizons were about to reopen, in part due to the reemergence of imperial power in Western Europe.

The revival of empire

In 962, Pope John XII called upon Otto I, duke of Saxony and king of the Germans, to protect him from Berengar II, margrave of Ivrea and upstart claimant to the royal title in Italy. As the contemporary observer Liudprand of Cremona described the situation in his work *Concerning King Otto,* John beseeched the king to "free the pope himself and his ward, the Roman Church, from the tyrant's fangs, and return them to their original health and liberty." Otto was more than up to the task. Building upon the successes of his father, Henry I, the Saxon ruler had consolidated his power over the major duchies of Germany, displaying his leadership and prowess when he crushed an invading Magyar army at the Battle of Lechfeld in 955. Otto had already subdued Berengar once before during a previous campaign in 951, when he had claimed the Italian crown for himself at Pavia. Responding to the pope's call, he marched once more against the margrave and forced him from the field before journeying in triumph to Rome.

On February 2, 962, Pope John crowned Otto as emperor, marking the first genuine revival of the imperial tradition since the collapse of the Carolingian Empire.[21] Weeks later, Otto confirmed the donations made by Pippin and Charlemagne to the Roman popes, enlarging the Papal States by adding more territories to them. He also swore to protect the papacy's rights, properties, and free elections, but, echoing the *Constitutio Romana*, he insisted that future popes immediately inform the emperor of their election and swear an oath of fidelity to him. Perhaps getting more than he bargained for, John XII soon turned against the new emperor, allying himself with his former enemy, Berengar. For Liudprand, the reasons behind this betrayal were quite simple. When Otto's messengers asked the Romans about John's change of heart, they replied that the emperor "loves what pertains to God, protects church and secular affairs with arms, improves them by his customs, and cleans them up with his laws; Pope John is against all these things."[22] Returning to Rome, Otto oversaw a council that deposed the pope, charging him with turning the Lateran into a brothel, incest, perjury, sorcery, and murder. Before again leaving Rome, the emperor installed a new pope, Leo VIII (963–65), but John subsequently drove him from the city, before dying from injuries he sustained in bed while having sex with another man's wife (or so his enemies claimed). The Romans elected a new pope, Benedict V (May–June 964), but he was forced to step down when Otto returned on the scene and restored Leo VIII.

From such episodes, the picturesque view of the papal Pornocracy endures, featuring the first of what E. R. Chamberlain colorfully called "Bad Popes."[23] One should never forget, however, to interrogate our sources of information for the scurrilous condition of the tenth-century papacy. In this case, Liudprand of Cremona, an Italian refugee at Otto's court restored to prominence by the emperor, had every reason to celebrate Otto's care for the Apostolic See, while painting Pope John XII with the darkest of colors. Viewed generously, the church at Rome at this time looked much like other churches around Europe, its clerical leaders serving the immediate interests of their friends, family, and city. In this regard, John XII represented what Kathleen Cushing describes as a "not untypical (if less than ideal) spiritual head of western Christendom."[24] Nevertheless, Rome's reputation suffered, in part since the standard for judging the city's bishops remained higher than that of their lesser counterparts. Everyone knew that the popes stood for something bigger and better. If nothing else, the fact that emperors came to Rome for their crowns made it impossible to forget this fact.

Otto and his heirs, Otto II and Otto III, had their own reasons to celebrate the privileges of the Roman Church. In a diploma issued in 1001, Otto III described Rome as the "royal city" and "mother of all churches," even as he complained about the questionable reputation of recent popes. Bestowing various Italian territories upon the papacy, an act sometimes called the "Ottonian Donation," the emperor praised Pope Sylvester II (999–1003), elected to the Apostolic See with Otto's open support.[25] For the young ruler, who presented his reign as a renovation of the Roman Empire, the emperor stood as the supreme head of the Christian world, reclaiming the city of Rome's imperial destiny, supported by the city's pontiffs. Sylvester II, originally known as Gerbert of Aurillac, possessed his own interesting ideas about the papal office. Highly educated, he had worked earlier as Otto III's tutor. Thinking back to his papal namesake, Sylvester I, this pope apparently saw himself as Otto's spiritual father, responsible for his soul and to some extent the governance of his Christian realm. As bishop of Rome, Sylvester did not hesitate to press the advantages of his exalted posistion, as seen, for example, when he forged a close bond between the Roman Church and the newly converted Hungarian king, Stephen, taking his kingdom under the protection of Saint Peter, sending him his crown to wear as a Christian ruler.

Even Sylvester II, however, for all his education and aspirations, could not escape the disruptive realities of his day. In 1001, a rebellion by the Tusculans and their supporters forced him and Otto III from Rome. Otto died before he could recover control of the city, marking the end of the Ottonian dynasty. Over a decade would pass before the new king of the Germans, the Salian ruler Henry II, came to Rome for his imperial coronation. Sylvester was permitted to return, but he died not long after. Whatever their partnership meant to pope and emperor, it came to a disappointing end, a sign of the persistent challenges to universal ambitions around the turn of the first millennium, whether imperial or papal.

Chapter 4: Reform and Crusade

Late in 1044, a faction of Romans drove the Tusculan Pope Benedict IX (1032–44) from office and chose a new pope, Sylvester III, elected in January 1045. Undaunted, Benedict expelled Sylvester from the city, but then decided to retire his office to yet another pope, Gregory VI (1045–46). Apparently, Benedict soon regretted his decision and tried to regain his position; not to be forgotten, Sylvester III refused to drop his claim to the papal office. In December 1046, the Salian Emperor Henry III intervened in this less than ideal situation, assembling a council at Sutri that deposed Benedict IX and Sylvester III, accepted Gregory VI's resignation, and approved the installation of a new pope, Clement II (1046–47). When Clement died the following year, Henry arranged for the appointment of the briefly lived Damasus II (July–August 1048), followed by Bruno of Toul, who took the name Leo IX (1049–54). Not long after the emperor selected him as pope, however, Leo insisted upon having the Roman clergy and people confirm his election. According to the contemporary *Life of Leo IX*, the new pope arrived in Rome in the manner of a pilgrim, entering the city barefoot and offering to leave if the Romans decided he was not fit to be their bishop. In response, the assembled clergy and people unanimously acclaimed him as pope.[1]

This portrait of Pope Leo revealed something important about his values and the priorities of those who supported him. Modern historians typically regard Leo as the first "reformer" pope – reform, in this instance, meaning an historical effort to transform the circumstances of the Roman Church and its place in European society. In concrete terms, such reformers targeted common practices of their day, such as clerical marriage and simony (that is, giving or receiving a gift or payment for a church office), viewed as sins that jeopardized the efficacy of the sacraments, imperiled ecclesiastical property, and threatened to pollute the faithful. Overall, they sought to secure the "liberty" of the Church, meaning its freedom from outside interference, including that of kings and emperors. At stake were the proper boundaries between the clergy and the laity, between priests and potentates, between the sacred and the secular. In this regard, the reform movement inaugurated what German scholar Gerd Tellenbach once described as a struggle for "right order" in the world.[2]

Although not inevitable, this transformation in the papacy resulted in open conflict between Pope Gregory VII (1073–84) and the German ruler Henry IV over the right to invest bishops with ring and staff, symbols of their sacred office. A native Roman who had left home earlier in his ecclesiastical career, Gregory had returned to Rome with Leo IX and served a series of reformist popes in their effort to purify the clergy of simony, fornication, and other violations of clerical sanctity. As the heir to Saint Peter, Gregory believed it was his right and duty to defend the Church's freedom from anyone who threatened it, including but not limited to Henry. The resulting Investiture Conflict divided much of Western Europe into two camps, supporting the papal and imperial causes, respectively. The struggle lasted for decades, both sides emerging with scars, and neither side claiming absolute victory. Pursuing their overarching vision of reform, however, the popes of Rome had deposed sinful clergy in their own ranks, reprimanded Eastern Christians for straying from Roman rites and teachings, vied with emperors for supreme leadership over Christendom, and declared holy wars that would lead Europeans to fight battles in God's name over a thousand miles from their homelands. As a consequence, the papacy and medieval Europe would never be the same.[3]

Reform and the Roman Church

On either side of the year 1000, beyond the immediate nexus of imperial and papal politics, important developments were underway with long-term significance for the Roman papacy. As the European political order, society, and economy recovered from the disruptions of the later Carolingian era, calls for the reform and reordering of the Western Church began to surface, the start of a veritable "apostolic revival" among contemporary Christians. By the mid-eleventh century, the papacy became an active agent for this reform of the Church, emphasizing the rightful place of the

Apostolic See as the head of Christendom. This drive to change the existing state of things, however, brought new conflicts in its wake, ranging from struggles over local church offices to disputes with far-off Constantinople.

Origins of reform

After the collapse of the Carolingian order, power in much of Western Europe had devolved to an extremely localized level. In places such as France, without strong royal leadership, dukes, counts, and petty lords dominated the scene, building castles as seats for their dominion over the surrounding countryside. Such castellans typically received military service from lesser lords, vassals who swore personal oaths to their superiors. The term "feudal" is sometimes used to describe this situation, wherein lords received fealty and service from their dependent vassals in return for a "fief," a grant of property and other forms of income. When they founded churches and monasteries for the salvation of their souls and those of their families, such landed aristocrats viewed them as their own property, choosing the clerics and monks – often their own relatives – who would watch over them. Standing among the mighty, bishops and abbots owed and received fealty and homage, just like other lords and vassals. In villages, humble parish priests commonly married, passing on their position to their sons. Through such ties of property and kinship, churches and monasteries became and remained embedded in the bonds of local society.

In Germany, the revival of strong kingship and empire also involved bishops and abbots in close-knit relationships with secular rulers, who issued privileges and immunities to the clergy, including such things as the right to collect tolls and taxes, permission to hold lucrative courts and markets, and freedom from certain fiscal burdens. The Ottonians and Salians, who relied upon clerics as agents for governance, commonly invested bishops with the symbols of their sacred office, typically a ring (the sign of the bishop's marriage to his see) and staff (the mark of his pastoral duties). Less exalted rulers in other regions of Europe did likewise. This ritual act of investiture disclosed the intimate relationship between secular and ecclesiastical powers that few questioned as a rightful part of their political and social order.

Over time, however, some churchmen and members of the laity came to believe that this situation needed changing, the untangling of the Church from its ties to the world. The foundation of Cluny in 910 by Duke William of Aquitaine provides a famous and early example of this phenomenon. In his charter establishing the new monastery, William declared that he established this religious house for the salvation of his soul, as well as the souls of his relatives, both living and dead. In this regard, he did nothing uncommon. After he nominated the first abbot, Bruno, William promised the monks of Cluny complete freedom to elect his successor without any outside intervention. He furthermore placed Cluny directly under the protection of the Roman pope, declaring that the monastery should not suffer any violation by secular princes, counts, and bishops, not even from the bishop of Rome. Enjoying this condition of monastic liberty, Cluny represented a compelling, innovative model for religious reform. Nor did it stand alone. Other monasteries, such as at Gorze in Lorraine, also called for a stricter obedience to the Benedictine Rule, a simplification and purification of their monastic life.[4]

As medieval Europe enjoyed increasing economic growth and material prosperity, sorting out the proper place of the Church – and its property – in the world must have seemed more and more urgent. Historians caution against describing these calls for reform as a "movement" or "program," words that imply coherence and coordination. Nonetheless, the proponents of such changes on a local level did communicate with each other, sharing common values and goals. In addition to speaking out against the violation of church goods, persons, and lands, they also began to insist that the clergy should be celibate, thereby extracted from the ties of marriage and family, and also that clerics should not give or receive any gifts or payment related to their position, condemned as the sin of simony. By such means, reformers sought – much like Cluny and similar houses had achieved – the proper liberty of the Church. As we will see, these sentiments possessed profound implications, invigorating and inspiring some, repelling and disturbing others.

Reform comes to Rome

Tenth-century popes did not stand entirely isolated from early calls to reform. As seen above, William of Aquitaine placed Cluny under the protection of the Apostolic See, demonstrating Rome's special appeal even in a balkanized, feudal world. In 931, Pope John XI issued a charter confirming Cluny's privileges and exemptions from oversight by outsiders. Pope Leo VII (936–39) issued a similar charter for Gorze in 938. It is unclear how much these tokens of papal support meant for their recipients, but they must have meant something or people would not have sought them. Throughout this period, in exchange for fees and annual payments, Rome's bishops continued to hear appeals from distant churchmen and bestow privileges on churches and monasteries, such as exemptions from certain forms of oversight or taxes. Supported by the Salian ruler Henry II, a supporter of Gorze, reformist impulses picked up speed. In 1022, the emperor and Pope Benedict VIII (1012–24) held a synod at Pavia that issued a number of reformist canons, anathematizing clergy guilty of simony and restating requirements for clerical celibacy.

Such reformist "dabbling" by the papacy, however, did little to satisfy figures such as Rodulfus Glaber, a monastic chronicler and admirer of Cluny. For Glaber, the Roman Church plainly displayed the very sins and shortcomings denounced by reformist circles. In his chronicle, he took particular aim at Pope John XIX (1024–32), including a story that the pope planned to recognize the primacy of Constantinople over the Eastern Church in return for bribes. The only thing that stopped John, Glaber declared, was the outrage caused when news of his plan leaked out. In his *Life of Saint William*, the abbot of Saint-Bénigne, Glaber included a letter written by the pious abbot rebuking one pope – again, most likely John XIX – because "throughout all Italy spiritual gifts were being sold on a large scale for gold and silver." Glaber held a similarly poor opinion of Pope Benedict IX, John XIX's nephew, claiming that he was only ten years old when he became pope through some well-placed bribes.[5] Whether these claims were true or not, they suggested to some reform-minded churchmen that the papacy represented part of the problem and not the solution.

Glaber ended his chronicle by praising Emperor Henry III for his opposition to simony, either dying or putting aside his work before Benedict IX, Sylvester III, and Gregory VI began their contest over the papal office. One imagines that he would have approved of how Henry resolved that unseemly situation at the Synod of Sutri. At first glance, Henry's subsequent appointment of Pope Leo IX seemed to fit the pattern of previous generations, a situation of strong imperial influence over the papal office and its occupant. Some contemporaries, however, strongly objected to the emperor's high-handed involvement in the choosing of popes. The anonymous French author of a tract called *On the Ordination of the Pope*, liberally quoting the *False Decretals* to make his point, called Henry "that most wicked emperor" on account of his actions, recalling past instances when rulers had unjustly interfered with the papacy.[6]

Before he became pope, Bruno of Toul had shown himself to be a committed monastic reformer in his own right. When he settled at Rome, he brought with him an entourage of people committed to a similar vision of reforming the Church, including Humbert of Marmoutier, named cardinal bishop of Silva Candida; Frederick of Lorraine, the future Pope Stephen IX (1057–58); and the young deacon Hildebrand, the future Pope Gregory VII. This circle enjoyed the support of other outspoken and like-minded churchmen, including the charismatic hermit and later cardinal bishop of Ostia, Peter Damian. Pope Leo shrewdly appointed such friends and like-minded figures as cardinal bishops and priests, often foreigners such as himself rather than local Romans, rightly viewing the cardinals as a resource for his reformist agenda.

Supported by such men, the pope put the principles of reform into action. Although based in Rome, he remained constantly on the move, journeying around Italy and north of the Alps. In this way, he embodied papal authority for people who had never seen a pope before. Leo summoned a series of reform synods between 1049 and 1053, issuing canons against simony and the selling of ecclesiastical goods, tightening restrictions upon who could become a priest, barring clerics from wielding weapons, and banning the acceptance of payment for burials, baptisms, and other pastoral tasks. In addition, such legislation took aim at lay violations of church canons, reiterating long-standing but largely ignored rules about marriage, incest, and divorce. Clergy and laity alike were being put on notice – no more business as usual.

At the Council of Reims in 1049, Leo stage-managed a dramatic scene over the course of three days when he insisted that bishops guilty of simony publically confess their sin. Some bishops immediately swore to their innocence, although others remained silent – including the host of the synod, the archbishop of Reims – and stalled for time. Bishop Hugh of Langres had an especially rough time at the council, accused not only of simony but several other crimes including murder. According to one account, the next day, when the bishop of Besançons rose to speak on Hugh's behalf, he was struck mute. Seeing the writing on the wall, Hugh secretly fled, resulting in his excommunication by the pope. On the third day, after prayers and processions around the church of Saint Remy, more bishops confessed their guilt. Leo reconciled most of them after their confession but stripped at least one bishop of his position. He also gave the archbishops clear instructions: If they knew that any bishops under their jurisdiction were guilty of simony, they must report this to the pope. Finally, Leo excommunicated in absentia several bishops who had failed to attend the council and had not written to explain their absence.

As he reminded the assembled clergy on the council's first day, Leo took such actions by virtue of the Roman Church's unrivaled status as the head of the universal Church.[7] His assertion of exclusive papal primacy cut to the heart of the reformers' developing strategy to secure their goals. Like a drum beat, Pope Leo, Humbert of Silva Candida, Peter Damian, and others in their circle insisted upon the dignity of the Apostolic See, conjuring images of the past to reshape their present, looking back to the origins of Rome as a Christian city. "The holy Roman Church ought to be loved and adored," wrote one sympathetic cleric, perhaps Humbert himself, "not because Rome was founded on the sand by Romulus and Remus, brought forth by a profane priesthood and who knows what kind of sacrilege, but rather because it was founded on the rock of Christ by Peter and Paul."[8] Over the coming years and decades, reformers highlighted the figure of Emperor Constantine as presented in the *Donation of Constantine*, a pious ruler who had humbled himself before bishops, showed deference to Pope Sylvester, and showered the Roman Church with property and imperial dignities. They compiled new canon law collections to support their claims, such as the *Collection in Seventy-Four Titles*, opening with a section "On the Primacy of the Roman Church." In a letter addressed to Hildebrand in 1059, Peter Damian compared such privileges of the Roman Church to weapons. Through its canonical rights and authority, Rome, the "head of the entire Christian religion through the chair of Saint Peter," marshaled the churches of the whole world just like a duke drawing up his soldiers into a battle formation. Recycling and reconfiguring these old building blocks, the reformers constructed their innovative vision of papal supremacy over Christendom.[9]

The schism of 1054

The papacy did not limit its ambitions to the Western Church on Leo's watch. In 1053, Humbert of Silva Candida brought to Pope Leo's attention a letter written by a Greek cleric that denounced several Western religious practices, including the Roman use of "azymes," unleavened rather than leavened bread, for the Eucharist. At this particular moment, tensions between Rome and Constantinople were running high due to the recent Norman conquests in southern Italy. The Normans, hard-scrabble descendants from earlier generations of Vikings, had first arrived as mercenaries fighting in petty squabbles between local Italian rulers and the Byzantines, who still ruled over portions of the peninsula. By the mid-eleventh century, the Normans had begun to carve out territories for themselves. Their growing clout destabilized the political and religious scene in the region, including churches and monasteries that followed Greek religious rules and practices. Reacting to Norman abuses of Greek clergy and property, the Byzantine Patriarch Michael Cerularius had closed Latin churches in Constantinople and probably approved the letter denouncing the Latin sacrifice.

Leo IX and Humbert were hardly the types to sit still for such an attack on the Western Church and its rites. The pope's circle fired off a number of letters to the Greek patriarch and Byzantine Emperor Constantine IX, defending the Latin celebration of the Eucharist and other traditions. If anything, they struck a more aggressive and uncompromising tone than they did when addressing Western audiences. In one letter to the Greek ruler, the pope and his ghost-writers included lengthy references to the *Donation of Constantine*, illustrating the first Christian emperor's supposed deference to the popes of Rome and reason for moving the imperial capital to Constantinople – a move made out of respect and reverence for Saint Peter and his heirs. As the successors to Peter, the popes of Rome enjoyed the "royal priesthood," a special insight into the workings of the Church, including the mysteries of the sacraments. In 1054, Humbert of Silva Candida led a delegation to Constantinople hoping to settle the matter. Further tracts and polemics were produced as the dispute widened to include Western complaints about the Greek allowance of clerical marriage and Eastern attacks on the Latin addition of *filioque* to the creed. In no mood to compromise, churchmen on both sides continued to press their positions. On July 16, 1054, Humbert deposited a bull excommunicating Michael Cerularius and his supporters on the high altar in the Church of Hagia Sophia. The Greek prelate responded in kind.

The resulting "Schism of 1054" did not create the lasting break between the Latin and Greek Churches, as historians sometimes assert. Over the following years, cooler heads prevailed and smoothed the dispute over. The underlying causes of this particular clash, however, did not go away. To the contrary, the episode offered a sign of things to come in the papacy's approach toward Constantinople, if not toward believers everywhere – a more assertive view of papal primacy, an emphasis on the superiority of the Roman rite and teachings, and a sense that opponents of the Roman Church in fact stood against the entirety of Christendom.

The Investiture Conflict

Although not necessarily clear at the time, the reform movement had also set popes and the German throne on a collision course, leading to a struggle that would divide Europe. Under Leo's successors, the papacy forged a new military alliance with the Normans, secured its grip on papal elections, and threw its support behind radical reformers in Milan. All of these moves challenged the existing balance of power between popes, Rome's aristocratic families, and the Salian dynasty, which claimed kingship over Italy and the imperial dignity. Under Gregory VII, the papacy identified clerical elections – for all bishops, not just the pope – as the defining issue of the reform movement. By denying the rights of investiture to King Henry IV, the uncompromising pope initiated a clash that would dominate the Roman Church for decades to come.

The Normans and the Election Decree of 1059

Despite his grand claims, Leo IX died after a humiliating defeat. In 1053, the pope had led a coalition of Roman troops into battle against the Normans, whose growing aggression in southern Italy threatened papal territories. Leo had apparently hoped to forge an alliance between Emperor Henry III and the Byzantine ruler Constantine IX against the Normans, but decided not to wait. At the battle of Civitate, the Normans routed the pope's army and took him prisoner. During much of the ensuing controversy with the Greek Church in 1054, the pope spent his time in "honorable" confinement as a prisoner at Benevento. After he acknowledged Norman rights over their conquests in Apulia and Calabria, he was allowed to return to Rome where he died before hearing about the outcome of Humbert's delegation to Constantinople.

Leo's ambitions did not perish with him. Although they faced stiff resistance from Rome's aristocratic families that stood to lose influence over the papal office, the reform party managed to elect Victor II (1055–57), followed by Stephen IX, men chosen from within their own ranks. Stephen also brought the reformers a powerful ally, his brother Duke Godfrey of Lower Lotharingia. When Stephen died, however, the Tusculan family made a bid to recover control of the papacy, electing their own pope, Benedict X. The supporters of reform, including a number of cardinal bishops, elected Pope Nicholas II (1059–61) at Siena, one of the first papal elections held outside of Rome without any input from the city's leading clergy and families. Backed by Godfrey of Lower Lotharingia, Nicholas drove Benedict X from Rome, excommunicating the anti-pope.

Nicholas oversaw two important developments for the future of the reform papacy. First, in need of further armed support against Rome's rebellious aristocrats, he pivoted on the papal relationship with the Normans. Rather than fighting against their growing power, he arranged an alliance with them, turning former enemies into a formidable source of muscle for the reformers. In 1059, Nicholas received oaths of allegiance from the Norman leaders Richard of Aversa, Richard of Capua, and Robert Guiscard, who swore to be faithful "to the holy Roman Church and the Apostolic See," and personally to Pope Nicholas, helping him to "hold the Roman papacy securely and honorably."[10] In effect, Guiscard and his fellow Normans became vassals of Saint Peter and his successors, acknowledging papal lordship in return for papal recognition of their conquests. For the papacy, this strategy quickly paid off when Richard of Capua subdued some of Nicholas's opponents and delivered Benedict X to Rome as a prisoner.

Second, Nicholas held a council at Rome that ratified the so-called "Election Decree of 1059." This legislation placed the authority to elect a new pope squarely in the hands of the cardinal bishops, who would determine papal succession before seeking the assent of the cardinal priests, followed by the remainder of the Roman clergy and people. In the case of a disputed election, the cardinal bishops possessed the final say and could hold their deliberations anywhere, not just in Rome (Nicholas, of course, had just been elected himself at Siena). By issuing these rules, the reformist party sought to secure control of papal elections and to stymie the influence of local Roman families over them. The decree also limited the role of the German king, Henry IV, in any future elections. At this point, the Roman reformers did not stand at odds with the Salians. Henry III, after all, had supported Leo IX throughout the entirety of his papacy and also supported his pro-reform successor, Victor II. When the emperor died in 1056, however, his son Henry IV was too young to assume the kingship of Germany and the imperial title, leading to the regency of his mother, Agnes. During this period of relative weakness for the imperial dynasty, the advocates of the reform papacy might have sensed an opportunity. The new Election Decree made no provisions for royal involvement beyond a vague reference to the "honor and reverence" owed to King Henry IV, who would one day "hopefully" become emperor.[11]

For all of its long-term consequences, the Election Decree of 1059 did not prevent future problems surrounding papal elections.

The decree itself created new controversies. An alternative version that circulated in imperial circles modified several key points, simply stating that the "cardinals" would manage the election of the new pope, thereby including the cardinal priests in the initial deliberations, not just the bishops. In time, the cardinal priests and deacons managed to secure their full participation in papal elections along with the bishops, yet another sign of the entire cardinalate's rising status. The alternative version also emphasized the need for the cardinals to confer with Henry, king of the Germans and future emperor, during the election proceedings.

Those opposed to the reformers tried to roll back such changes. When Nicholas died in 1061, a delegation from the Roman opposition – undoubtedly smarting from their failed election of Benedict X – made their way to the German court to lobby for their choice of his successor. This dissident group elected a new pope, Honorius II. The reformers in Rome chose Anselm of Lucca, a longtime member of their circle, who took the name Alexander II (1061–73). The following year, when a synod met to investigate the double election, the reformist party stood well positioned to guide its deliberations and secured Alexander's recognition as pope. Honorius, who never abandoned his claim to be the rightful pope, died in obscurity about a decade later. The reformers and their transformative goals, it seemed, had come to stay.

The papacy and the Patarenes

During the 1050s, the city of Milan had emerged as a laboratory of reformist sentiment in its own right. Under the leadership of two clerics, Ariald of Varese and Landulf Cotta, a movement of pious citizens demanded an end to simony, clerical marriage, and other abuses among the clergy. They took their demands to extreme ends, forcing clerics to sign agreements to live in chastity, barring some from the altar entirely. They also swore oaths not to recognize the validity of any cleric who obtained his office by simony. Eventually they drove Archbishop Guido of Milan from the city when he failed to support their cause. Resistant to such radical changes, their enemies began to call these men and women "Patarenes," perhaps meaning "the ragged ones," indicating their origins with a group of cloth-weavers. Whatever the named originally meant, the label stuck.

As this dispute in the city worsened, both sides appealed to Rome. In 1059, Nicholas II had sent Peter Damian and Anselm of Lucca as legates to settle the situation. For the more conservative elements in

Milan, the growing clout of the reform papacy posed an unwelcome source of interference in their own church's venerable traditions and rights, traced back proudly to Saint Ambrose of Milan. Perhaps not surprisingly, the papacy generally sided with the Patarenes. Several prominent bishops from the surrounding region of Lombardy joined the Roman faction that elected Honorius II in 1061, demonstrating their opposition to the papal reformers. As the years passed, the situation grew more and more violent, including riots and street-fighting between the opposing parties. In June 1066, one faction murdered Ariald, leaving Landulf's brother Erlembald in charge of the movement. A layman and warrior, Erlembald intensified the armed conflict in Milan, acting like a veritable warlord who ran the city. As a sign of papal support, he even bore the "banner of Saint Peter" given to him by Alexander II.

Eventually, this struggle in Milan became the flash point for a wider contest between the papacy and Henry IV, when the king reached maturity and came to exercise his sovereign rights in northern Italy. When Archbishop Guido resigned his office in 1072, he tried to secure the position of his successor Godfrey by appealing to Henry. The Patarenes, however, elected their own candidate, Atto. Alexander II threw his weight behind Atto and excommunicated five of Henry's counselors, who, he declared, had wrongfully participated in Godfrey's consecration. After his election in 1073, Alexander's successor, Pope Gregory VII, continued to ratchet up the pressure in Lombardy. Accusing various bishops in the region of suppressing earlier papal legislation, including the Election Decree of 1059, he deposed some of them and summoned others to Rome for judgment. Gregory also dispatched the banner of Saint Peter to Erlembald, openly displaying his sympathies for the Patarenes.

The situation in Milan continued to deteriorate. Faced with a rebellion against his rule in Saxony, Henry maintained a conciliatory tone toward the pope, who responded in kind. In 1075, however, the German king delivered a devastating blow against the rebels and began to reassert his position in Lombardy. That same year, the Patarenes suffered their own military reverses when Erlembald was killed and Milan's cathedral burned. After this latest round of chaos, some of the city's citizens called upon Henry IV to intervene. Eager to reassert his prerogatives in the city and region, the German king appointed a new archbishop, Tedald, disregarding both Atto and Godfrey's existing claims to the office. He also appointed new bishops in Spoleto and Fermo. Although his actions fell well within the traditional rights of German rulers in the region, Pope Gregory VII's unflinching commitment to the reform of the Church provoked a strong reaction against this act of secular intervention.

The Investiture Conflict

More than any other figure, Gregory VII placed a lasting stamp upon the reform papacy of the eleventh century. Modern scholars sometimes refer to the papal reform movement as the "Gregorian" reform, a somewhat inaccurate label that has stuck. A former monk, Gregory brought an ascetic sense of devotion to the papal office, continuing to wear a monastic habit even after his election. His view of the papacy and his own role in the Church can be seen at a glance in the so-called *Dictatus Papae*, a famous and puzzling document. Written in 1075 for an unclear purpose and never circulated, it made stark, point-by-point claims for the authority of Saint Peter's successors. A few of its statements included the claim that "only the Roman Pontiff may rightly be called universal," that "he alone can depose or restore bishops," that "he may depose emperors," and that "he may be judged by no one." It also flatly stated that "someone not in concord with the Roman Church may not be held catholic."[12] Even if Gregory did not broadcast this particular text, such language signaled his lack of inclination to compromise.

At the beginning of his papacy, Gregory professed his love and concern for Henry as a Christian ruler and beloved son. When the German monarch installed Tedald as archbishop of Milan, events began to take on a momentum of their own. In a letter written to Henry on December 8, 1075, Gregory rebuked him for continuing to communicate with men "under the censure of the Apostolic See," breaking his promises and appointing "persons entirely unknown to us" as bishops in Spoleto and Fermo. Reminding Henry about the pope's power to "loosen and bind," granted through Saint Peter, Gregory warned him not to imperil the "freedom of the Church." Early the following year, Henry responded by assembling a council of bishops and lay rulers, who denounced their obedience to the "false monk, Hildebrand." In a widely circulated letter to the pope, the emperor decried Gregory's recent actions with regard to Milan and elsewhere: "By the sword you have come to the throne of peace," the king thundered, "and from the throne of peace you have destroyed the peace." In February 1076, Gregory responded in kind by excommunicating Henry during a synod held at Rome, releasing all of his subjects from any oaths of allegiance and fealty owed to the

anathematized ruler. For good measure, the pope also excommunicated all of the bishops in Lombardy who supported Henry.[13]
As one pro-imperial observer wrote about this turn of events and
Pope Gregory, "The Christian people is divided in two, with some
saying he is good and others calling him an imposter and false monk
and an anti-Christian."[14] As his struggle with Henry escalated, the
pope depicted their combat in apocalyptic tones – history, Gregory
implied, had reached a new and perhaps final stage in the ongoing
battle between good and evil, with the forces of God's followers on
one side and the servants of Antichrist on the other.

By 1077, faced with a fresh rebellion against his authority in Saxony
and losing his propaganda war with the relentless pope, Henry inter-
cepted Gregory at the mountain castle of Canossa in Tuscany as
the pope traveled to Germany to meet with the Saxon rebels. He
appeared in the snow outside the castle, barefoot and wearing penitential garb. After days of mediation involving Abbot Hugh of Cluny
and Mathilda of Tuscany, a longtime supporter of the reformers at
Rome, the pope and emperor were reconciled on terms that seemed
favorable to the papacy. Among other things, Henry swore to obey
the pope's future commands, to allow Gregory safe passage into
Germany to meet with the rebellious princes, and to face judgment
by them and the pope about whether he should retain his royal title.
The two parted in peace, leaving the resolution of their differences
to the future months.

On the surface, Canossa marked the high point of Gregory's influence. At a synod held during Lent in 1078, he drove his point home,
issuing the first explicit prohibitions against lay investiture, decree-
ing "that no one of the clergy shall receive the investiture with a
bishopric or abbey or church from the hand of an emperor or king
or of any lay person, male or female." In reality, Gregory's apparent
victory marked the beginning of a slide into defeat. Although the
pope later tried to qualify what he did at Canossa, saying he had
only restored Henry to communion with the Church and did not
validate his royal status, their reconciliation put the German king in
a position to suppress the rebellion against him. The Saxon rebels
felt betrayed by the pope. Henry easily defeated their newly elected
"anti-king," Rudolf of Swabia, and continued to appoint loyal bishops
in Germany and Lombardy without consulting Gregory. In 1080, the
pope renewed his excommunication of the German king. Writing to
Bishop Hermann of Metz the next year, Gregory offered a compelling
defense of papal primacy and the ultimate authority of popes over
secular rulers, referring to Pope Gelasius's view on the two powers,

as well as the moment when "another Roman pontiff deposed the king of the Franks," meaning when the papacy supported Pippin's displacement of the Merovingian dynasty.[15]

Despite these bold claims, the pope's second excommunication of the German king did not have the same dramatic impact as the first. In June 1080, an assembly of bishops in Lombardy elected an opposition pope, Guibert of Ravenna, who took the name Clement III. Over the following years, many of Rome's noble families, tired of the ongoing conflict, began to side with Henry and his anti-pope. In 1084, Henry marched on the city. While Gregory took refuge in the Castel Sant'Angelo, Clement crowned Henry emperor and his wife empress. Many of cardinals in the city also transferred their loyalty to the new pope in residence at the Lateran. Later that year Norman soldiers drove the German emperor from Rome and plundered the city, taking Gregory with them when they left. He passed away at Salerno on May 25, 1085, reportedly saying on his deathbed, "I have loved righteousness and hated iniquity, therefore I die in exile."

The conflict continues

After Gregory's exile and demise, one might have easily imagined a grim future for the reform papacy. Henry IV's apparent triumph, however, did not spell an end to the overall contest between popes and emperors. Despite imperial opposition and a relatively well-established anti-pope, Gregory's successors Victor III (1086–87) and Urban II (1088–99) continued to assert the reformist vision of leadership over the Roman Church insistently, if somewhat more moderately than Pope Gregory – the days of boycotting sinful priests and dragging them from the altar were over. Supporters and opponents of papal reform continued to churn out letters and polemical tracts, each side denouncing the other, although everyone now seemed to agree that simony and clerical marriage were abuses needing correction. In the 1090s, Henry faced a rebellion by nobles who elected his disaffected son Conrad as their anti-king with support from northern Italian cities that included Milan, Cremona, and Piacenza. Taking advantage of this situation, through negotiation and compromise, Urban II skillfully managed to swing most of the bishops in Lombardy around to his side. As discussed below, he also managed a show-stopping demonstration of papal leadership in 1095 when he summoned an expedition to free Jerusalem from Muslim hands, known as the First Crusade.

By late summer of 1097, backed by Mathilda of Tuscany's troops, Pope Urban finally reclaimed Rome for his papacy, driving Clement III from the city. Urban passed away in July 1099 and Clement died just over a year later. Meanwhile, Pope Paschal II (1099–1118) continued to press his advantage against Henry IV, who died in 1106 after facing another rebellion by his other son, Henry V. The moment seemed ripe for reconciliation between the papacy and empire. Paschal had supported Henry when he rebelled against his father; now king, Henry V showed himself open to compromise with the pope. In 1110, Henry marched to Rome with a large force of soldiers, apparently planning to reconcile with the pope. Paschal greeted the emperor and they celebrated mass together in Saint Peter's basilica. Apparently, Paschal proposed that the Roman Church would renounce all the *regalia* – properties, goods, and other benefits – received from imperial sources in the past, leaving the Church only in possession of places and things that it did not owe to the empire (including, presumably, a good portion of the Papal States). In return, the emperor would surrender the right of investiture, linked to the imperial bestowal of such temporalities. According to later accounts, Henry secretly agreed to this plan, most likely as a temporary expediency to secure his coronation, but when Paschal announced it, people on all sides objected to this unworkable idea. As the French chronicler Suger of Saint Denis described the scene, violence soon broke out due to the "treacherous Germans." Whatever exactly happened, the emperor seized the pope and imprisoned him outside of Rome. Under these circumstances, Suger reports, Henry "extorted another privilege, which he stole from the hand of the lord pope: that he might continue to perform investitures." In addition, the pope swore never to excommunicate the German ruler. On April 13, Paschal crowned Henry as emperor, after which the German monarch released the pope and headed home.[16]

The Concordat of Worms

Paschal quickly denounced these coerced concessions and the controversy continued off and on for the remainder of this papacy. His successor, Gelasius II (1118–19), finally took the step of excommunicating Henry V. The emperor elected an unconvincing anti-pope, Gregory VIII, who enjoyed little support from anyone. By this time, the exhausted parties on both sides seemed ready to compromise, based on some level of distinction between the sacred and secular components of the bishop's position. This practical solution to the dilemma had been taking shape for some time, first explored in the works of the prominent French canon lawyer, Ivo of Chartres. As Ivo noted in a letter to Hugh of Lyons, "we see many disquieted, many churches despoiled, many scandals arisen, and a division between the kingship and the priesthood without whose harmonious cooperation there can be no sound and secure conduct of human affairs."[17] His answer to this problem lay with the difference between the handing over of the bishop's office, a "sacramental act" not fit for a layperson, and the temporalities attached to the office, which could be rightfully bestowed by a king or emperor. By 1107–8, both the English and French kings had agreed to a settlement along these lines, surrendering the right of investiture with ring and staff, but continuing to receive homage from newly elected bishops for the properties, privileges, and other material benefits that came with their offices.

In 1122, Pope Callixtus II (1119–24) finally reached a similar agreement with Henry V. In the Concordat of Worms, the pope swore to the emperor:

> We hereby grant that in Germany the elections of the bishops shall be held in your presence, such elections to be held canonically and without simony or other illegality. In case of disputed elections you shall have the right to decide between the parties after consulting with the archbishop of the province and his fellow bishops.

On his side, Henry took the following oath:

> I, Henry, by grace of God, emperor of the Romans, hereby surrender to God and his apostles, Saints Peter and Paul, and to the holy catholic Church, all investiture by ring and staff. I agree that elections shall be conducted canonically and shall be free from all interference.[18]

In 1123, the First Lateran Council ratified this compromise. Although seen by many as a temporary solution, the Concordat of Worms began a decades-long truce between the papacy and empire. Both sides had won and lost something. By giving up investiture but receiving oaths of allegiance from clergy for the temporalities bestowed with their offices, the German emperor retained considerable influence over clerical appointments. At the same time, through their struggle over investiture, the popes of Rome had indisputably asserted their influence over secular rulers, forcing them to concede long-standing rights over the Church. In a period of roughly seventy years, the Roman papacy had gone from being a local bishop with a tarnished claim to universal authority to acting as the supreme pontiff of Christian Europe. Just as importantly, the reformist vision of Christendom had secured its hold on the imagination of the Western Church, affecting how the clergy and the laity understood the role of their faith in everything from kingship to daily religious life.

The Origins of the Crusades

Alongside the Investiture Conflict, the reform papacy contributed to another dramatic transformation in medieval European society through its call for an innovative kind of holy war, the crusades. The idea of fighting in God's name was hardly unknown to contemporary Christians. Starting with Pope Urban II and the First Crusade, however, the popes of Rome united the idea of sanctified violence with the penitential ethos of pilgrimage, carried out with the promise of spiritual rewards granted by the authority of the Apostolic See. In this way, the Roman Church carved out new space for its priestly leadership over Christian Europeans, creating an inspiring if bloody outlet for Europe's expansionary energies.

Reform, peace, and violence

In addition to combating clerical marriage and simony, reformist sentiment around the turn of the millennium also shaped the so-called Peace and later Truce of God. Starting on a regional level, particularly in Aquitaine, Burgundy, and Languedoc, churchmen began to denounce the predatory violence of secular lords against the weak and defenseless, including the poor, widows, and children, but above all members of the clergy and their property. Modern historians debate the actual level of violence in Western Europe around the year 1000 – monks and church chroniclers might have exaggerated such devastation to make their point. Regardless, at assemblies such as the Council of Charroux in 989, churchmen promised the excommunication of those who plundered churches, robbed peasants of their livestock, or attacked clerics. By the same token, the Peace movement forbade clergy to fight or bear weapons. Chroniclers reported that large crowds of peasants joined churchmen to call for "Peace!" By staging popular assemblies, invoking the power of the saints, and passing ecclesiastical legislation, bishops, abbots, and sympathetic laypersons sought to constrain and redefine the legitimacy of armed conflict. By declaring some forms of violence illicit, moreover, the Peace and Truce of God suggested that other uses of force might be legitimate, perhaps meritorious. Clergy must not bear arms, but the laity could and in some cases should, such as when they fought to protect ecclesiastical property or to defend the weak from the depredations of wicked men. Rather than an unavoidable evil, a soldier wielding the sword could do the Lord's work.[19]

From its beginnings, the reform papacy had signaled a shift in attitudes toward armed force, seen when Leo IX led his own army into battle against the Normans at Civitate in 1053. Popes before Leo had personally led troops to defend papal territories. For Leo and his successors, however, such fighting transcended earthly politics – according to some observers, the men who died at Civitate fighting for the pope were nothing less than martyrs. Later popes such as Nicholas II, through his alliance with the Normans, and Alexander II, who dispatched the papal banner to Erlembald in Milan and also to William the Conqueror before his invasion of England in 1066, sent similar signals about the legitimate nature of warfare under certain circumstances. On more than one occasion, Gregory VII referred to secular rulers who fought to protect papal interests as the "soldiers" or "militia of Saint Peter." When the Investiture Conflict erupted into armed conflict between the pope and the emperor, Gregory insisted that open violence was far better than a false peace, the willingness to compromise with the powers of the world that lulled believers into a false sense of security and complaisance that imperiled their salvation. Surrounded by opponents whom he described as schismatics and heretics, the fiery pope believed it better to struggle than submit to those who opposed the Church.[20]

As the eleventh century progressed, the popes of Rome identified another theater for sanctified warfare along Christendom's expanding frontiers: fighting against "pagans" and "infidels," meaning Muslims, mostly in Spain and Sicily. In such regions, fueled by Europe's demographic, economic, and political takeoff, Christian powers had begun a process of piecemeal conquest, annexing such territories to their kingdoms. They hardly needed the pope's encouragement to do so. Nevertheless, the reform papacy eagerly embraced and narrated such campaigns as part of God's plan for history.

For example, before the Spanish campaign to capture Barbastro in 1063, Alexander II promised the remission of sins for soldiers fighting against infidels. In 1073, Gregory VII made a similar proclamation to a band of French warriors heading south to battle against Muslims in the region. In their letters to Spanish kings and bishops, Gregory and Urban II looked back centuries to a time when the "Saracens" had unjustly seized Spain, reducing the liberty of the Church to a state of bondage. Now, by God's grace, Spanish princes were restoring Saint Peter's patrimony to Rome, reclaiming lands that belonged to the obedience of the Roman Church. In addition to confirming the privileges of restored bishoprics in the region, the popes encouraged Spanish rulers and prelates to implant the proper Roman liturgy in the "liberated" Spanish churches, displacing the local rites followed by Christians who had lived for generations under Islamic rule. In their correspondence with Norman conquerors and clergy in Sicily, Popes Gregory and Urban offered a similar vision of history's progress as Christian soldiers freed such territories from nonbelievers.

The call of Jerusalem

Looking farther afield, European Christians saw that Muslims ruled over the very land where Christ had lived, died, and returned to life before ascending into Heaven, including the Church of the Holy Sepulcher in Jerusalem. According to one source, Pope Sergius IV (1009–12) had issued a call for Christians to march eastward and rescue Christ's tomb from the "pagans" after the erratic Fatimid caliph al-Hakim ordered the razing of the Holy Sepulcher in 1009. Chronicler Rodulfus Glaber later reported rumors that Jews in Europe had conspired with the Muslims to bring about the destruction of the Holy Sepulcher. Declaring his intention to sail with an Italian fleet to Syria and avenge "our Redeemer and his tomb," Sergius promised the "eternal kingdom" for those who defended God along with him. Nothing came of the pope's call to arms, assuming people knew about it. (Some scholars even believe this document to be a forgery dating from the time of the First Crusade.) Regardless, Jerusalem remained at the forefront of Western Christians' imagination over the following generations. Pilgrimage to the city increased over the course of the eleventh century, which featured several mass pilgrimages to the holy places, sometimes numbering in the thousands.[21]

The idea of recovering Jerusalem emerged (or reemerged) under Gregory VII. After the Byzantine Empire suffered a crushing defeat by Turkish forces at the battle of Manzikert in 1071, the pope received letters from Christians in the East describing their plight and calling for aid. Writing to all the faithful, including some of his closest supporters, like Countess Mathilda of Tuscany and even Emperor Henry IV (this happened before their dispute over investiture), Gregory informed his readers about the evils besetting their Christian brothers. Calling upon the "faithful men of Saint Peter" to assist him, Gregory summoned an armed expedition of Christian princes, led perhaps by the pope himself, that would march to the East, free their fellow Christians from oppression, and press onward to the Church of the Holy Sepulcher. This so-called Crusade Plan of 1074 never happened and soon enough the pope had his hands full with the Investiture Conflict. Nevertheless, Gregory's vision of an armed expedition to free the Eastern Church and restore Jerusalem for Christendom foreshadowed the dramatic events set in motion by Pope Urban II just over twenty years later.

Urban II and the First Crusade

In November 1095, while traveling in France, Urban II delivered a rousing sermon at Clermont before a crowd of clerical and lay listeners, calling upon them to take up arms and liberate the Eastern Church from bondage. Multiple reports of his address have survived, some written by attendees and others by chroniclers who later read or heard about his words. Although the details vary, the basic message stayed the same. Channeling sentiments from the Peace of God, the pope called upon the warriors present to stop being the "oppressors of children, plunderers of widows … guilty of homicide, robbers of another's rights, who await the pay of thieves for the shedding of Christian blood." Instead, he proposed a better use for their arms – to march eastward and defend Christendom. Urban described in exaggerated detail the abuse and slaughter of Eastern Christians at the hands of the "Turks" and "Saracens," who subjected them to rape, theft, torture, and other violations. Jerusalem, he declared according to one report, "situated at the center of the world" was "in subjection to those who do not know God, to the worship of the heathens." Another account of Clermont attributed apocalyptic sentiments to the pope, who suggested that the expedition to free Jerusalem might mark the beginning of the end of the world. By restoring the Christian Church in the holy places, the crusaders would ensure that Antichrist found plenty of Christians there to persecute during his reign of evil, as foretold by the Bible.

Not long before Clermont, Urban had received a call for military assistance from the Greek emperor, Alexius I, who probably imagined that a small army of professional warriors would be sent to his aid.

This appeal might have inspired the pope's later call for the crusade. Yet Urban clearly envisioned something quite different. At Clermont he coupled his appeal with the promise of spiritual rewards for those who heeded his call and swore a vow to complete their pilgrimage, instructing them to sign themselves with the cross as a symbol of their vow. "Undertake this journey," he exhorted his listeners, "for the remission of your sins, with the assurance of the imperishable glory of the kingdom of Heaven." In addition, the pope promised earthly protection for the soldiers, their families, and their property while they were gone. His evocative portrait of Christian suffering and assurance of salvation proved highly effective. Urban's audience, we are told, greeted his appeal with a cry of "God wills it!," setting in motion what became known as the First Crusade.[22]

Trying to exercise some direct control over the expedition, Urban quickly assigned his legate Adhémar, bishop of Le Puy, as the spiritual leader and advisor for the armed pilgrimage. Events soon took on a life of their own, as waves of Christian Europeans – lay and clerical, rich and poor, men and women – set out for Jerusalem over the following months. The first major crowd of crusaders, consisting of lesser elite and poorer elements without effective organization, met with disaster in Anatolia, destroyed by Turkish forces. The next group – of well-armed bands led by major princes and nobles – marched eastward to assemble at the imperial capital of Constantinople. These forces progressed in fits and starts across Anatolia and Syria toward Jerusalem. At points, such as during the protracted siege of Antioch in summer 1098, it seemed as if the expedition might collapse entirely. The crusaders, however, enjoying some lucky breaks and not facing any unified resistance from the fractious Muslim powers in the region, reached Jerusalem after roughly three years of privation and warfare. A sense of apocalyptic destiny filled the air. Following a siege and a ritual procession around the city by the penitential warriors, the army captured Jerusalem on July 15, 1099.

The miraculous success of the First Crusade staggered the imagination. One crusade chronicler, Robert the Monk, declared it the biggest thing since Christ. Popular enthusiasm for the crusade to Jerusalem cannot be attributed solely to the papacy. Without a deep-seated and widespread desire for salvation, a belief among the laity in the power of penance and the merits of pilgrimage, the expedition would never have caught fire as it did. Some reported that a charismatic preacher named Peter the Hermit really started the crusade. After experiencing a heavenly vision during a pilgrimage to Jerusalem, Peter returned home bearing a letter from the city's patriarch calling for Western aid and sought out the pope for assistance. Nevertheless, most contemporaries remembered Urban as the one who set the crusade in motion and viewed it as a product of papal leadership. Indeed, writing to Urban from Antioch in 1098, the leading nobles of the crusader army had even called upon the pope to join them and take charge after the death of Adhémar of Le Puy. "You started this expedition," they wrote. "Your sermons made us all leave our lands and what was in them, follow Christ by taking up the cross and exalt the Christian name ... If you do come to us to complete with us the expedition you began, the whole world will obey you."[23]

By calling for the liberation of Jerusalem, Urban had gambled on his position of spiritual leadership and achieved a dramatic win. The successful result of the crusade represented a triumph for the papal vision of Christendom at a time when the reform papacy still confronted opposition from its opponents, including Henry IV and Guibert of Ravenna, the anti-pope Clement III. As crusader and chronicler Fulcher of Chartres remembered Urban II, he "restored peace and re-established the rights of the Church in their former condition. He also made a vigorous effort to drive the pagans from the lands of the Christians. And since he endeavored in every way to glorify everything which was of God, nearly everyone freely submitted in obedience to his paternal authority." Nearly everyone, Fulcher qualified, because Guibert had tried to usurp the papal office, convincing some people to follow him – even the Romans, who had barred Urban from entering the holy city. Confusion reigned and Christendom suffered from this disorder. "It was necessary to put an end to all these evils," Fulcher continued, "and in accordance with the plan initiated by Pope Urban, to turn against the pagans the fighting which up to now customarily went on among the Christians." The plan more or less worked. Ironically, Urban died two weeks after the crusaders captured Jerusalem, before the news of the city's fall reached him.[24]

Aftermath of the First Crusade

In 1101, Pope Urban II's successor, Paschal II, sent a letter to the faithful Christians still remaining in Palestine, praising their recent deeds whereby God had scattered those who oppressed Christians and restored the Eastern Church to its liberty. In the territories captured by the crusaders, the conquerors installed Western clergy into existing churches or established new ones, creating a Latin clerical hierarchy in the holy places. Problems, however, had already begun to emerge. A dispute soon broke out over who would be the Latin patriarch in Jerusalem, the first of many such squabbles that would require the papacy's attention. Even more pressing, the crusader kingdoms desperately needed manpower for their protection. After fulfilling their vow, most of the crusaders had gone home. In response, Paschal summoned a new crusading army, including soldiers who had sworn to go on the first expedition but had failed to depart or had returned to Europe before its conclusion. Islamic forces wiped out this so-called Crusade of 1101 before it ever reached Jerusalem. For contemporaries, the message of this defeat seemed clear – these sinful crusaders, unlike the first ones, had not walked with the Lord.

Pope Paschal learned that crusades did not always go as planned. Even during the First Crusade, the call to holy war had produced some unintended consequences and left unforeseen legacies. During their passage through Germany, some of the crusaders on the first wave of the expedition had attacked and plundered local Jewish communities, seeing those "killers of Christ" as enemies of Christendom living within their very midst. In cities along the Rhine, the crusaders slaughtered and forcibly converted Jewish men, women, and children, some of whom took their own lives before they could be baptized. It is not clear what Pope Urban thought about this turn of events, which ran contrary to church teachings about Jews (that they should be denigrated but not slaughtered) and baptism (a voluntary act). Facing the crusaders, some German bishops had helped the Jewish inhabitants of their cities while others fled and abandoned them to their fate. One crusader chronicler, Albert of Aix, viewed the crusaders who violated the Jews as wrongful sinners who got their just reward when most of them perished en route to Jerusalem. Others, however, judged the attacks the righteous actions of God's army against the non-believers in their midst.

The First Crusade also created friction between the Latin crusaders and the very people that they marched forth to rescue, Eastern Christians, especially in the Byzantine Empire. Despite all of their disagreements, including the schism of 1054, Western and Eastern Christians generally viewed themselves as fellow believers, members of the same universal Church. From the beginning of his papacy, Pope Urban had attempted to reconcile Latin and Greek Christians, settling their disputes over differences of doctrine, rites, and church discipline. The main stumbling block remained papal primacy, which the Greeks refused to recognize. The First Crusade, however, caused deep mistrust between the crusade leaders and Alexius I, whom the crusaders accused of betraying the army and favoring his Muslim neighbors. In 1107, Bohemond of Taranto, Norman warrior, former crusader, and ruler of Antioch, led a crusading army on its way to Jerusalem into an unsuccessful attack on the Byzantine Empire. In a letter to Pope Paschal, the Norman leader had complained about the need to settle Rome's disagreements with Constantinople, mentioning azymes, *filioque*, and clerical marriage specifically. Although the pope did not seem to view the army's unsuccessful assault on Alexius as a holy war against the Greeks, he eagerly supported Bohemond's effort to drum up support for a new crusade and did nothing to prevent the army's turn against Byzantium, revealing the dangers posed by crusading to harmony between Eastern and Western Christians.

With the crusades, the reform papacy had invented a new and compelling kind of warfare for medieval Europe, transforming Christian sensibilities with regard to sin, redemption, and violence. Over the following decades, popes, canon lawyers, and theologians began slowly to systematize crusading, creating rules and regulations for crusader vows and privileges, dispatching crusade preachers, and organizing the careful collection of funds for further expeditions. Through the redemption of crusade vows, that is, swearing a vow and then paying for someone capable to redeem it, everyone – women and children, the elderly and unfit – could participate in these holy wars and enjoy their spiritual blessings. Nor did the papacy limit this enterprise to Jerusalem. Popes starting with Urban II promised Christians fighting in Spain the same protections and spiritual benefits as soldiers who made the journey to Jerusalem. Such privileges and rewards were later offered to those fighting pagans in the region of the Baltic Sea. Authorized by the pope, crusades could happen on any of Christendom's frontiers and inside its borders, such as when popes declared crusades against heretics or Rome's political opponents. For the papacy, entering into the era of its greatest prestige and influence over Christian Europe, the crusading movement represented one of its greatest enterprises, for better and for worse.

Chapter 5: Papal Monarchy

In his book *On Consideration*, the charismatic Cistercian abbot Bernard of Clairvaux reflected on the powers, obligations, and burdens of the papal office for Pope Eugene III (1143–53). Writing to his former pupil, Bernard emphasized the unique position of Rome's bishop as the heir of Saint Peter: "Others are called to share part of the responsibility for souls," Bernard addressed to the pope, "you are called to the fullness of power." Saint Peter, the Cistercian monk continued, showed himself to be the unique "vicar of Christ," as seen in the Gospels when Peter walked on the many waters of the storm-tossed sea beside the Lord (Mt. 14: 29). The "many waters," Bernard explained, "signifies 'many peoples.' Thus, although each of the others has his own ship, to you is entrusted the greatest of all, made from all others, the universal Church which is spread throughout the whole world." The key to holding this exalted position, however, lay with humility. Carrying such an awesome burden, Bernard reminded Eugene, the pope must act as the servant for the downtrodden, avoiding pride in order to exercise a spiritual dominion. Unimpressed by all the lawsuits reaching Rome, he decried the fact that the Supreme Pontiff had to "sweat over such affairs" for the likes of lawyers and litigants. "Clearly your power is over sin and not property," he wryly addressed Pope Eugene," since it is because of sin that you have received the keys of the heavenly kingdom." Bernard also took aim at elaborate papal ceremonial and dress. Saint Peter, he observed, was "known never to have gone in procession adorned with either jewels or silks, covered with gold, carried on a white horse, attended by a knight or surrounded by clamoring servants." Commenting on such display, the Cistercian abbot simply disapproved: "In this finery, you are the successor not of Peter, but of Constantine."[1]

Bernard's advice to Pope Eugene, a celebration and critique of the papal office, captured the papacy's dilemma during the so-called High Middle Ages. Both men lived in the middle of what modern scholars sometimes call the "renaissance of the twelfth century." Alongside continued economic vitality and urban growth, Christian Europeans experimented with new kinds of strong, centralizing government, secular and ecclesiastical, as well as innovative forms of intellectual inquiry into the nature of God, the Church, and the world. In the study of theology and law, scholars codified and systematized knowledge for practical ends; architects constructed monumental Romanesque and later Gothic churches that dominated the skylines of bustling cities. The twelfth century also experienced its own "reformation," the rapid proliferation of new religious orders that challenged the traditional models of monasticism, calling for an embrace of the apostolic life – poverty, simplicity, preaching, and evangelical renewal. Bernard of Clairvaux's Cistercian order represented only one successful example of this phenomenon.

Historians also call the High Middle Ages the era of "papal monarchy," a term that describes the power of the Roman papacy at its greatest extent, when popes stood as potent figures at the apex of an ecclesiastical hierarchy that reached into every corner of Europe. To function as an effective center for ecclesiastical business, the papal curia developed increasingly effective forms of bureaucracy, or at least as effective as possible within the constraints of medieval governance. Canon lawyers justified papal authority with increasing rigor and precision. Popes dressed and in some ways acted like worldly rulers, setting armies in motion, defending church offices and property, offering judgment in disputes. Sitting on the Apostolic See, they made binding decisions in matters of faith, and witnessed the countless numbers of churchmen who journeyed to their city, the spiritual capital of Christendom, as pilgrims, litigants, favor-seekers, or some combination of these things.

As Saint Bernard well understood, however, success brought its own challenges and problems. Just like secular monarchs, popes confronted limits to their effective power. Contemporaries took aim at the papacy's growing bureaucracy and the endless thirst for money, questioning why the heirs of Saint Peter lived in opulence rather than humble poverty, why they bloodied themselves fighting to protect their earthly possessions. Disputed papal elections and revolts in the city of Rome disrupted papal attempts at governance. Crusades failed, and failed again. Through its clashes with kings and especially emperors, the papacy made crucial advances for its claims of primacy, but also expended its resources and spiritual capital. Starting during the twelfth century, one begins to see the paradox of the medieval papacy on full display – popes acting as the successors to both Peter and Constantine, claiming the "fullness of power" as spiritual and temporal figures, experiencing their greatest successes and setbacks.

The Machinery of Papal Business

With the Investiture Conflict resolved, the papacy settled into a period of sustained growth, building upon earlier developments in ecclesiastical administration. Through the development of the papal curia, the rise of the College of Cardinals, the use of legates, and the holding of general councils, the Roman Church actualized its claim to be the center of Christendom in ways that earlier generations of popes could never have imagined.

The papal curia

By the time of Pope Urban II, a formal papal curia had begun to emerge for the purposes of church governance, mirroring other royal and princely courts around Europe. Ironically, the fact that Urban spent years outside of Rome while the anti-pope Clement III occupied the city forced him to innovate and refine the administrative mechanisms available to him. Growing out of the pope's household staff, the curia evolved into three distinct branches: the chamber (*camera*), handling financial matters; the chancery, producing and storing documents; and the chapel, overseeing the papacy's elaborate liturgical duties. The position of papal chamberlain emerged as one of considerable power and importance, as did the chancellor, whose office became a stepping stone for future popes. This growth and formalization of the Roman curia responded to – and, in turn, encouraged – a massive expansion of ecclesiastical business directed toward the papacy. As we have seen, the idea that the Roman Church represented a final court of appeals for "major cases" dated back to the fourth century. During the twelfth century, the volume of such appeals to Rome grew in leaps and bounds, the product of an increasingly literate and litigious European society. Rather than seeking a final decision from Rome, people turned there first, trying to circumvent local authorities and win their case with a preemptive judgment from the Apostolic See. Various popes encouraged this state of affairs by granting churches and monasteries exemptions from judicial oversight and other immunities.

Seeking to bolster these centralizing tendencies, the papacy also staged more frequent ecclesiastical councils, yet another venue for pursuing reformist impulses since the days of Gregory VII. During almost every year of his papacy, Gregory held Lenten synods at Rome that issued canons for the reform of the clergy and, eventually, the prohibition of lay investiture. Increasingly, the papacy looked to general councils as opportunities for determining church policy and legislation, as seen at the First Lateran Council in 1123 that confirmed the Concordat of Worms and issued a series of canons covering everything from clerical celibacy to the remission of sins promised to crusaders. As we will see, above all after times of schism or disruption in the papal office, popes turned to such general councils held at the Lateran as a symbolic and administrative means of demonstrating Rome's primacy over the Church.

As a visible marker of these changes, the twelfth-century popes cultivated their office's ceremonial life, publically displaying their sovereign power through elaborate dress and ritual much as described in the *Donation of Constantine*. Starting in the time of Paschal II, a typical papal election might include the donning of a purple mantle before the newly chosen pope would make a procession to the Lateran church, where he received a set of keys and a scepter, symbols of his temporal dominion over the Papal States. Popes also began to wear an ornate tiara, in effect an imperial crown, as another sign of their earthly authority, and sometimes sat for the prostration of visitors, who ritually kissed the pope's feet (an act traditionally performed before the Byzantine emperor). Rather than the persona of a local landowner and the leading figure of liturgical worship for the city of Rome, twelfth-century popes adopted the idiom of a veritable monarch, ruling over the lands of Saint Peter, claiming authority over the Western Church.

The College of Cardinals

As part of this transformation in papal bureaucracy, cardinal bishops, priests, and deacons emerged as a critical governing body within the Roman Church. As described above, the status of cardinal bishops and priests originated with their performance of special liturgical functions in the Lateran and Rome's major basilica churches. Starting in the 1050s, however, the cardinal bishops began to form a source of critical support for the reform papacy, offering a counterweight to the influence of Rome's aristocratic families over the papal office.

Reform popes starting with Leo IX appointed their closest supporters and advisors as cardinal bishops, joined by cardinal priests and later deacons, whose precise numbers expanded and contracted over time. The Election Decree of 1059 that gave the cardinal bishops (and later, after some protest about their exclusion, the other cardinals) control over papal elections provides one major example of their growing clout. During the protracted struggle over investiture, parties on both sides seeking legitimacy – including Urban II and anti-pope Clement III – appealed to the cardinals, expanding the rights of cardinal priests and deacons as a means of bolstering their own positions.

Recognizing the cardinals' growing importance as agents of church governance and reform, contemporaries sometimes described the College of Cardinals as a "new Roman senate." Among other changes, cardinal clergy began to play a more active role in the chancery, claiming the right to act as signatories on papal bulls, privileges, and immunities, involving themselves in the awarding of special grants and other favors. By the mid-twelfth century, a separate body called the consistory developed to manage the ever-increasing number of appeals and exemptions flooding into Rome. Assembling in the Lateran, sometimes with the pope joining them, the cardinals would hear cases and adjudicate disputes, giving them a direct hand in ecclesiastical business. Outside of Rome, the cardinals also acted as the long arm of Rome's growing bureaucratic reach, acting as papal legates. Such envoys had become increasingly important for the reform papacy during the later eleventh century. From the time of Pope Gregory VII until the close of the twelfth century, with a handful of exceptions, every pope had acted at some point in his ecclesiastical career as a papal legate. During the Investiture Conflict, Gregory started the practice of appointing permanent legates to represent the papacy abroad during its struggle with Henry IV and his supporters. Over time, popes began to assign such permanent envoys in France, England, and elsewhere, often natives of the country in question. During the twelfth century, however, Rome began to rely more and more on cardinal bishops, priests, and deacons as their legates, viewing them as less invested in local affairs and more dependent upon the Roman papacy for their position.

Renaissance and reformation

Beyond the papal curia and College of Cardinals, wider trends in Europe's intellectual and religious life favored such innovation and expansion in governance. In burgeoning cities, cathedral schools began to complement and eventually replace monasteries as the primary centers of education, sites for the training of "scholastic" thinkers, theologians, and biblical commentators, intellectuals who invoked the power of reason and logic to grapple with the nature of the Trinity, the working of the sacraments, and the organization of the Church. Paris, home to an exceptional school founded at the abbey of Saint Victor, developed into a particularly important hub for the study of theology and related disciplines. Over the course of the twelfth century, high-profile intellectuals, such as the French theologian and teacher Peter Abelard, subjected the Bible and other sources of Christian authority to new forms of scrutiny, as seen in Abelard's work *Yes and No*, which set forth apparently contradictory statements by patristic authors and offered guidelines for their reconciliation. Others, such as Peter Lombard in his *Four Books of Sentences* or Peter Comestor in his *Scholastic History*, tried to summarize the constantly expanding body of Christian knowledge for students and their masters. In practical terms, these schools also produced preachers to disseminate the increasingly refined norms of the Christian faith to the laity, and clerics to work in the growing ecclesiastical and secular bureaucracies of the era, including that of the papacy.

This same period witnessed equally momentous changes in the study and application of both civil and ecclesiastical law. The city of Bologna emerged as a particularly important center for legal studies and education. As noted above, the development of the reform movement in the Roman Church, and resultant clash between popes and emperors, had provided a strong impetus for renewed attention to canon law, a critical source of support for papal claims to primacy over Christian society. During the twelfth century, this legal revolution continued to build up steam. Around 1140, a lawyer from Bologna named Gratian created the *Concordance of Discordant Canons*, also called the *Decretum*. In this highly influential legal tome, he attempted to systematize centuries of canon law, resolving apparent contradictions between patristic theologians, conciliar decrees, papal decretals, and other sources of traditional authority. The *Decretum* quickly became an indispensible resource for the management of the Roman Church, creating a new breed of lawyers who constantly added their own commentaries and glosses on the legal text.[2]

Described as an era of "renaissance" due to such developments, the twelfth century also witnessed its own "reformation," that is, a period of rapid innovation and diversification in the forms of religious life, challenging traditional monasticism as embodied by Cluny. New orders burst on the scene with startling frequency. Founded in 1098 at Cîteaux by Robert of Molesme, the Cistercians represented one such group, committed to renewing the original spirit of the Benedictine Rule, rejecting Cluny's elaborate liturgy and wealth. Additional orders included the Carthusians, Premonstratensians, and the Templars, secular warriors who lived much like monks, devoted to the protection of pilgrims and the preservation of the crusader presence in the Holy Land. The unexpected emergence of such orders disturbed some and thrilled others. Seeing an opportunity, the twelfth-century papacy generally endorsed these religious innovators, granting them protections and exemptions. In return, these vibrant communities provided new networks of communication and sources of financial support for the papacy. The close working relationship between Bernard of Clairvaux and Pope Eugene III, Bernard's former pupil and the first Cistercian pontiff, provides just one example of how the twelfth-century reformation affected the Roman Church and fueled its growing clout around Europe.[3]

Paying for papal monarchy

Not surprisingly, this growing machinery of papal business cost ever-increasing amounts of money. Popes had a variety of resources at their disposal to pay for these financial obligations, some long-standing and others new, although the amount of funds never seemed to match the papacy's needs. Close at hand, popes drew upon the resources of the Papal States, receiving direct income from property owned by the church at Rome, along with various payments and forms of tribute made to the popes by their nominal subjects around the Italian peninsula. Fees paid for carrying out business at the curia and consistory – less charitably, bribes – added a vast and ever-expanding source of income for those involved in papal administration. Looking further afield, the Roman Church relied more and more upon the so-called *census*, a kind of payment made to the papacy for various protections, exemptions, and benefits (including, for example, the offering of "Peter's pence" by the English king among others). Numerous monasteries owed Rome similar payments, as did archbishops who received their *pallium* from the pope. In 1192, the papal chamberlain Censius – future pope Honorius III (1216–27) – compiled a record of such obligations, the so-called *Liber Censuum*, listing the hundreds of payments, tributes, tithes, and fees owed to the papacy from around Europe.[4]

As one might imagine, Rome's seemingly inexhaustible thirst for coin created a great deal of resentment. For litigants, navigating a case through the papal court required the payment of considerable legal fees and straightforward bribes. As a satirical poem from this period put it, "Blessed are the wealthy, for theirs is the Roman curia." The duty for collecting fees and revenues abroad typically fell to papal legates, another one of their important roles, making them into a subject of considerable scorn. In his *Book of the Pontiffs*, the English cleric John of Salisbury, who spent a number of years at the papal curia, described the shameful behavior of two legates in Germany, Jordan of Saint Susanna and Octavian of Saint Cecilia. "Each was at heart a wolf in sheep's clothing," John wrote about the two men, who robbed the poor and oppressed the innocent. "Quarrelling over everything, they made the church a laughing-stock." Eventually, they were recalled to Rome, "leaving hatred and contempt for the papacy."[5] The influx of wealth into the curia created new tensions and problems at the heart of papal governance, as the cardinals pushed for a greater share of such revenues, as did various aristocratic factions and noble families in Rome. In short, everyone wanted a piece of a constantly growing but never sufficient pie.

The papacy's involvement in such worldly matters represented nothing new. What had changed was the scope and tempo of such legal and economic business. In this regard, the Roman Church wrestled with changes similar to those faced by secular monarchies such as the kingdoms of England and France, which benefited from rapid growth in bureaucratic forms of governance, courts, and fiscal revenues – likewise generating severe criticism from disgruntled contemporaries. We should also remember that litigants and those seeking privileges were largely responsible for making Rome into the center of ecclesiastical business that others condemned. The vast majority of the time the Roman papacy did not impose its judgments unasked for upon local communities. Clerics, monks, and others came to the popes, seeking immunities, exemptions, and justice. While present in Rome, such petitioners still acted as pious pilgrims, praying and venerating the apostles. Devotion and the business of running the Church did not always stand at odds with one other. On a day-to-day basis, papal monarchy worked not because popes ruled like kings, but rather because members of the Roman Church saw their own material advantages and spiritual well-being as linked to the papal project.

The Price of Success: Schism, Commune, and Crusade

Accompanying its growing reach and bureaucratic efficiency, the papacy during the middle decades of the twelfth century faced serious upheavals, linked to its expanding ambitions. First, a division between two Roman families and among the cardinals produced a contested papal election, a schism that revealed new fault lines in the Roman Church. Second, the citizens of Rome declared a commune, a form of civil governance that directly challenged the pope's control of the city. Finally, the papacy set another major crusade in motion, the Second Crusade, a dramatic demonstration of papal leadership that came to a disappointing end.

The schism of 1130

During the period after the First Lateran Council, two factions had emerged among the cardinals centered on rival aristocratic Roman families, the Pierleoni and the Frangipani. The Pierleoni family and its allies might be described as "old school" Gregorian reformers, committed to pursuing the reformist agenda begun in the eleventh century. The Frangipani and their circle, by contrast, might be called "post-Gregorian," new men who had come into their positions after the settlement at Worms and who were less interested in fighting old battles. When a portion of the cardinals elected a Frangipani-backed pope, Gregorio Papereschi, who took the name Innocent II (1130–43), the opposing side staged their own election of Pietro Pierleoni, known as Anacletus II. Neither man possessed a compelling majority in the College of Cardinals. Looting and disorder broke out in the city. Through their connections and some generous, well-placed "gifts," the Pierleoni family soon secured Anacletus's position in Rome, while the Frangipani backed off from their support of Innocent, forcing him to flee the city.

Subsequent events showed how much the times had changed from the days when local interests largely determined who became the bishop of Rome. Anacletus controlled the city and forged an alliance with the Normans in southern Italy, meeting with King Roger II in 1130 and recognizing his family's claims to the greater kingdom of Sicily, including Apulia and Calabria. Innocent, however, rallied the remainder of major European powers to his side, meeting over the following years with the German, French, and English kings. He also enjoyed considerable financial and moral support from the Cistercian order, including the charismatic and influential Bernard of Clairvaux. In this case, the pope abroad made a more compelling case for his legitimacy than the pope in Rome. During their meeting at Liège in 1131, King Lothar III of Germany performed "groom service" for Innocent, humbly leading the pope seated on horseback much as described in the *Donation of Constantine*. In 1132–33, Lothar showed his support for Innocent by marching into Italy with the pope and entering Rome, forcing Anacletus to barricade himself in the Church of Saint Peter. Innocent crowned Lothar as emperor, holding the ceremony in the Lateran. After the coronation, however, Lothar returned to Germany, leaving the pope without much support in Rome. Innocent once again took flight from the city until Lothar returned with another display of force in 1137, restoring control of Rome to Innocent and pressuring the Normans in Apulia. The following year, when Anacletus died, his supporters elected another anti-pope, Victor IV, but he soon submitted to Innocent. By this time, Innocent's position in Rome was far more secure. Through a series of promises and bribes to the Pierleoni – in effect, assuring them of their share of the monies flooding into the Lateran – Innocent finally brought them over to his side.

In 1139, at the Second Lateran Council, the uncontested pope presided over an end to the schism dividing the Roman Church. Nearly one thousand clergy from Europe attended. Much like the First Lateran Council, the assembly reiterated and clarified long-standing reformist canons that prohibited clerical marriage, simony, and other clerical abuses. The council also provided Innocent with a high-profile chance to remind his listeners about the primacy of Rome and the heirs of Saint Peter, not to be forgotten or questioned despite the recent schism in the papal office. As Innocent declared at the council's opening: "You recognize that Rome is the head of the world and that the highest honor of an ecclesiastical office is received by the permission of the Roman pontiff."[6] At the council, the pope also excommunicated Roger II, Anacletus's former ally, whose territorial ambitions threatened papal rights and properties in southern Italy and Sicily. Later that year, apparently forgetting the lesson of Civitate and the fate of Pope Leo IX, Innocent led his own troops into battle against the Normans south of Rome. Beaten on the battlefield, the pope was taken prisoner. Roger soon released him but only after Innocent recognized Norman rule over the kingdom of Sicily on the same favorable terms as Anacletus. The humiliated pope died several years later in 1143, a stark reminder of the papal monarchy's limits.

The Roman commune

By this time, further troubles lay on the horizon for the Apostolic See. During the brief papacies of Celestine II (1143–44) and Lucius II

(1144–45), a group of citizens declared a commune in Rome. This episode formed part of a wider trend among twelfth-century Italian cities, which sought to cast off forms of traditional lordship by bishops and secular nobles, installing alternative forms of civil government in their city-states. Among other moves, the instigators of this civil movement created a new Roman senate and tried to limit the papal role in city governance, rejecting the authority of the papal prefect, the pope's primary representative in Rome's municipal affairs. The papacy did not back down from this new challenge. Lucius II died from wounds received during a skirmish with some of the commune's forces. Due to the ongoing violence, his successor Pope Eugene III could not be consecrated in Rome and fled the city. He returned in 1145, after making a deal with the commune's leadership: the pope recognized their right to exist, while the commune accepted some papal involvement in the city's governance. By early 1146, however, this truce fell apart and Eugene again left the city.

In 1146, the civic movement elevated a new and controversial leader, Arnold of Brescia. Arnold had already been excommunicated years earlier for his supposed heretical beliefs and his agitated speeches in Brescia against the city's bishop. According to the contemporary German chronicler Otto of Freising, Arnold denied the papacy any role in governing Rome, declaring that "nothing in the administration of the city was the concern of the Roman pontiff; the ecclesiastical courts should be enough for him." He also denounced the College of Cardinals as "not the church of God, but a place of business and den of thieves."[7] In his *Book of the Pontiffs*, John of Salisbury recorded Arnold's equally fiery denunciation of Eugene III. The pope, Arnold proclaimed, "was not what he professed to be – an apostolic man and shepherd of souls – but a man of blood who maintained his authority by fire and sword, a tormentor of churches and oppressor of the innocent, who did nothing in the world save gratify his flesh and empty other men's coffers to fill his own."[8]

The constant growth of papal bureaucracy, and the funds needed to pay for it, fueled such accusations. Years of almost constant warfare, first under Innocent II during his struggle against Anacletus, and then by successive popes against the Roman commune, also cost immense sums of money. So too did payments and bribes needed to secure the support of Rome's various aristocratic families such as the Pierleoni. As more and more money flowed through the papal curia to meet these and other demands, the stakes grew greater in managing the Lateran complex, the mechanisms for papal governance, and the revenues that supported it, not to mention securing control of the Papal States. Arnold's denunciations of Eugene and the cardinals echoed those of others, who far more gently chided the bishops of Rome for similar reasons. Even the papacy's friends and admirers saw and lamented the burdens placed on Saint Peter's heirs by their earthly ambitions.

The Second Crusade

Facing such criticisms in Rome, unable to sit securely in his own city, Pope Eugene III nonetheless demonstrated the powerful appeal of his office by summoning another crusade. Shocked by the Muslim capture of crusader-held Edessa in 1144, the pope called the following year for another major effort to aid Eastern Christians and protect the holy places. As Eugene declared in the bull *Quantum predecessores*, deliberately harkening back to the First Crusade:

> We know by the history of past time past, and by the traditions of our fathers, how many efforts our predecessors made for the deliverance of the Church of the East. Our predecessor, Urban of happy memory, sounded the evangelical trumpet and asserted himself with unexampled zeal in summoning the Christian nations from all parts of the world to the defense of the Holy Land. At his voice the brave and intrepid warriors of the kingdom of the Franks and the Italians, inflamed with holy ardor, took arms and delivered at the cost of their blood the city in which our Savior deigned to suffer for us, and which contains his tomb, the monument of his passion.[9]

In present times, by contrast, as punishment for their sins Christians had lost Edessa, once again experiencing death and destruction at the hands of the infidels. Exhorting those who heard his call to "take up the cross and arms," Eugene promised them the same spiritual rewards and earthly protections that Urban II had offered to that previous generation of warriors.

The crusade started off with considerable enthusiasm and promise. Speaking on Eugene's behalf, Bernard of Clairvaux traveled around France and Germany preaching in support of the new expedition. Eventually French King Louis VII and German King Conrad III swore crusading vows. As the crusade took shape, the participants viewed the campaign as a multiple-front war against the non-believers threatening Christians, not just in the Holy Land but also in Spain and against the pagan Wends along Germany's eastern frontiers. Regardless of where they fought, the warriors would receive the same spiritual rewards and protected status.[10]

The Second Crusade, however, proved to be a crushing disappointment for Christian Europe. Although the crusaders who attacked the Wends and captured Lisbon could claim victories, the main German and French armies met with a series of setbacks en route to the Holy Land. Once there, joined by troops from the Latin kingdom of Jerusalem the crusaders attacked Damascus in 1149, despite the fact the city had allied itself with Jerusalem against other Muslim powers in the region in the recent past. The siege failed miserably and the crusaders ignominiously retreated, spelling an effective end to the entire expedition. As the public face of the crusade, Bernard and Eugene III faced withering criticism after its failure. Indeed, such complaints partly motivated Bernard to write *On Consideration* for Pope Eugene, starting in 1149. "It is a watchtower," Bernard wrote about the papal throne. "From it, you oversee everything though the office of your episcopacy. Why should you not be placed on high where you can see everything, you who have been appointed watchman over all?" In aftermath of the Second Crusade, however, the burdens and dangers of holding such an exalted position clearly weighed on Bernard's mind. Speaking about the crusade itself, the Cistercian monk invoked God's inscrutable will and the inability of mere humans to understand the divine plan. He also insisted that the barbs of his own critics meant little to him. He had followed his conscience in calling for the crusade and could take refuge in that fact. Eugene should do likewise.[11]

Conflict Renewed between Church and Empire

As described above, the Concordat of Worms in 1122 initiated a relatively stable peace between the papacy and the German emperors, ending their immediate conflict over investiture. The underlying issues that fueled their sometimes violent disagreements, however, had not been resolved. In the realm of ideas, popes and emperors continued to dispute their relative preeminence in Christendom. In the arena of local politics, they struggled over competing territorial claims and rights in central and northern Italy. With the rise of the strong Hohenstaufen ruler Frederick I, open war once again resulted between papacy and empire.

The two swords

In his work *On Consideration*, Bernard of Clairvaux also turned his attention to the Gelasian idea of the two powers, that of secular rulers (*regnum*) and the priesthood (*sacerdotium*), commenting specifically on Luke 22: 38, wherein the apostles say, "Lord, behold here are two swords," and Christ replies, "It is enough." According to Bernard, this passage referred to the "spiritual sword," the pastoral authority of the Church, and the "material sword," the use of force by secular princes in the Church's service. Although not the first to offer such an interpretation of the two swords, Bernard signaled a renewed interest in political significance of this notion. As he put it:

> Both swords, that is, the spiritual and material, belong to the Church; however, the latter is to be drawn for the Church and the former by the Church. The spiritual sword should be drawn by the hand of the priest; the material sword by the hand of the knight, but clearly at the bidding of the priest and at the command of the emperor.[12]

In his work the *Policraticus*, John of Salisbury offered a similar assessment: "The sword is therefore accepted by the prince from the hand of the Church ... The prince is therefore a sort of minister of the priests and one who exercises those features of the sacred duties that seem an indignity in the hands of priests."[13] Despite their emphasis on the ultimate superiority of the spiritual sphere, neither Bernard nor John seemed to draw the conclusion that popes should enjoy dominion over emperors. Reacting to the recent violence between the papacy and the Roman commune, Bernard's primary concern seemed to be the direct use of violence by popes, which he viewed as a corrupting force for the Roman Church. Popes, ultimately, should turn to secular rulers to wield the material sword. Others, however, did suggest that the possession of the "two swords" by the pope – not the Church more generally – indicated his superiority over secular rulers.

Developments in twelfth-century canon law, including the dissemination of the *Decretum*, provided another venue for Christian thinkers to explore the relative authority of popes and emperors. Perhaps shrewdly, Gratian offered a conservative view of the "two powers," avoiding any controversial conclusions. Later commentators on the *Decretum*, however, the so-called Decretists, offered a wide range of opinions on the matter. The canon lawyer Rufinus, an instructor at

Bologna, asserted around 1157 that popes possessed authority over emperors, since they consecrated imperial rulers and could impose penance upon them. Years later, Huguccio of Pisa declared by contrast that "each power, the apostolic and imperial, was instituted by God, and neither is derived from the other," meaning that the emperor did not "have the sword" from Saint Peter or his successors. His contemporary, Alanus Anglicus, thought otherwise, stating that the emperor "is subject to the pope in spiritual matters and also receives his sword from him, for the right of both swords belongs to the pope."[14] In the debate over *regnum* and *sacerdotium*, Christian intellectuals agreed to disagree, revealing the persistent uncertainties that surrounded fundamental questions of political and religious authority in twelfth-century Europe.

The papacy and Frederick I

These academic debates over the two powers corresponded to real world events. After the death of Eugene III and the brief papacy of Anastasius IV (1153–54), the newly elected Hadrian IV (1154–59) made some progress in his relations with the Roman commune, placing the city under a sentence of interdict that halted most religious services until the Romans expelled Arnold of Brescia and his followers. Although Hadrian pushed back the more radical threat posed to papal rule over the city, the commune had come to stay. Over the following decades, popes had to compromise and negotiate with the civil body, much as they contended with the aristocratic families that dominated Rome's local political life. An effective organizer, this English pope – the only one ever elected to the Apostolic See – set about tightening and reorganizing Rome's rule over the Papal States, helped by his efficient chamberlain, Cardinal Boso. Keeping careful records and wisely managing his revenues, Hadrian used the funds to pay off important Roman families and placate communal governments in papal territories. He also made greater use of "feudal" bonds to secure papal dependencies, receiving personal oaths of fealty from nobles and civic leaders who became "vassals" of Saint Peter.

In the fall of 1154, two years after his coronation as king of the Germans, Frederick I marched into Italy to claim his Italian and imperial crowns. During his campaign, he captured Arnold and handed him over to the papal prefect. The papal nemesis was hung, burned, and his ashes scattered into the Tiber. During the previous year, Frederick had already met with Eugene III and signed the Treaty of Constance, swearing to recognize the lands claimed by Rome as part of the Papal States and to protect them from harm. He also agreed never to align himself with the Norman kingdom of Sicily, an alliance that would squeeze the papacy between two formidable powers on the Italian peninsula. Meeting at Sutri the following summer, Frederick and Hadrian renewed the Treaty of Constance. At the pope's insistence, the German ruler – reluctantly, some sources reported – acted as his groomsman, reenacting the scene between Sylvester and Constantine, as previously done by Innocent II and Lothar III at Liège. Proceeding to Rome, Hadrian crowned Frederick emperor on June 18, 1155. Riots broke out as Roman citizens objected to this display of imperial rule in their city. Frederick and his soldiers forcibly crushed the opposition. When the dust settled, Hadrian left Rome with the new emperor, judging it unsafe to remain in the city due to his still rocky relations with the commune.

To Hadrian's disappointment, Frederick soon returned to Germany. As a result, the pope accused him of failing to honor the Treaty of Constance. In an about-face, after some inconclusive fighting between them, Hadrian and King William I of Sicily reached their own compromise, signing the Treaty of Benevento in 1156. Hadrian acknowledged William's rights of lordship in the kingdom of Sicily, while William agreed to pay homage to the pope, rendering an annual tribute and providing military aid when needed. At first, a majority of the cardinals had tried to oppose this change of policy toward the Normans, a sign of how the pope's desires did not always meet with the approval of the College of Cardinals. Eventually, Hadrian gathered enough support among them to move forward with his plans. By 1157, he was able to return to Rome. With this new Norman alliance and the commune more or less at peace with papal rule, Hadrian stood in a more secure position than any of his predecessors had for decades.

Frederick, however, viewed the Treaty of Benevento as a betrayal by the pope. In October 1157, imperial–papal relations took a turn for the worse at the imperial diet of Besançon, where papal legates delivered a letter to the emperor from Hadrian claiming that he held his crown as a "benefit" from the lord pope. It is not entirely clear what the pope meant by this statement – he later denied its implication that the emperor ruled only as a vassal of the pope. The damage was done. According to Otto of Freising, the Germans and papal envoys also argued over a mural at the Lateran church that depicted Lothar III with the words: "Coming before our gates, the king vows to safeguard the city; then, a liegeman to the pope, by him he is granted the crown." At one point in this debate, a frustrated papal supporter cried out about the emperor: "From whom then does he have the empire, if not from our lord, the pope?" Not long after Besançon, Frederick issued a letter tearing into Hadrian for making such claims, declaring that "Divine Sovereignty, from which is derived all power in heaven and earth, has entrusted unto us, His anointed, the kingdom and the empire to rule over, and has ordained that the peace of the churches is to be maintained by the imperial arms." Invoking the notion of the "two swords," the emperor made it clear that he received his sword directly from God – not the pope.[15]

In 1158–59, the confrontation between papacy and empire worsened as a result of a dispute over the appointment of a new archbishop in Ravenna and a revolt against Frederick's lordship in Milan. The two sides also continued to argue over Frederick's right of imperial taxation in northern Italy, the so-called *fodrum*, one more sign of the emperor's increasingly aggressive claims to rule over the region. Just before he died, Hadrian considered an alliance with some of the Lombard cities opposed to Frederick, making plans to excommunicate the emperor if he did not back down. After the pope's death the divided College of Cardinals could not agree upon a candidate. The majority elected Roland of Siena, one of Hadrian's close advisors, who took the name Alexander III (1158–81). A pro-imperial faction, however, chose their own pope, Octavian of Saint Cecilia (the former legate to Germany, mocked by John of Salisbury), who took the name Victor IV. Among other things, Victor's supporters accused Alexander and his party of conspiring with the Normans against the emperor. Seeing an opportunity, Frederick intervened and summoned a council at Pavia to settle the schism. Not surprisingly, this assembly decided in favor of Victor IV. Alexander renounced the council and the emperor as an "oppressor" rather than "protector" of the papacy. Fighting broke out as the revolt against Frederick in Lombardy picked up steam. Militarily speaking, Alexander and his advocates did not stand a chance against the imperial forces and fled to France. The pope and his legates, however, steadily gathered support from the English and French kings, who generally opposed the Hohenstaufen emperor's ambitions. The Cistercians and the Templars also drew upon their considerable wealth to support the exiled pontiff, largely deprived of his income from the Papal States.

The struggle dragged on, involving the major powers of Europe as well as tangled and shifting alliances between the Italian communes, looking to preserve their independence between the competing claims of the papacy and the empire. When Victor IV died, the pro-imperial cardinals elected another anti-pope, Paschal III. In 1176, however, an alliance of northern Italian cities – the so-called Lombard League – delivered a devastating military blow against Frederick at the battle of Legnano, forcing him to reach an accommodation with Alexander III and his allies. In July 1177, the two sides and their supporters agreed to the Peace of Venice, ending overt hostilities. Frederick denounced anti-pope Paschal III and performed groom-service for Alexander, although insisting that he did not regard the pope as his feudal lord. Far from a decisive outcome, the Peace of Venice effectively declared a truce among the worn-out parties, leaving many of the disputes between the papacy, the emperor, and Lombard cities unresolved.

The Third Lateran Council

Nevertheless, Alexander III must have looked on his situation with some satisfaction. The pope had enjoyed another triumph of sorts in England through his posthumous support for the fiery archbishop of Canterbury, Thomas Becket. Earlier in Alexander's papacy, Becket had opposed English King Henry II's attempts to extend his authority over church offices and institutions, above all over clergy guilty of crimes who avoided royal justice through their trial in ecclesiastical courts. At the time, worried about a possible alliance between Henry and Frederick I, the pope had hesitated to intervene, contributing to Becket's decision to flee to France in 1164. After he returned in 1170, perhaps with Henry's approval, some of the king's retainers cut down the redoubtable archbishop in Canterbury Cathedral. The story of Becket's martyrdom swept through Europe, forcing a penitent Henry to make concessions to Rome and swear a crusade vow before Alexander would reconcile him with the Roman Church. At Canterbury Becket's shrine quickly became a pilgrimage destination of extraordinary popularity. In 1173, Alexander formally canonized Thomas Becket as a saint, reminding everyone about the pope's ability to bring powerful monarchs to heel.

With the schism behind him and the conflict with Frederick I temporarily resolved, the pope convened the Third Lateran Council in 1179. Hundreds of churchmen from around Europe attended. Rufinus, bishop of Assisi, opened the first session on a celebratory note with praise for the Apostolic See. "The holy Roman Church," he proclaimed, "since she is the apex of all episcopal thrones and since she is the mother of all churches and the mistress of all, has most worthily deserved to obtain a unique monarchy of all churches."[16]

Much like the preceding general councils at the Lateran, the synod issued a number of canons regulating clerical behavior. It also nullified any ordinations made by the recent string of anti-popes. In an attempt to avoid the sort of situation that had led to the last two schisms in the Roman Church, the assembly also reformed the election procedures in the College of Cardinals, requiring that a candidate have backing from a two-thirds majority of the cardinals to be elected, the first major changes in papal elections since the Decree of 1059.[17]

Thinking long term, the council also showed a growing papal concern with the problem of heresy in the Roman Church. During the previous decades, various popes had played a minor role in dealing with suspect theologians, scholastic thinkers who pushed the boundaries of their faith through academic speculation. Pope Innocent II, for example, had denounced the controversial master Peter Abelard for his "perverse teachings," while Eugene III had supported the condemnation of Gilbert of Porée for his disturbing claims about the Trinity. The papacy, however, did not possess – and apparently, did not feel that it needed – any systematic means of identifying or investigating possible cases of heresy, leaving such matters in the hands of local authorities. The innovative religious climate of the twelfth century, however, began to charge the borders between popular heresy and orthodoxy with a greater voltage. Calls to follow the "apostolic life" did not always remain safely behind monastery and church walls, as seen when the former monk Henry of Lausanne delivered public and fiery sermons against clerical corruption in Le Mans in 1116, or when a merchant from Lyons named Peter Waldo preached the virtues of apostolic poverty in 1174. Catholic churchmen, including Bernard of Clairvaux, also identified somewhat mysterious groups of "Good Christians" in southern France and northern Italy, whom they accused of dualist beliefs, that is, dividing the cosmos into a corrupt material world ruled by an evil deity and a pure spiritual realm reigned over by God. For these unconventional Christians, lumped together and called Cathars or "Pure Ones" by the Roman Church, Christ never assumed a human body, nor did material sacraments such as baptism and the Eucharist impart any grace.[18]

At the Third Lateran Council, the twenty-seventh canon denounced the so-called Cathars, also called Patarenes, promising the protection of the Church for those who combated such heretics and others like them. In the case of Peter Waldo and his followers, Pope Alexander III approved of the Waldensians' commitment to poverty but prohibited them from preaching – not a fitting occupation for the laity. Five years later at the Council of Verona, Alexander's successor, Pope Lucius III (1181–85), condemned the Waldensians for failing to observe this prohibition. At the same council the pope and Frederick I jointly issued the decree *Ad abolendam* to combat the threat of heresy more generally. "We have risen up against those heretics," the bull stated in 1184, "to whom diverse names have ascribed the profession of various errors, and, by the tenor of this constitution, with apostolic authority, we condemn all heresy, however it may be named."[19] Working together, clerical and lay authorities were called upon to identify heretics and take measures against them, including excommunication, seizure of their property, and other forms of punishment including exile and execution by the "secular arm." A new phase had begun in the Roman Church's effort to police the boundaries of the orthodox community.

The papacy at a crossroads

Although Alexander III emerged in a position of relative strength from his conflict with Frederick I, his successors did not possess the energy or resources to press their position. Italy stood in a state of exhaustion and the Papal States in a condition of disarray after the recent war. Alexander also confronted renewed tensions with the Roman commune, forcing him to spend the remaining years of his papacy outside of the city. After he died in 1181, his successor, Lucius III, adopted a conciliatory attitude toward Frederick, as seen during their meeting at Verona and agreement to work together for the suppression of heresy. Lucius also made plans for a new crusade at Verona, planning on the emperor's participation. In addition, the pope tried to address an ongoing dispute with Frederick over the so-called "Mathildine" territories in Tuscany, estates left by Mathilda of Tuscany to the papacy when she died in 1115, but never successfully claimed by Rome. Complicating the situation, Mathilda had also delegated certain privileges in the region to Henry V. During the schism of 1130, in return for Lothar III's support, Pope Innocent II had yielded custody over the Mathildine lands to the German king, while retaining their nominal ownership. Not surprisingly, this intractable matter remained impossible for Lucius to resolve.

By the time that he died in 1185, Lucius's relations with Frederick had started to sour, in part because he refused to crown Frederick's son, Henry VI, as co-emperor. His successor, Urban III (1185–87), supported by cardinals who wanted to see a firmer hand with the

emperor, immediately began to resist the German ruler's interests, opposing his candidate for the archbishopric of Trier, and
complaining about the common royal practice – also performed
by the French and English crowns – of claiming revenues from
vacant church offices. The situation deteriorated to the point where
Frederick ordered Henry VI to invade the Papal States, effectively
sealing the pope up in Verona, where he spent most of his papacy,
also unable to return to Rome due to resistance from the commune.
When Urban died, Pope Gregory VIII (October–December 1187)
changed course again, seeking to placate the emperor. Despite his
brief time as pope, Gregory VIII confronted a shocking blow for the
Western Church, the loss of Jerusalem to the Muslim ruler Saladin
in 1187. That same year he issued the call for what became the Third
Crusade, asking not just warriors but Christians everywhere to support the crusade through prayers, fasting, and other acts of penance.
Waged by King Richard I of England and King Philip Augustus of
France, the Third Crusade failed to recover Jerusalem.

The papacy's longtime foe, the aging Frederick I, died on the
crusade before ever reaching the Holy Land. Before Frederick had
set out on the expedition, Pope Clement III (1187–91) had completed the papal reconciliation with the emperor, crowning his son
Henry, who pulled his forces out of the Papal States. Clement also
made peace with the Roman commune, allowing him to return to
Rome. The city's senators agreed to recognize papal sovereignty and
restored seized assets and estates to the pope, while retaining daily
administrative control over Rome. Clement agreed to make substantial payments to the commune, placing another layer of financial
obligations on the curia (one reason that he asked his chamberlain,
Censius, to compile the *Liber Censuum*, completed in 1192). Although
Frederick was out of the picture, Clement's successor, Celestine III
(1191–98), faced growing problems with his young and assertive heir
Henry VI. In 1186, Henry had married Constance of Sicily, daughter of the Norman ruler, Roger II, making Henry the heir to the
Sicilian throne when Constance's nephew King William II of Sicily
died childless in 1189. Henry thereby possessed the German and
Sicilian crowns, a union feared by the papacy, one that would hem
in the Papal States on both sides. In 1191, Celestine III nevertheless
crowned Henry and his wife as emperor and empress, the first of
many conciliatory gestures he made toward the German monarch.
Over the following years, as Henry attempted to subdue rebellious
forces in Sicily that resisted his claim to the crown, Celestine found
war on his doorstep, but took little action to restrain Henry, even

when the ambitious ruler disregarded papal rights and claims in the region. Henry's unexpected death from malaria in 1197 forestalled further troubles for the elderly pope, who himself died months later. As the twelfth century drew to a close, after a series of elderly and accommodating popes, the papacy seemed to be in a holding pattern. In fact, a renewed round of strong papal leadership lay just around the corner, the capstone of the papal monarchy.

Chapter 6: The Whole World to Govern

On January 8, 1198, the very same day that Pope Celestine III died, the College of Cardinals elected the young and energetic Lothar of Segni as the bishop of Rome. He took the name Innocent III (1198–1216). Lothar came well prepared to the papal throne. Early in his ecclesiastical career he had spent years studying liberal arts and theology in Paris. After that, he probably studied canon law in Bologna. In 1189 or 1190, Clement III elevated him to the status of cardinal deacon, and he later became cardinal priest of Saint Pudentiana. During these years, showing his education and keen mind, Lothar penned a number of influential theological tracts, including *The Misery of the Human Condition*, which reflected on the turmoil and troubles people face in the world, and *The Sacred Mysteries of the Altar*, a commentary on the mass and sacraments. In a sermon delivered after his election, Innocent stressed the themes of papal primacy and the pope's universal responsibilities, invoking what became one of his favorite biblical passages, Jeremiah 1: 10, "I have set you this day over the nations, and over the kingdoms, to root up and pull down, to waste and to destroy, and to build and to plant." Echoing Bernard of Clairvaux, the new pope – who first began to use the title "Vicar of Christ" with regularity – proclaimed that the Lord had given to the papacy not just the Church, but the "whole world to govern." Innocent immediately set about that task, "rooting up" abuses and "planting" the seeds of the faith. With his theological training and practical experience he knew how things worked and the problems that the clergy faced. At the start of his papacy he personally sat in on the consistory several days a week, hearing appeals, requests, and litigation. He also kept a systematic register of all his letters, paying more attention to the papal archives than his predecessors.[1]

Most modern scholars of the papacy seem to agree that Innocent III's time as pope represented the high-water mark of papal monarchy. Benefiting from the lack of a strong imperial competitor, the ambitious pope frequently intervened in secular politics and tightened Rome's administrative grasp on the Papal States. He declared multiple crusades and targeted heretics, seeking to expand and defend the catholic Roman Church. Over the following decades, his equally motivated successors maintained similar levels of activity in the governance of the Church, battling the resurgent imperial power of the Hohenstaufen ruler, Frederick II, disciplining the faithful, declaring even more crusades, and sending out missionaries to non-Christian lands. By these measures, popes took seriously their claim to govern the whole world.

By the later thirteenth century, however, the papal monarchy began to run out of steam and confronted intractable problems. Defeating Frederick II, in particular, had represented a costly endeavor, draining the papacy's resources and using up a great deal of the contemporary good will toward Rome. Searching for allies on the Italian peninsula after the final defeat of the Hohenstaufen dynasty, a series of less compelling popes looked to Charles of Anjou, a member of the French royal family, as their new champion. The arrival of the Angevins, however, brought disruptive wars in its wake and introduced another strong competitor in the region contesting papal rule. On farther horizons, events likewise did not favor papal plans and projects, as seen when the final crusader stronghold in the Middle East, the city of Acre, fell to Muslim armies in 1291. The "seeds" that Innocent III and his successors planted, it would seem, did not always bear the fruit that they wanted.

The Vicar of Christ

In many ways, Innocent III recovered the earlier "Gregorian" enthusiasm to reform the Church by asserting papal leadership over Christendom. Innocent, moreover, had resources at his disposal that Gregory VII could only have imagined, including an active College of Cardinals, a well-developed body of canon law, and a relatively effective papal bureaucracy. For these reasons and more, Innocent's papacy redefined the possible for the Roman Church, although even this powerful pope experienced his own disappointments.

Secular powers and the Papal States

In 1197, Emperor Henry VI had died at the age of 32, leaving his young son, Frederick, as his heir in Sicily. In Germany, a struggle broke out between two claimants to the royal throne and imperial title, Philip of Swabia and Otto of Brunswick. Innocent backed Otto, viewing him as the more suitable choice, although Philip emerged as the stronger candidate. Meanwhile, the pope faced a new threat to the Papal States by one of Henry's former vassals, Markward of Anweiler. Innocent declared a virtual crusade against Markward, promising soldiers who fought against him on the papacy's behalf the same spiritual benefits and protections as warriors going to Jerusalem. Markward died in 1202, but uncertainty persisted. As Innocent prepared to reach an accommodation with Philip of Swabia, someone murdered the imperial hopeful. At this point, the pope turned back to his preferred candidate Otto of Brunswick, who made all sorts of promises in return for papal support, including not to interfere with episcopal elections or appeals to the pope, not to appropriate incomes from vacant churches, and never to attempt to unite the kingdoms of Germany and Sicily under his power. In 1209, Innocent offered the imperial crown to Otto, who quickly reneged on most of his pledges. The following year the pope excommunicated him and threw his support behind the young but ambitious Hohenstaufen heir, Frederick, now old enough to begin pursuing his father's legacy.

This turmoil caused Innocent his share of problems, but it also created a window of opportunity for the pope. During the entire controversy over Henry VI's succession, he stressed repeatedly the role of the pope as the rightful arbiter of the imperial dignity, pointing back to the role of the Apostolic See in transferring the power of empire from the Greeks to the Germans in the first place during the age of Charlemagne. Popes, Innocent reminded everyone, bestowed the imperial crown for a reason. He also stressed that he sought the "conservation and exaltation" and not "destruction" of the Christian Empire. Both popes and emperors were necessary for protecting the faith, creating peace and justice, and battling against unbelievers, as long as secular rulers paid proper deference to the bearers of sacred authority. With empire in such a state of disarray, the outspoken pope's possession of the "two swords" seemed incontrovertible.[2]

The lack of a strong emperor also created breathing room for Innocent to reorganize the governance of the Papal States. Reaching back to the era of Carolingian donations to the papacy, Innocent carefully marshaled his sources for Rome's claims to places contested for generations or never successfully realized in the past. In return for Innocent's support in his struggle against Philip, Otto had issued the "Promise of Neuss" in 1201, recognizing papal lands including the duchy of Rome and its surroundings, along with Spoleto, the former exarchate of Ravenna, the March of Ancona, and even the contested Mathildine lands. One scholar has called this document the genuine "birth certificate of the Papal State."[3] Over the following years, Innocent appointed clerical rectors to oversee these regions, called assemblies to pass statutes governing papal rights, privileges, and jurisdictions, and received countless oaths of fealty from his Italian subjects. Although Otto later repudiated his "promise" and tried to reassert his authority in Italy, Innocent had placed Rome's administration of papal territories on more secure footing than ever before.

Dealing with other European powers, Innocent showed a similar assertiveness, with mixed success. Like many of his predecessors he enjoyed relatively warm relations with the French crown, although he denounced King Philip Augustus for repudiating his wife, Ingeborg of Demark, and illegally marrying his mistress. The pope pressured Philip into grudgingly taking Ingeborg back, but he struggled in vain to reconcile the two in any meaningful way. He also experienced difficulties brokering peace between Philip and King Richard of England. Ending their conflict, Innocent believed, formed a necessary condition for any further attempt to recover the Holy Land. After Richard died in 1199, Innocent pursued his agenda with Richard's successor, John I. Relations between the pope and English king, however, soured due to their conflict over the vacant archbishopric of Canterbury. When Innocent rejected two of John's preferred candidates for the office and promoted Stephen Langton, John prevented Stephen from entering England. In 1208, not one to pull punches, the pope placed the kingdom under interdict and excommunicated John the following year.

Faced with growing unrest among his own barons and threatened by the pope with deposition, in 1213 John finally caved in, reversing his position and accepting Stephen Langton. In addition, he yielded the kingdoms of England and Ireland as a fief to the papacy, obligating him to make considerable payments in lieu of his feudal service, and even swore a crusade vow. The king's concessions to the pope represented another moment of political triumph for Innocent. As the pope wrote to John two years later, Christ, the "King of kings" and "priest forever after the order of Melchisedech," had set the pope over all, the one

> whom He has appointed as His Vicar on earth, so that, as every knee is bowed to Jesus, of things in heaven, and things in earth, and things under the earth, so all men should obey His Vicar

and strive that there may be one fold and one shepherd. All secular kings for the sake of God so venerate this Vicar, that unless they seek to serve him devotedly they doubt if they are reigning properly.[4]

John's strategy of submission to the pope, however, also had its benefits for the English monarch. Innocent withdrew his support for the rebellious barons and clergy in his kingdom, declaring their charter of aristocratic liberties and privileges issued in 1215 – the Magna Carta – null and void. This move created considerable resentment among the English nobility and clergy toward Rome. In a turnabout, the pope also rebuked Stephen Langton for his continued aid of the rebels against King John, Innocent's former foe, but now his "well beloved son in Christ." The pope's worldly successes did not come without compromises.

Innocent and the crusades

More than any other pope except perhaps Urban II, Innocent III remains associated in modern times with the commitment of the medieval papacy to the crusading movement. As a deacon in the circle of Gregory VIII, the young Lothar of Segni no doubt never forgot hearing the traumatic news of Jerusalem's loss to Saladin. Immediately after his election, Innocent began to gather support for a new expedition to free the Holy Land. Picking up on themes from the call for the Third Crusade, Innocent lamented the loss of Jerusalem as a blow against all of Christendom. "For behold," the pope wrote in 1198, drawing upon the Book of Lamentations, "our inheritance has been given over to strangers, our houses have gone to foreigners." Everyone had a role to play in the recovery of Christ's tomb through donations, prayers, fasting, and other forms of penance. Over the following years, Innocent dispatched legates and preachers around Europe to raise enthusiasm and funds for his crusade, putting aside a tenth of papal incomes for this purpose.[5]

Answering this call in 1202, a combined force of French warriors and Venetian sailors known as the Fourth Crusade set out for the Eastern Mediterranean. Due to a miscalculation regarding the number of ships they would require, the French army accrued a substantial debt to the Venetians, a financial situation that jeopardized the entire expedition. Despite papal instructions to the contrary, at Venice's behest they headed first to attack Zara, a city on the Adriatic resisting Venetian rule, and next to Constantinople, lured by the promise of much-needed funds if they helped to place the young Byzantine prince-in-exile Alexius on the throne alongside his deposed and imprisoned father, Isaac II. In 1203 the crusaders captured the city. Although he had fulminated against the decision to divert the crusade to Byzantium in the first place, Innocent greeted the news of the city's fall with cautious acceptance after the fact, insisting that Alexius submit the Greek Church to Roman authority. Much like his predecessors, Innocent believed that the Greeks had strayed into schism by refusing to acknowledge papal primacy, persisting in their erroneous rejection of *filioque*, and maintaining other divergences from the Roman Church. Alexius, however, had already begun to fall short of his agreements with the crusading army. A usurper soon deposed and murdered the short-reigned emperor. When fighting broke out again between the Greeks and the crusaders, the French and Venetians seized the Byzantine capital for themselves in April 1204, establishing the Latin Empire of Constantinople.

Innocent reacted to the second capture of the city in far stronger terms, viewing it as a providential event. God, the pope addressed the crusading clergy in November 1204, "has transferred the empire of Constantinople from the proud to humble, from the disobedient to the obedient, from schismatics to catholics, namely, from the Greeks to the Latins." In this remarkable letter Innocent drew inspiration from the apocalyptic prophecies of the Italian monastic reformer and prophet Joachim of Fiore, whose commentaries on the Bible led him to predict the future conversion of the Jews and the restoration of the Greeks to the Roman Church before the transformative age of the Holy Spirit on earth. Before he died in 1202, Joachim had met with Popes Lucius III and Urban III, and had submitted his works for approval from Celestine III and Innocent III. The popes of Rome clearly felt the attractions of his prophecies. In this case, the abbot's predictions convinced Innocent that the capture of Constantinople represented an apocalyptic event, a sign that the conversion of the Jews and recovery of the Holy Land might not be all that far away.[6] As time passed, however, the pope grew increasingly disillusioned about the sack of Constantinople when he heard about the crusaders' violent mistreatment of the Greeks, although he never abandoned his belief that the conquest of Constantinople represented a step toward the union of the Latin and Greek Churches and the capture of Jerusalem.

Despite the outcome of the Fourth Crusade – certainly, not everyone agreed with the pope about its divine nature – Innocent's enthusiasm for crusading remained strong, and not just when directed toward the recovery of Jerusalem. As noted above, earlier in his papacy, he had declared a crusade of sorts against Markward of Anweiler, who threatened the Papal States after Henry VI's death. In 1204, the pope also called upon Philip Augustus or his son Louis to take up arms against the supposed "Cathars," a clear example of the material sword working in defense of the Church at the bidding of its spiritual superior. When the French king – apparently more eager to fight the English than heretics – failed to act, Innocent called more widely upon northern French nobles to head south against the Cathars in November 1207, promising them the same spiritual rewards and protections as knights bound for the Holy Land. Tepid at first, enthusiasm for this new expedition took off after the murder of Innocent's legate, Peter Castlenau, in southern France, initiating the Albigensian Crusade.

Over the course of his papacy, Innocent also showed his support for theaters of crusading in Spain and the Baltic region. In 1212, for example, he staged an elaborate liturgical celebration at Rome following news of an unhoped-for victory by the kings of Castile, Aragon, Navarre, and Portugal over Muslim forces at the Battle of Las Navas de Tolosa. Jerusalem, however, remained the ultimate crusading prize. Reenergized by the Christian victory in Spain, in 1213 Innocent issued the bulls *Quia maior* and *Vineam domini*, summoning what became the Fifth Crusade. In his call for a new expedition to recover Jerusalem, Innocent once again channeled apocalyptic expectations. Referencing the number 666 from the Book of Revelation, he declared that almost six hundred and sixty-six years had passed since the time of Muhammad. The moment for Christian triumph, he reasoned, must be at hand. Newly confident, the pope even dispatched a letter to the Ayyubid sultan of Egypt, al-Kamil, asking him to surrender the holy places and avoid further bloodshed. The sultan declined, as one must suspect Innocent knew he would. Plans for the crusade continued.[7]

The Fourth Lateran Council

Gearing up for the new crusade, Innocent also called for an ecumenical council to meet at the Lateran in November 1215 to pursue the twin goals of ecclesiastical reform and the liberation of the Holy Land. Well over four hundred bishops and over nine hundred abbots attended the synod, some coming from as far afield as the Latin Empire of Constantinople and crusader-held territories in the Levant. The canons of the council offered a wide-ranging, comprehensive set of reforms and regulations for governing the lives of Christians, including rulers and ruled, clergy and the laity, men and women. Combating heresy, providing pastoral care for Christians, properly managing clerical offices, planning for the future crusade – at the Fourth Lateran Council, Innocent III oversaw these and other initiatives for the strengthening and defense of Christendom.

Seeking to refute the so-called "Good Men" in southern France and other heretics, the council's first canon reasserted the basic tenets and sacraments of the Christian faith with new clarity and precision, including the doctrine of the Trinity, the creation of the world by God the Father, the Incarnation of Christ in the flesh, the saving grace of the Eucharist and baptism by water, and the resurrection of the body after Christ's return in the Final Judgment. Canon three tackled the problem of heresy directly, reiterating many of the provisions from *Ad abolendam* and calling upon bishops to root up heretics in their dioceses. Other canons stressed the need for prelates to monitor the morals and behavior of clergy, especially those accused of corruption, drunkenness, fornication, or otherwise abusing their position. The legislation of the council placed a special emphasis on the need for well-trained and efficient preachers, to spread the word of God among the laity. As for the laity themselves, the canons addressed a host of issues, focusing on the need to regularize central sacraments in the life of the Church. In addition to refining the rules for marriage, the twenty-first canon mandated that men and women confess their sins at least once a year and receive the Eucharist at Easter. In the wake of the council, confessor manuals began to circulate around Europe, providing detailed instructions for this task and the assigning of penance. The pastoral maintenance of Christendom had become an increasingly professional job.

The council's thirteenth canon placed a cap on the creation of new religious orders. By Innocent III's day, still more groups had emerged with a compelling – and, to some, disturbing – devotion to apostolic living, including the Beguines, women residing together for the purposes of prayer and spiritual reflection, and the Humiliati, men and women devoted to a penitential lifestyle and acts of charity. Neither of these communities or others like them took formal vows, and they engaged in "suspect" behavior, such as reading the Bible in the vernacular without clerical supervision. Confronting this dynamic landscape of religious piety, Innocent III showed a remarkable flexibility and willingness to find points of accommodation with such potential heretics, keeping them in the orthodox camp. In 1201, he reconciled Humiliati communities in northern Italy with clerical authorities, creating around 150 formal houses under an official rule. Innocent also embraced a band of Waldensians who pledged obedience to Rome as the "Poor Catholics." Although he could not have known it at the time, he laid the foundations for an even greater revolution in the Church through his support for Dominic of Caleruega and Francis of Assisi, along with their respective followers. By living lives of apostolic devotion, the Dominicans sought to beat heretics at their own game, providing the laity with inspirational and orthodox models of religious piety in action. The Franciscans dedicated themselves to poverty and preaching after the model of their founder, who had experienced a religious awakening much like Peter Waldo. Although it fell to his successor, Honorius III, to recognize the rules of the wildly popular mendicant orders, Innocent set them on the road to approval. Indeed, the canon against new orders at the Fourth Lateran Council might have represented the work of certain cardinals, nervous about the pope's recent accommodations toward the Humiliati, the friars, and others.

Defining the norms of orthodox believers also meant heightened scrutiny of those who did not belong within the Christian community, not just heretics but also Jews and Muslims. Generally speaking, the anomalous position of the Jews in medieval Christian society had grown increasingly uncomfortable if not downright dangerous over the course of the twelfth century. Canon sixty-eight addressed a concern that in some places Christians could not distinguish, based on appearance, between themselves and these non-believers, resulting in "prohibited intercourse" between them. To prevent this, the legislation decreed that Jews and Muslims "shall be marked off in the eyes of the public from other peoples through the character of their dress." This same canon also called for them not to appear in public during the three days before Easter to prevent them from mocking Christians. Canons sixty-nine and seventy took further steps, prohibiting Jews from holding public office and calling upon bishops to prevent, forcibly if needed, any Jews who did convert to Christianity from "backsliding" into the practices of the Jewish faith. Before closing, the council finally turned to the business of crusading, calling upon future crusaders to fortify themselves "with spiritual and material arms" through their humility and acts of repentance, as well as their military and financial arrangements. Ratcheting up the pressure on everyone to support the expedition, the legislation promised the excommunication of pirates who plundered crusading vessels and those who traded with Muslim powers in timber, weapons, and other supplies.[8]

Innocent must have been pleased with the outcome of his enterprise, although he died in Perugia on July 16, 1216, before he could see any results from the council or his planned crusade. One eyewitness to these events, James of Vitry, arrived at Perugia just after the pope passed away. James was en route to Acre, where he had been appointed bishop. An enthusiast for lay devotion, during his travels in Italy James had observed the Humiliati and the Franciscans with great interest and approval. He later joined the Fifth Crusade and accompanied the army to its ultimate destination in Egypt. In these and other ways, James inhabited a world that Innocent had helped to create. Arriving in Perugia, however, he found the great pontiff in a decidedly humble state. "During the night," James wrote to his friends back in Liège, "some thieves had stripped his body of all the precious vestments with which he was to be interred, and left it there in the church virtually naked and already decaying. I went into the church and saw with utter faith how fleeting and empty is the deceitful glory of this world."[9] For all of his ambitions and accomplishments, one suspects that Innocent III would not have disagreed with this assessment.

Christendom in the Thirteenth Century

Over the following decades, Innocent III's successors continued to act with exceptional energy and effectiveness as the self-proclaimed Vicars of Christ, legislating over the Church, declaring crusades, suppressing heresy, and taking other actions in the name of the Apostolic See. Popes again battled an ambitious emperor, vying for supremacy in the ongoing struggle between secular power and priestly authority. Tapping into the enthusiasm of the mendicant orders, they sent missionaries to places as far away as China and imagined Rome's universal spiritual government in wider terms than ever before.

The papacy and Frederick II

In 1214, Otto of Brunswick and his English allies had suffered a crushing defeat by French forces at the Battle of Bouvines. The following year Otto abdicated the imperial throne, opening the door for the Hohenstaufen heir, Frederick II. As described above, Frederick had enjoyed Innocent III's support since the pope's falling out with Otto. In 1213, the would-be emperor had signed the "Golden Bull of Eger," making the same promises to the papacy as Otto before him, recognizing and swearing to protect the Papal States. In 1215, Frederick was crowned king of the Germans at Aachen. To Innocent's delight, the new ruler also swore a crusading vow. It took time for Frederick to secure his position, but in 1220 he journeyed to Rome where Honorius III crowned him emperor. At the time, Frederick also renewed his crusading vow at the hands of Hugolino di Conti, cardinal bishop of Ostia and future Pope Gregory IX (1227–41), promising to join the Fifth Crusade in Egypt the following summer.

When Frederick failed to do so, many in Europe and what was left of the crusader kingdoms blamed him for the expedition's eventual military collapse in 1221. Hopeful of a better outcome, Honorius continued to press the emperor to fulfill his crusading vow, but Frederick seemed more bent on securing his rule over Sicily than leaving for the Holy Land. In 1225, Frederick proclaimed himself king of Jerusalem after marrying Isabella, daughter of the city's Latin ruler-in-exile, John of Brienne. Delayed by illness, however, he still refused to depart on crusade, prompting Honorius III's successor, Gregory IX, to excommunicate him in 1228. When Frederick finally fulfilled his crusading vow later that year, he technically remained under a sentence of excommunication. By signing a controversial ten-year truce with the Egyptian sultan, al-Kamil, the audacious emperor succeeded where generations of crusaders before him had failed, regaining Christian control of Jerusalem in 1229. Despite efforts to stop him by Jerusalem's Latin patriarch, Gerold, the excommunicate ruler entered the Church of the Holy Sepulcher and staged his own coronation ceremony.

While navigating the complicated political landscape in the crusader East, Frederick had made numerous enemies, who wasted little time spreading the word about what they saw as his disgraceful behavior and coziness with the Muslims. Gerold penned a vitriolic diatribe against him that circulated around Europe. As for the pope, Gregory IX remained unimpressed by what he saw as a hollow triumph. After Frederick returned to Sicily in 1229, confronting military pressure from enemies backed by the pope, he reconciled with Gregory. His ambitions, however, above all his unification of the kingdoms of Sicily and Germany under a single ruler – a Hohenstaufen goal long feared by the papacy – seemed to ensure future conflict. In 1231, for example, Frederick issued a new law code for Sicily, the Constitutions of Melfi, which restricted the property rights of bishops in the kingdom, and made prelates subject to secular courts. After several years of an effective truce, the pope grew increasingly antagonistic toward the emperor due to such "abuses" of church liberties, offices, and persons.

In 1239, the pope again excommunicated Frederick and declared a crusade against him, accusing him of further crimes including attacks on the clergy, impeding the crusades, and blasphemy against Christ. A state of all-out war resulted on the Italian peninsula, as communes lined up on either side, the so-called "Ghibellines" supporting the imperial cause, the "Guelfs" backing the papacy. According to some apocalyptic-minded clerics, inspired by Joachim of Fiore, Frederick represented nothing less than Antichrist, although imperial supporters made similar accusations against the papacy. At one point, in February 1240, the emperor threatened Rome itself, revealing divisions even among the cardinals and the Romans, some of whom declared their hope that Frederick would seize the city. In response, Gregory staged an elaborate procession with Peter and Paul's relics from the Lateran to the Church of Saint Peter, calling upon the apostles' protection, presenting the defense of Rome as a holy war. Frederick, lacking the strength to attack the well-fortified city, withdrew for the time being.[10]

When Gregory died in 1241, the Hohenstaufen ruler claimed that he still desired a peaceful resolution to his dispute with the Roman Church. Due to contention among the cardinals and uncertainty about their next move, the election of Gregory's successor dragged on. Finally, the Roman senator and effective dictator, Matteo Rosso Orsini, forcibly confined the cardinals in a broken-down palace called the Septizonium until they made a decision. This papal "conclave" elected an elderly, sickly compromise candidate, Celestine IV, on October 25, 1241, but he died weeks later. Eager to avoid another stint in the conclave, the cardinals fled Rome to Anagni, taking another eighteen months to elect Sinibaldo di Fieschi, who took the name Innocent IV (1243–54).

Picking up where Gregory left off, the new pope adopted a hard line against the emperor. When imperial armies again gathered near Rome, trying to seal off the city, Innocent fled to Genoa and then Lyons. In June 1245, he convened the First Council of Lyons. Among other business, the council renewed the emperor's excommunication, accusing him of perjury, breaking the peace, sacrilege, violating ecclesiastical property and persons, and heresy (not to mention spending time with Muslim concubines. The imperial representative Thaddeus of Suessa protested in vain. Before the end of the council, Innocent deposed Frederick, stripping him of all his titles. The emperor denounced his actions and the devastating war in Italy between imperial armies and papal allies continued until Frederick II unexpectedly died in 1250. When his heir Conrad died four years later, the Hohenstaufen dynasty stood in a state of uncertainty, leaving Frederick's illegitimate son Manfred and his grandson Conradin as beleaguered claimants to his titles and territories. The papacy had received an unexpected reprieve, apparently opening the door to another round of strong papal leadership over Europe.

Disciplining Christendom

The reopening of conflict between papacy and empire did not mean an end to papal ambitions for the reform and regulation of the faith. Gregory IX and Innocent IV advanced a number of projects with long-lasting consequences, turning to members of the rapidly growing mendicant orders to execute their plans. In 1230, Gregory commissioned his confessor, a Dominican friar named Raymond of Penyafort, to compile a definitive edition of canon law including recent papal decretals. Updated, revised, and commented upon by subsequent popes (including Innocent IV) and later generations of canon lawyers, the so-called *Decretals* became the standard collection of Roman ecclesiastical law. In addition, the pope also showed his support for the University of Paris, a training ground for theologians and clerical administrators, issuing a bull of privileges for the school's masters and students in 1231. On Gregory's watch, the papacy also took its first steps toward centralizing the investigation of heresy, the origins of medieval inquisition. In 1231, the pope appointed the first inquisitor directly empowered by the Apostolic See to find and eradicate heretics in German lands, Conrad of Marburg. Gregory assigned other papal inquisitors in southern France, still hunting the so-called Cathars in the region. In 1252, Innocent IV formally established the inquisition in Italy, dividing the Papal States into Franciscan and Dominican zones of jurisdiction.

The powers and reach of medieval inquisition should not be exaggerated. The legal procedures in question – including hearings and tribunals, the deposition of witnesses (sometimes under torture), and the keeping of careful records – remained a largely local affair, dependent upon bishops and cooperative secular figures. Under certain circumstances, Christians did not hesitate to protest or resist invasive or overly zealous inquisitors – Conrad of Marburg, for example, was murdered in 1233. Nevertheless, the development of inquisitorial procedures and agents represented another stage in the papacy's attempt to define, target, and suppress heresy on a European-wide scale. Starting in 1236, the papacy even tackled what it saw as a Jewish "heresy," supporting an investigation into the Talmud after a Jewish convert to Christianity, Nicholas Donin, denounced the Hebrew religious writings in a letter to Gregory IX. Years later, urged on by Rome, French King Louis IX ordered copies of the Talmud burned by the cartload in Paris. On other occasions, however, Pope Gregory and Innocent did speak out against the slanderous "Blood Libel," the Christian accusation that groups of Jews kidnapped and sacrificed Christian boys on Passover.

This era also witnessed a sensational controversy over the apocalypse. Inspired by the works of Joachim of Fiore, some Franciscans showed a particular interest in predictions about the future of their own order, the papacy, and empire, creating and circulating new works under Joachim's name that sometimes became more popular than his authentic writings. At Paris, a Franciscan friar named Gerard of Borgo San Donnino created a considerable stir when he published his *Introduction to the Eternal Gospel*, a guide to Joachim's major works. Gerard, moreover, declared that the future age of the Holy Spirit would see a coming spiritual Covenant, superseding the New Testament, rendering the ecclesiastical hierarchy and sacraments of the current age null and void. In the future, an order of spiritual preachers, associated by Gerard with the Franciscans, would form a new priesthood, surpassing the clergy of the present age. In addition, he predicted the rise of a "pseudo-pope" around the time of Antichrist, but also the arrival of a new leader for God's Church after the trials of the end times, a universal pontiff for the New Jerusalem. Condemned by Franciscan authorities and a panel of investigators commissioned by Innocent IV's successor, Alexander IV (1254–61), Gerard spent his final days in prison. Just like other forms of supposed heresy, however, apocalyptic critiques of the Roman Church proved difficult to suppress and persisted over the coming years.

Expanding Christendom

Looking further afield, Gregory IX and Innocent IV enlisted members of the mendicant orders as diplomats and missionaries to non-Christian lands. The Franciscans in particular viewed their commitment to preaching as extending beyond the borders of Europe, drawing inspiration from their founder's attempt to convert the Egyptian ruler al-Kamil during the course of the Fifth Crusade. Rather than fearing death as a result of their proselytizing among the infidels, they positively embraced it as a way of achieving martyrdom. The friars also hoped to reach various Eastern Christian peoples living under Islamic rule, viewed as heretics who failed to observe Roman teachings and practices. Issuing bulls in support of mendicant missions, the papacy suggested that the friars' efforts possessed an apocalyptic significance, signaling the conversion of peoples around the world before the end of time. Popes also dispatched Franciscans and Dominicans as envoys to Islamic rulers ranging from northern Africa to Syria and beyond. In their correspondence with Muslim sultans and emirs, the popes acknowledged that both Christians and Muslims worshipped the all-powerful Creator God, maker of heaven and earth – Christians realized, however, and Muslims did not, that God had assumed the flesh as Jesus Christ, the son of God, for the redemption of humankind. Not surprisingly, Muslim rulers replied that Christians had failed to recognize God's revelation to Muhammad, as revealed in the Qur'an.[11]

Starting in the 1240s, the opportunities for converting non-believers and schismatic Christians widened immeasurably with the rise of a new Mongol dominion, stretching from China to the edges of Europe. Initially, the growing power of the Mongols (or Tartars, as Europeans called them) terrified the self-proclaimed residents of Christendom. As the insatiably curious English chronicler Matthew Paris described their arrival in the region of Hungary, the Tartars "burst forth from their mountain-bound regions ... overrunning the country, covering the face of the earth like locusts, they ravaged the eastern countries with lamentable destruction, spreading fire and slaughter wherever they went." Rumors and panic spread. Some claimed that Frederick II had secretly arranged the invasions, part of his plan to rule the world. Others told stories about the Jews helping the Tartars, trying to smuggle weapons to them hidden in wine casks. Before the First Council of Lyons, Pope Innocent IV called for a crusade against these unexpected invaders of Christian lands. Not to be outdone, Emperor Frederick II also circulated letters around Europe, declaring his intention to defend the faithful from this new threat.[12]

From Lyons, Pope Innocent dispatched envoys to the Mongols, in part to spy on them but also hoping for their possible conversion. One of his representatives, the Franciscan friar John of Plano Carpini, bore papal letters to the Mongol ruler Güyük, which explained the basic tenets of the Christian faith, including Christ's incarnation, resurrection, and ascension. The Lord then left behind his "vicar" on earth with the keys to the kingdom of Heaven. "Wherefore we," the pope addressed the khan,

> though unworthy, have become by the Lord's disposition the successor of this vicar, do turn our keen attention, before all else

incumbent on us in virtue of our office, to your salvation and that of other men, and on this matter especially do we fix our mind, sedulously keeping watch over it with diligent zeal and zealous diligence, so that we maybe be able with the help of God's grace to lead those in error into the way of truth and gain all men for Him.

As pope and a trained canon lawyer, Innocent IV recognized the rights of infidels to wield political power under natural law. As the pope put it on another occasion, God had created "lordship, possession, and jurisdiction … not only for the faithful, but for every rational creature." Nevertheless, he added, "we do believe that the pope, who is the vicar of Jesus Christ, has power not only over Christians but also over all infidels, for Jesus Christ had power over all."[13] Although they did not know it, Frederick II and the distant Mongol khan had something in common – both should rightly submit to the pope of Rome. Güyük remained unimpressed. In his letters of response to Innocent, he declared that divine power obviously favored the Mongols, who had conquered everything from the East to the West. Rather than seeking his conversion, the pope and Christian princes should surrender and make peace with him.

The Limits of Papal Monarchy

At the First Council of Lyons, Innocent IV had spoken about the "five wounds" plaguing Christendom: the heretical emperor Frederick, the Mongol invasion, the need to defend Latin Constantinople from the schismatic Greeks, the suffering of Jerusalem at the hands of Muslims, and the perennial concern of reforms, abuse, and corruption in the Church. His words, in some ways, were prescient. After Innocent died in 1254, the apparent opportunity for continued papal leadership over Christendom began to slip away, as his relatively uninspired or ineffective successors faced mounting troubles close to Rome and abroad.

Rome's "Sicilian" problem

Despite its favorable outcome, the papacy's clash with Frederick II did not come cheaply. Although the machinery for raising revenues from the Papal States and other sources around Europe worked more effectively than ever before, the protracted war against the emperor and his allies had placed incredible strains on Rome's finances. Much of the worst fighting took place in the papacy's own backyard. Even by the standards of the day, the war struck contemporaries as devastating and particularly nasty. In addition to expending material capital, Innocent IV had leveraged a great of his spiritual authority in the fight against Frederick, calling upon Christians everywhere to support his holy war against the emperor as an enemy of the Church. By doing so, he further exhausted the emotional appeal of crusading vows and privileges.

Whatever benefits it brought for the papacy, Frederick's death generated new problems, creating serious political instability in the neighboring kingdom of Sicily. In 1258, Frederick's son Manfred invaded papal territories, putting pressure on Alexander IV, who remained somewhat hobbled by his rocky relations with various factions in Rome. The next pope, Urban IV (1261–64), a former French cardinal named Jacques Pantaléon, pursued an unsuccessful peace with Manfred. In 1263, seeking a strong ally to bring order to the region, Urban declared his support for the conquest of the kingdom of Sicily by Louis IX's brother, Charles of Anjou – in retrospect, a fateful decision. Urban's successor, another French pope, Clement IV (1265–68), likewise favored this alliance with Charles, although some of the cardinals continued to oppose this plan. Regardless, Charles defeated Manfred at the Battle of Benevento in 1266; two years later, after Conradin fell into his hands, he executed the last Hohenstaufen heir.

Elected to a ten-year term as a Roman senator, Charles swore to respect the papacy's rights and territorial claims, and not to interfere in papal government. The coming of the Angevin dynasty, however, introduced another competitor for papal control of the region, one that challenged Rome's immediate authority as much as the Hohenstaufen dynasty. After Clement died, a divided College of Cardinals could not settle upon a successor, provoking another conclave when the churchmen were effectively locked up in the Lateran. After nearly three years of wrangling, the cardinals elected Gregory X (1271–76), who put up considerable resistance to Angevin ambitions. (Trying to prevent future delays in papal elections, Gregory also mandated that conclaves must commence within ten days of a pope's demise.) After a series of short-lived popes – Innocent V (January–June 1276), Hadrian V (July–August 1276), and John XXI (1276–77) – Nicholas III (1277–80) pushed back even more against Charles of Anjou, for example, refusing to renew Charles's term as senator. A member of the powerful Roman Orsini family, Nicholas openly turned to his relatives for assistance in running the curia and governing the Papal States, an increasingly common pattern among later thirteenth-century popes.

Nicholas's successor, the French-born Martin IV (1281–85), reversed course yet again and embraced the Angevin cause, even after the Sicilians drove Charles from the island in 1282 during an uprising called the Sicilian Vespers, threatening his grip on southern Italy. Seeking support against the house of Anjou and its papal allies, the Sicilians invited Manfred's son-in-law, Peter III of Aragon, to rule the island. The pope promptly excommunicated Peter and even declared a crusade against him. The crusade never happened, but the papal involvement in this expensive and protracted war between French and Aragonese interests in the Mediterranean cost the Roman Church considerable sums of money, as the papacy funneled resources around Europe into the conflict. Despite Charles of Anjou's death in January 1285, Martin's successors Honorius IV (1285–87) and Nicholas IV (1288–92) continued to back the Angevins, trying in vain to dislodge the Aragonese from Sicily. By the end of the thirteenth century, the kingdom of Sicily had become a quagmire for the papacy's revenues, energies, and attention.

Christendom's contracting horizons

Facing the wider world, the papacy encountered similar setbacks and disillusionment. Although the immediate Mongol threat to Europe had abated, the khans had declined to embrace Christianity and remained a source of possible danger. In 1261, the Greeks recaptured Constantinople, spelling an end to the Latin Empire of Byzantium. Urban IV duly called for a crusade to recapture the city, with little result. As for the Holy Land, despite repeated calls for crusades, the region remained in the hands of the "infidels." Even the pious crusader-king Louis IX of France had failed to make any headway in that direction during his ill-fated crusades, the first in Egypt from 1248 to 1250, and the second in Tunisia in 1270.

Pope Gregory X briefly rekindled some spark of earlier papal aspirations for church reform, union with the Greeks, and the recovery of Jerusalem. Summoning the Second Council of Lyons in 1274, Gregory and the assembled churchmen declared a new crusade, celebrated a joint liturgy with Greek clerics, including the controversial *filioque* clause, and issued a number of reformist canons. Several Mongol ambassadors in attendance were baptized, fostering hope for a new alliance with them against Muslim powers. Apocalyptic sentiments and prophecies once again filled the air, foretelling the union of the world's people under the Apostolic See. The following decades, however, proved equally disappointing for these plans. The reunion with the Greeks proved short-lived. The vast majority of Greek clergy rejected any accommodation with the Roman Church, even if Byzantine emperors hoped to secure an alliance with the papacy as a counter-balance to the growing influence of French and Aragonese power in the Mediterranean. Gregory's called-for crusade never happened. Popes Honorius IV and Nicholas IV indulged in some hopeful plans to ally Christian forces with the Mongol ruler of Persia, Arghun, exchanging ambassadors and letters with him. Nicholas expressed his desire that the khan would receive baptism, perhaps even in Jerusalem after the Mongols and crusaders recovered the city. Nothing came of these proposals, however, and Arghun died in 1291. That same year, Mamluk forces captured Acre, the final crusader bastion in the Holy Land. Although the crusading movement continued, the city's fall marked an effective end to the crusades envisioned as large-scale expeditions for the recovery of Jerusalem.

Even contemporaries could see that things had gone terribly awry with the papacy's claim to govern the world. Writing his *Knowledge of the Ages* in Cologne, Alexander of Roes looked back to the Second Council of Lyons as a time of promise, when Christian kings and princes, Jews, Greeks, and Tartars had all recognized the bishop of Rome "as the monarch of the world." Since then, the Greeks had withdrawn from unity with the Roman Church, the Tartars had begun to attack Christian lands once again, the "Saracens" were on the rise in Africa, and war had erupted in Europe. In particular, Alexander denounced Martin IV for favoring the French at the expense of papal interests and alienating the Greeks. The picture he painted was a gloomy one. Alexander died sometime around the turn of the fourteenth century. If he had lived any longer, as we will see, his pessimism would likely have grown worse.[14]

Chapter 7: The Papacy in Crisis

In 1346, a bridge in Avignon over the Rhone River collapsed. According to the Franciscan prophet John of Rupescissa, this event symbolized the future tribulations facing the papal curia, which had been installed in the city for several decades and showed no signs of returning to Rome. John was also in Avignon at the time, kept under lock and key in a papal prison, viewed as too dangerous to roam about while making his apocalyptic predictions. In his numerous writings about the state of the Roman Church and its place in the world, John criticized the clergy of his day, including the pope, as greedy and corrupt. Soon God would scourge his wayward flock through war, plague, famine, and social unrest, as the lowly would rise up against the mighty and cast them down. The figure of Antichrist would appear on the scene, perhaps more than one of them, wicked rulers in the East and the West, together with an evil "false pope." Looking beyond these trials, however, the Franciscan friar saw peace and renewal for the Church in the future age of the Holy Spirit. Among other developments, an "angelic" pope would arise from among the Franciscans to combat heretics, console the poor, defeat Islam, and expand the Christian faith to embrace all the peoples of the world.[1]

John of Rupescissa showed an uncanny knack for capturing the sensibilities of his age. Famine and plague, social upheaval and war – these are the signs of the fourteenth century, commonly described by modern historians as an era of "waning," "decline," or "catastrophe." After the population growth and economic expansion of the preceding centuries, Europe entered a period of economic and demographic contraction. Much of the available and fertile land for agricultural cultivation had been used up. Climate also played a role in these developments: the so-called "Little Ice Age," a period of cooling temperatures, contributed to the outbreak of the "Great Famine" from around 1315 to 1322, a series of crop failures that killed thousands from starvation and disease. This disaster paled in comparison to the arrival of the Black Death in 1346–48, a form of bubonic plague which had spread along trade routes from Asia into Europe, where it wiped out a third to half of the population. Adding to these troubles, in 1337 a sporadic but protracted and devastating conflict broke out between England and France, known as the Hundred Years War. These disruptive events contributed to further economic and social unrest, including large-scale peasant rebellions as a form of violent protest.

The fourteenth century also stands as a period of crisis in the history of the papacy. Two developments in particular mark this era as a turning point for the Roman Church and the Apostolic See. First, coming on the heels of a bitter dispute between the papacy and the French crown, successive popes permanently settled in the city of Avignon, located in southern France. Lasting from 1309 to 1376, the Avignon papacy contributed to unease and complaints about the Roman bishop's prolonged absence from the city of Saint Peter. For some contemporaries, Avignon became known as a "new Babylon," a place of captivity and corruption for bishops of Rome. Second, after a disputed papal election in 1376, the emergence of two popes – one at Rome, the other at Avignon – inaugurated the so-called Great Schism that lasted until 1417, a turn of events that did severe damage to the Roman Church's prestige, authority, and institutional effectiveness.

In theory, after the resolution of the Great Schism, the popes of Rome still claimed their position of universal primacy over all Christians. In reality, however, the ground had shifted beneath their feet. After decades of scandal and internal division, the papacy had lost much of its political clout, yielding effective control over churches around Europe to kings and princes, viewed as the only rightful sovereigns fit for earthly governance. To resolve the Great Schism, some churchmen had come to claim that ecclesiastical councils, not the Apostolic See, possessed true and binding authority over the Church, an open challenge to the notion of papal monarchy. After centuries of claiming supremacy over Christendom, with a considerable degree of success, the popes of Rome found themselves questioned and pressured like never before.

Church and State in the Later Middle Ages

Around the turn of the fourteenth century, controversy surrounded the Roman papacy on multiple fronts. For some, involved in a bitter debate over the role of poverty in the Franciscan order, the corrupt popes of their own day represented nothing less than Antichrist, a sign of the imminent apocalypse. Other critics of the papacy argued vehemently that the pope should limit his actions to spiritual matters and should play no role in temporal governance. For the increasingly powerful monarchs of the era, armed with innovative ideas about the natural authority of the "State," popes had no business interfering in the finances or governing of their kingdoms. Never resolved, the relationship between the ecclesiastical and secular spheres entered into a new and contested phase.

Papal Antichrists and angelic popes

Decades after the death of their founder, the Franciscans had begun to experience a bitter dispute over the centrality of poverty to their order that more or less split the friars into two camps, typically labeled Conventuals and Spirituals. Although neither side denied the importance of apostolic poverty to the Franciscan way of life, Conventuals accepted legal technicalities that allowed the friars to enjoy considerable wealth, technically owned by "spiritual friends" of the order, but used by the mendicants themselves. The Spirituals rejected such accommodations as a betrayal of Francis's vision and emphasized the centrality of rigorously observed poverty for their order. Disputes broke out as Spiritual friars resisted and rejected Conventual authorities, viewing themselves as a persecuted minority, suffering at the hands of the corrupt and avaricious Roman Church.

In 1294, a miracle seemed to happen. To break a deadlock after the death of Nicholas IV, the cardinals elected the pious hermit Peter Morone, who took the name Celestine V (July–December 1294). The Spirituals greeted him as the answer to their prayers. Celestine's ineffective papacy, however, ended a few months later when he renounced his position. A faction that had opposed him from the start imprisoned the retired pope, who died in 1296. The Spiritual Franciscans numbered among those who refused to recognize Celestine's abdication and rejected his successor, Benedetto Caetani, who took the name Boniface VIII (1294–1303). Drawing upon the apocalyptic tradition inspired by Joachim of Fiore, Spiritual circles proclaimed that Celestine had represented a true spiritual leader for

God's Church, followed by Boniface, a veritable Antichrist. The following years witnessed an outpouring of prophecies and apocalyptic tracts, including the so-called "Pope prophecies," which presented a series of wicked popes – including Boniface – but also predicted the coming of an angelic pastor to guide the Church, a messianic shepherd who would preside over a future time of peace and renewal. One Franciscan apocalyptic thinker, Peter John Olivi, predicted the coming of a "mystical Antichrist" who would sit on the Apostolic See before the emergence of a true, spiritual pope. Meanwhile, Spiritual Franciscans in exile among Jews, Mongols, and Muslims would bring about the conversion of non-Christians everywhere. At some point, Olivi speculated, the successors of Saint Peter might even move from Rome to Jerusalem, restoring the head of the Church to the center of the world.

Measured against such an imagined and longed-for spiritual pontiff, the current papacy must have seemed lacking indeed, although clearly not everyone felt this way about the bishop of Rome. As demonstrated by the Jubilee Year of 1300, the Apostolic See had not lost its wide-ranging appeal for the people of Christian Europe. Considered Antichrist by some, Boniface VIII demonstrated Rome's ongoing spiritual appeal when he declared that Christians who made a fifteen-day pilgrimage to the city's holy places before Christmas of that year would enjoy a plenary indulgence, the full remission of penance for their sins in this life and the next. Believers by the thousand set out for Rome from around Christendom, making the jubilee into a wild success, perhaps more than Boniface had anticipated. Prophecies and a sense of apocalyptic expectation filled the air, a sense of religious inspiration and revival. In this sense, the Jubilee Year revealed the Apostolic See's continued appeal to pious believers and its ongoing spiritual attractions, even as the current pope miscalculated the strength of his position during an ongoing conflict with the French crown.[2]

Boniface VIII and Philip IV

Focused on their imperial rivals, thirteenth-century popes had not always recognized the increasingly serious challenge posed to their position by Europe's kings, who lacked the theoretical grandeur of emperors, but exercised a more direct and far-reaching power over their territories. When war broke out between the English and French in 1294, the monarchs of both countries, Edward I and Philip IV, began to aggressively tax ecclesiastical properties to pay for their military expenses, demanding that clergy yield up half or more of their annual incomes. For Edward and Philip, who styled themselves as defenders of the English and French churches, respectively, it made sense that they might levy similar taxes on the churchmen in their kingdoms to support their wars, cutting Rome out of the picture entirely. Philip, in particular, emerged as a strong, centralizing monarch who tightened royal control over France in both political and fiscal terms. Over the previous decades, in fact, the papacy had facilitated this growing royal control over church finances by splitting crusading tithes with rulers who fought for the papal–Angevin cause in southern Italy.

As noted above, Benedetto Caetani had risen to papal office under less than ideal circumstances after the resignation – followed by the suspicious demise – of the "hermit pope" Celestine V, whose avid supporters refused to recognize his resignation or Boniface's election. By his subsequent actions, Boniface did little to insulate himself from further criticisms. To secure his position and control of the curia, he relied openly upon his family connections, endowing the Caetani with key positions and properties in the papal patrimony. As pope, he also became known for enlarging the papal crown and erecting statues of himself in churches around the city of Rome. He made particular enemies of the well-to-do Colonna family, who stoked rumors about Celestine's unusual resignation and cast doubt on Boniface's legitimacy. In 1296, Boniface became involved in a virtual war between the Caetani and Colonna, even declaring a crusade against his family's aristocratic rivals before they grudgingly submitted in 1299. Meanwhile, he continued the papal effort to restore the Angevins in the kingdom of Sicily, racking up further debts by supporting their military cause in the region.

In sum, Boniface was hardly the sort to take royal encroachment on ecclesiastical properties and revenues lightly. In 1296, he issued the bull *Clericis laicos*, declaring that rulers possessed no such rights to tax church properties, threatening excommunication of any "emperors, kings, or princes, dukes, earls, or barons, powers, captains, or officials, or rectors," who "arrest, seize, or presume to take possession of things anywhere deposited in holy buildings, or command them to be arrested, or taken, or receive them when taken, seized, or arrested."[3] Philip responded by forbidding the export of gold and silver from France, effectively denying the papacy incomes from ecclesiastical properties in the kingdom. Facing debts from his unsuccessful ventures in Sicily, as well as opposition from the Colonna family, Boniface backed down. In July 1297, he issued the bull *Etsi de statu,* an effective truce with Philip that allowed subsidies and "gifts" from the clergy to the king's coffers when an emergency threatened the realm, even without prior papal approval. In 1301, however, when the French crown arrested the bishop of Palmiers for heresy and slandering the king, Boniface demanded his release, setting in motion a bitter clash between the pope and French ruler. Modern historians have even speculated that the success of the Jubilee Year in 1300 might have gone to Boniface's head, causing him to overplay his hand. Issuing the bull *Asculta filii* in December 1301, Boniface restated the major principles of *Clericis laicos,* reminding the French ruler of his subordination to the Church hierarchy, accusing him of "devouring" church incomes, and insisting upon the pope's power over clerical offices, benefices, goods, and other properties.[4]

On November 18, 1302, the pope went a step further and issued the bull *Unam sanctam,* offering one of the most forceful, concise statements of papal primacy ever made. Emphasizing the unity of the "Holy Catholic and Apostolic Church," he proclaimed "in this one and only Church, there is one body and one head – not two heads as if it were a monster – namely, Christ and Christ's vicar, Saint Peter, and Peter's successor, for the Lord said to Peter 'feed my sheep'." Describing the Church's ultimate power to dispose both the material and the spiritual swords, Boniface flatly stated that "one sword should be under the other, and the temporal authority subject to the spiritual power." To avoid any confusion on the matter, Boniface concluded with the words: "Therefore we declare, state, define and pronounce that it is altogether necessary to salvation for every human creature to be subject to the Roman pontiff."[5]

Philip remained unimpressed, forbidding French bishops from attending a forthcoming council planned by the pope at Rome. The king also assembled the "three estates" in support of his position, including the nobility, the clergy, and, for the first time, the well-to-do urban classes, which collectively rejected Boniface's claims. The following year, the king's advocate William of Playsian crafted a series of charges against the pope, including the accusation that he denied the immortality of souls and transubstantiation, encouraged idolatry, and also that he consulted a "private demon" for advice. Boniface, William wrote, "does not seek the salvation of souls, but their perdition." Things came to a head in September 1303. French troops led into Italy by the king's counselor William of Nogaret, assisted by one of the pope's vengeful foes, Sciarra Colonna, surprised the pontiff during his stay at Anagni and placed him under arrest. Although the townspeople rallied and freed the pope days later, Boniface soon died, traumatized by the experience. The consequences of this event, not necessarily evident at the time, were far reaching. Despite Boniface's strident claims in *Unam sanctam*, papal claims to wield spiritual authority over temporal rulers suddenly seemed more like a facade than a reality of Christian political life.

Sovereignty, kingship, and priesthood

While this showdown developed between Philip IV and Boniface VIII, clerical intellectuals on both sides of the fence had turned once again to the theoretical question of the proper relationship between kings and popes, the bearers of temporal power and priestly authority. In the latest iteration of this debate, royal supporters or sympathizers possessed new weapons at their disposal, including the philosophical teachings of the Greek philosopher Aristotle and his notion of the State as a corporate body of citizens, a rational product of man's condition as a social being subject to natural rather than Christian law. Aristotle's teachings, which sometimes contradicted the Bible, did not come without their share of controversies. By the dawn of the fourteenth century, however, more and more Christian Europeans had come to recognize the possibility of the civil State as a natural, sovereign entity, not just the result of humanity's fallen condition as taught by patristic theologians such as Augustine of Hippo.

In intellectual circles, of course, the papacy still had its defenders. In his 1302 work *On Ecclesiastical Power*, Giles of Rome strongly reiterated the themes of ultimate papal jurisdiction over temporal affairs, writing that earthly powers must answer to clerical authorities, above all to "the Supreme Pontiff, who, in the ecclesiastical hierarchy, has attained the summit of the Church, and under whom all men – kings, as excelling, and all others – must be subject." That same year, James of Viterbo declared in his tract *On Christian Governance* that the pope represented "king of all spiritual kings, the shepherd of shepherds, the father of fathers, the head of all the faithful and of all who rule the faithful."[6] Such arguments in favor of papal monarchy, however, seemed less and less convincing in the face of changing ideas about the nature of political sovereignty. In his 1302 treatise *On Royal and Papal Power*, the university master John of Paris reworked the traditional Gelasian view of the two spheres, emphasizing the need for both kings and priests, the former for governance over the "natural" world, and the latter for the "supernatural" care of souls and their eternal salvation. The king stood as the single leader to rule the community for the common good; the pope represented the head of the

Church and the unifier of the Christian people. Yet the pope, John insisted, did not possess any temporal jurisdiction over the laity and only limited rights over ecclesiastical property. Refusing to subordinate one power to the other, John declared the priority of kingship in time (that is, there were kings before there were priests) and the superiority of the priesthood in dignity, but he also insisted that both powers "rise directly from a single supreme power: the divine power."[7]

Celestine V's resignation had also raised questions about whether it was even possible for a pope to resign his divinely given office. Others wondered if a heretical or otherwise sinful pope could be deposed from the Apostolic See. Despite their spiritual power, John argued, popes could resign and could be deposed under certain circumstances. Although their office came from God, popes remained part of – not above or outside – the Church, the true source of Christian authority, exercising their power for the good of the faith. An individual pope who violated that good and abused his spiritual position could be removed by the cardinals or a church council. Canon lawyers had made this claim before, but never with so much certitude. For John, the idea that the pope stood above any form of earthly judgment simply did not make sense. Given his views on the pope's lack of temporal authority, John also took aim at the *Donation of Constantine* and its claim that the "pope is emperor and lord of the world ... and can install and remove kings just as an emperor can." Although he did not question its historical authenticity, John flatly denied the *Donation*'s implications for papal monarchy, insisting that Constantine actually had no legal right to diminish his office this regard, and that its terms referred only to certain properties in Italy, not the entire Roman Empire. Referring back to the *Legend of Saint Sylvester*, John wrote that angels cried out in Heaven at the moment of Constantine's donation, "Today poison has been poured into the Church."[8]

Complaints about the *Donation of Constantine* were not limited to theologians. The famous Italian poet Dante Alighieri, a citizen of Florence who suffered exile for his opposition to the pro-papal Guelph faction that dominated the city's politics after the year 1301, offered his own critiques of the emperor's "poisonous" gift to the Church. Dante is best known for his masterpiece *The Divine Comedy*, which describes the author's journey through Hell, Purgatory, and Heaven, where he encounters – among many other saints and sinners – various popes, including a damned Boniface VIII (despite the fact that Boniface still lived when Dante wrote this part of his work). During the poet's visit to paradise, none other than Saint

Peter denounces Boniface as a "usurper of my place," who "made my burial ground a sewer of blood and of stench." The *Divine Comedy* also expressed sentiments that the *Donation of Constantine* – even if well intentioned – had caused incalculable damage to the Church. In his Latin tract *On Monarchy*, written between 1310 and 1314, Dante drew upon Aristotelian ideas to celebrate the idea of a universal leader, an emperor who might restore peace and order to Europe. At the time, the Italian poet apparently hoped – without cause, as it turned out – that the rising power of the German ruler Henry VII might restore his fortunes in Florence. Taking aim specifically at the *Donation of Constantine*, Dante did not deny its authenticity, but he declared that the emperor in fact had no right to divide imperial power, an act antithetical to the emperor's duty to unify mankind. By the same token, the pope had no business accepting such temporal goods from Constantine. Like John of Paris, Dante thereby cast the exchange between Constantine and Sylvester as an historical wrong turn for the Roman Church.[9]

The Popes at Avignon

After the brief papacy of Benedict IX (1303–4), the cardinals elected the archbishop of Bordeaux, who took the name Clement V (1304–14). After his election, Clement began to plan his journey to Rome, but for various reasons – including his own poor health and disturbances caused in the city by the ongoing dispute between the Caetani and Colonna families – he never left southern France. By 1309, the pope and papal curia had settled in the city of Avignon, located in the territory of a papal enclave. His successor, Pope John XXII (1316–34), abandoned any pretense of leaving the city, expanding the papal palace; the next pope, Benedict XII (1334–42), began the construction of a vast new complex for the papal curia. The papacy, it must have seemed clear to everyone, was not about to leave Avignon.

The "Babylonian Captivity"

Although not just a puppet of the French crown, Clement V proved generally friendly to King Philip's interests. In 1307, for example, after a subdued protest, the pope endorsed the king's violent dissolution of the Templars, accused of heresy, blasphemy, and other crimes. Destroying the wealthy and powerful military order and seizing its assets proved a lucrative proposition for the French crown, abetted by the papacy. The growing number of French clergy appointed to the College of Cardinals further cemented these bonds between the king and the pope. Eventually, after making certain concessions to Philip, Clement convinced him to drop the ongoing charges of heresy made against his dead predecessor, Boniface VIII. A great deal of damage, however, had been done to the reputation and prestige of the papal office.

Considered dispassionately, there were many sensible reasons for the prolonged stay in Avignon. The city lay in a more central location than Rome with respect to northern Europe, well connected with the outside world by the Rhone. Residing in Avignon also meant that the popes and cardinals did not have to deal with the constant infighting of Rome's aristocratic families. For that matter, previous popes had spent a considerable amount of time outside of Rome, traveling on ecclesiastical business or fleeing the city because of civil strife or imperial oppression. As the fourteenth century passed, however, contemporaries began to perceive that the papal residence in Avignon represented something different and disturbing. The Italian writer and scholar Petrarch, who spent time as a young man at the papal court in Avignon, had little doubt that the papacy had entered into a new "Babylonian Captivity," just like the ancient Israelites carried into bondage in Babylon during the time of the Old Testament:

> I know by experience that there is in this place no piety, no charity, no faith, no reverence for God, no fear, no holiness, no justice, nothing of equitableness, nothing trustworthy, finally, nothing human ... who could ever imagine it in a place where everything is filled with lies: the air, the earth, the homes, the towers, the hamlets, the entry halls, streets, arcades, the vestibules, the courts, the bedrooms, the panels of ceilings, the cracks of walls, the rooms of inns, the sanctuaries of the temple, the benches of judges, the thrones of popes.

Avignon, as the Italian writer put it, had become "the modern Babylon, heated, raging, obscene, terrible." Perhaps not surprisingly, Dante echoed such sentiments.[10]

Modern scholars have sometimes been quick to follow Petrarch's lead, presenting the Avignon papacy as particularly corrupt and decadent. Taking a more balanced perspective, one can recognize important developments in the institutional life of the Roman Church during this period and also see how those changes fueled contemporary criticism – sometimes warranted, sometimes not – of the Avignon popes. In the first place, the fourteenth-century papacy continued to build upon the administrative machinery of previous generations, expanding the bureaucracy and finances of papal governance over the Church, including its chancery and registers, the hearing of appeals and petitions, the granting of exemptions and more. Certain circumstances facing the Avignon popes, however, demanded the even more intensive exploitation of such ecclesiastical resources. With the popes absent from Rome, Italian city-states and aristocratic factions had far greater latitude to ignore papal oversight and financial demands. Largely cut off from the direct revenues of the Papal States, the papacy increasingly relied upon fees from appeals and taxes levied on church properties from around Western Europe. Starting under Clement V, the papal curia reserved the right to fill any vacant benefice, anywhere, claiming a portion of the first year of its revenue – also called "annates" – from its newly appointed holder. In some cases, the papacy left benefices deliberately vacant and claimed the resulting revenues, regardless of the impact that such an empty office might have on the pastoral care of a local community.

The popes at Avignon also incurred exceptional expenses, including the exorbitant cost of building the new papal complex in the city on the Rhone. Under John XXII, the papacy began to wage a series of military campaigns in Italy, trying – without much success – to reassert control over papal territories in the region. Before the pope could even consider returning to Rome, so the logic went, he had to regain some measure of stability and order in central Italy. Following the collapse of Hohenstaufen rule and the failed Angevin effort to secure the kingdom of Sicily, power in the region had fragmented worse than ever, falling into the hands of local strongmen (*signori*) served by mercenary captains (*condottieri*). These wars continued under Benedict XII, Clement VI (1342–52), and Innocent VI (1352–62), who appointed the relentless archbishop of Toledo, Gil Albornoz, as his main agent to pacify papal opponents on the Italian peninsula. For well over a decade, Albornoz spent vast sums of money on bribes, alliances, and mercenaries, pushing the papal cause at all costs, making him a hero to some and a villain to others.

The financial needs and machinery of the popes at Avignon intensified age-old criticisms of the papal court as corrupt and avaricious, a more suitable place for cutthroat lawyers than pious men. Contemporaries complained in particular about the papacy's perceived abuse of crusading tithes, starting with the Council of Vienne in 1311 that mandated a tax on all benefices over the following six years for a crusade that never happened. One aspiring French official, Pierre Dubois, composed an entire treaty about his plans for an ideal crusade, *The Recovery of the Holy Land*. In this proposal, he recognized the pope as the "mirror of the whole world" and the "Vicar of Christ," but argued that the present-day papacy had squandered its moral authority and wealth on its own petty struggles for dominion in Italy. A morally correct pope would bring peace to the Church, purifying Christendom and aiding kings – above all, the French king – in the effort to liberate Jerusalem once and for all. "The pope," Dubois wrote, "who ought to be the author and promoter of world peace, will then no longer instigate wars ... the most holy pope will no longer strive to amass riches, nor will he be hampered in the duty of caring for things spiritual."[11] In a letter written in 1332, by contrast, John XXII flatly defended his right to reappropriate revenues meant for crusading to other causes, including wars to control the papal patrimony in Italy, with these words: "Why therefore was it wrong, and how could it be wrong, for the High Pontiff to divert to one use money dedicated to another one, when the common cause is threatened?"[12]

The Avignon popes did make efforts to curb abuses. John XXII, for example, tried without much success to limit the holding of multiple benefices by a single individual along with the growth of so-called sinecures, benefices awarded without any pastoral duties attached to them. None of his attempts slowed the flood of people coming to Avignon to secure benefices, armed with fees and bribes. In addition, the fourteenth-century papacy continued to dispatch missionaries to various parts of northern Africa and Asia, continuing the effort to spread the Gospel around the world much like their thirteenth-century predecessors. The fragmentation and progressive collapse of Mongol power, however, accompanied by the devastations of the Black Death, discouraged the continuing vitality of such missionary activities. When some Christians blamed the outbreak of the plague on the Jews in their midst, accusing them of poisoning wells, Clement VI tried in vain to prevent attacks on Jewish communities. Everywhere they turned, the Avignon popes encountered mounting challenges and criticisms along with successive blows to their prestige, even as they manipulated the machinery of papal business for their endless expenses more intensively than ever before.

Poverty, property, and power

During John XXII's papacy, the ongoing crackdown by Franciscan and papal authorities on the Spiritual friars continued to roil the Roman Church – four recalcitrant friars were burned at the stake in

1318 – and created even further controversy about the place of poverty in Christian life. In 1322, Pope John declared it a heresy to claim that Christ and the apostles had not possessed goods or enjoyed rights over property, overturning earlier papal support for the Franciscan way of life. This turn shocked and dismayed even many of the Conventuals. Some of the papacy's most outspoken critics rallied around the current Roman emperor, Louis the Bavarian, no friend of the pope, since John XXII had backed Louis's former rival for the throne, Frederick of Austria. In 1328, after being crowned emperor by the Roman commune, Louis secured the election of a Franciscan anti-pope, Nicholas V. By this time, his court was becoming a center of anti-papal propaganda, home to figures like Marsilius of Padua, a former rector at the University of Paris, and William Ockham, an English Franciscan who had fled the curia at Avignon.

Between the two of them, Marsilius and William leveled devastating attacks on the notion of papal monarchy. In his 1324 work *The Defender of the Peace*, written two years before his arrival at Louis's court, Marsilius picked up where thinkers like John of Paris had left off, drawing upon Aristotle to present the State as the "perfect community having full limit of self-sufficiency." In this tract, he directly targeted papal claims to exercise any sort of dominion over the State or temporal goods. The pope of Rome, Marsilius declared, just like other bishops and clergyman, did not posses any rights of "rulership or coercive judgment or jurisdiction over any priest or non-priest, ruler, community, group, or individual of whatever condition." Instead, he argued that the earliest bishops of Rome drew their authority from the consent and obedience of the faithful, a situation abused by popes after Constantine through their assertion of powers and claims that did not belong to them.[13] In particular, Marsilius targeted papal claims to the "fullness of power," an expression open to a variety of interpretations, ranging from the "unlimited power to perform every possible act and to make anything at will," a power enjoyed only by Christ, to the "general pastoral cure of souls." Secretly, he claimed, the popes of Rome had twisted and abused this notion to assert their fullness of power in every sense of the word, "thereby committing very many monstrous crimes in civil order against divine and human law, and against the right judgment of every rational human being." By turning its back on apostolic poverty and usurping the control of temporal goods, the papacy had overstepped the bounds of its priestly office, violating the natural governance of the State and its ruler.[14] For good measure, Marsilius heaped criticism upon the Avignon popes for abuses of their authority, such as issuing crusading indulgences to soldiers who fought other Christians in Italy, not infidels, wasting church resources that should be spent on the needy, or ransoming hostages seized by Muslims overseas.

Much like Marsilius of Padua, William of Ockham celebrated the prerogatives of secular sovereigns while denying the right of the papacy to interfere in temporal governance in works such as his *Dialog on the Rights of the Roman Empire* and his *Eight Questions on the Power of the Pope*. In 1338, around the time of a proposed alliance between Louis the Bavarian and the English King Edward III, William penned a tract with the lengthy title, *Whether a Ruler can Accept the Goods of the Church for his Own Needs, Namely, in the Case of War, even against the Wishes of the Pope*. The answer to this query was a resounding yes. "Some think that the pope possesses from Christ such fullness of power in temporal matters as he has in spiritual," Ockham wrote, "so that he can do everything, and that everything which is not found contrary to human or divine law is subject to his power." The English friar denied this proposition. Drawing upon Bernard of Clairvaux's *On Consideration* among other sources, he declared it absurd that the pope could claim lordship of any kind over kings and emperors. Returning to the long-standing allegory of the two swords, William conceded that the popes might have the right to encourage secular powers to wield their might in defense of the Church or other causes, but denied the papacy any right to infringe upon temporal jurisdiction.[15]

Papal infallibility

In an apparent contradiction, Ockham also turned the notion of papal infallibility against the contemporary papacy. Churchmen starting with Peter John Olivi had played a crucial role in exploring the idea that the true Roman pope could not err in his judgments. With his apocalyptic anticipation of the papal Antichrist, Olivi clearly envisioned a time when a false pope might try to undo the "infallible" work of his predecessors. Despite his sympathy for the Spiritual Franciscans, Olivi had also defended Celestine V's right to resign his office. Any individual pope, he declared, could renounce his office and be deposed by others. Genuine popes, such as those who had defended the Franciscan order, were infallible; a present or future pope who made decisions contrary to the faith of the universal Church revealed himself to be a heretic – and therefore lost his power and legitimacy. Ockham, who had watched John XXII reverse course on the question of apostolic poverty and the Franciscan way of life, turned the notion of papal infallibility against the current pope in precisely this manner. As soon as the pope became guilty of heresy, Ockham and others like him insisted, violating the unerring decisions of his pious predecessors, he ceased to be the true supreme pontiff of the Apostolic See. Perhaps not surprisingly, other churchmen who supported John XXII tried to enlist the notion of papal infallibility to their side, declaring that God would not let a pope make heretical decisions about the Christian faith in the first place.[16]

Around this time, the legend of Pope Joan began to circulate in the Roman Church, linked to contemporary debates over papal infallibility, along with the rights of popes to resign or be deposed. Originating in a Dominican chronicle in the thirteenth century, this tradition claimed that a nameless woman had secretly entered the priesthood and risen through the ranks to become pope during the middle of the ninth century. The tale grew more elaborate with each subsequent telling, naming the pope Joan and claiming that eventually she died in public after giving birth to an illegitimate child sired by her lover. Later versions of this story insisted that medieval popes afterwards had to sit in a special chair, where another cleric could inspect and confirm their male genitals from below. A serious question lay behind this salacious tale: What happened if a pope was canonically elected, but turned out to be incapable or ineligible for the position? Although God directly granted the Apostolic See its spiritual power, any given person claiming the chair of Saint Peter could be found lacking – in the case of Pope Joan, even lacking the necessary manhood to be a true pope.

The return to Rome

After John XXII died, his successor Benedict XII largely repaired the papacy's relationship with Louis the Bavarian. Formerly known as Jacques Fournier, a relentless inquisitor against heresy in southern France, Benedict tried to negotiate a peace treaty between England and France, cracked down on nepotism at the papal curia, and made plans to return to Rome. His successors, Clement VI and Innocent VI, likewise indicated their intentions to move the papal curia back to the resting place of Saints Peter and Paul. The Avignon popes, after all, were not entirely tone deaf to the growing distain caused by their prolonged residence in southern France. In 1367, Pope Urban V (1362–70) actually journeyed to Rome and installed a diminished version of the papal curia in the Vatican palace, since the Lateran complex had fallen into such disrepair. During his stay, Urban even met with Byzantine Emperor John V Palaeologus to discuss the long-cherished goal of reunion between the Latin and Greek Churches, linked to a new crusade. These ambitious plans, however, came to nothing. The pope experienced so much trouble with Rome's unruly aristocratic families and factional politics that he left the city and returned to France in 1370.

The idea nevertheless persisted that the popes should abandon the city on the Rhone for their city on the Tiber. Among others, the well-known mystic Catherine of Siena called for the papacy to reform its ways, embrace spiritual renewal, declare a crusade, and return to Rome. As Catherine appealed to Urban V's successor, Gregory XI (1370–78), "Come, come and no longer resist the will of God who calls you. Your languishing flock awaits your coming to take and to guard the place of your predecessor and your model, the apostle Peter. As Vicar of Christ, you are obliged to reside in your own place. Come, and delay no longer."[17] Seven years later, at the urging of Catherine of Siena and others like her, Gregory XI traveled to Rome and likewise took up residence at the Vatican, only to die shortly after. Perhaps under popular pressure to do so, the conclave in Rome elected an Italian pope, Urban VI (1378–89), an apparently arrogant figure who quickly alienated many of the cardinals. A dispute over the election erupted, involving members of the Roman nobility and a number of the cardinals who claimed that they had been coerced into choosing Urban in the first place. A dissenting majority of the cardinals left the city for Anagni, where they annulled Urban's election and chose a new pontiff, Clement VII. Urban and Clement promptly excommunicated each other. Clement soon withdrew to Avignon, where the business of ecclesiastical governance had never really stopped despite Gregory XI's departure for Rome.

Catherine of Siena lamented this latest turn for the worse in papal affairs, exhorting Clement VII's supporters among the cardinal bishops to acknowledge Urban VI's election, lawfully undertaken without fear or compulsion. As Catherine put it:

> Thus, I say that you along with the antipope have done evil, and I can say that he was elected a member of the devil. If he had been a member of Christ, he would have chosen death rather than consent to so great an evil because he knows the truth and cannot plead ignorance ... You have departed from the light, entered into darkness and, in truth, have joined yourselves to a lie.[18]

Despite such pleas, both sides dug into their positions as powers across Europe began to line up behind their respective popes, France and its allies supporting Clement; England, Italy, Germany, and others throwing their weight behind Urban VI. In 1389, when Urban VI died, the cardinals in his camp elected a new pope, Boniface IX (1389–1404). When Clement VII passed away at Avignon in 1394, a conclave in that city elected his successor, Benedict XIII. In this way, the two lines of popes persisted beyond the lives of the original disputants. Christendom stood divided against itself.

The Great Schism and Its Aftermath

A schism in the papal office was nothing new. The precise circumstances of what became known as the "Great Schism," however, created an unprecedented situation in the Roman Church – two popes, established in two more or less functioning centers of ecclesiastical governance, served by two papal courts, staffs, and archives. Extreme confusion resulted in the hearing of appeals, the appointment of benefices, and the issuing of indulgences. Beyond such institutional chaos lay a fundamental crisis of salvation. Prophecies and apocalyptic visions multiplied. Confronting two papacies claiming their loyalties, Christians had to make a choice about whom to follow and obey. The wrong decision could mean eternal damnation.

Religious protest

Among other consequences, the Great Schism intensified existing religious criticisms of the fourteenth-century papacy. Two figures in particular, the English theologian and Oxford master John Wyclif and the Bohemian reformer Jan Hus, presented critiques of the papal office that went far beyond the split between Rome and Avignon, offering scathing attacks on the Roman Church's teachings, clerical hierarchy, and widespread religious practices such as the issuing of indulgences for the forgiveness of sins. Both men pushed for a deeper, more involved commitment by the laity to their own salvation (for example, encouraging the reading of the Bible in the vernacular). In the climate of the Great Schism, their attacks struck a powerful chord among those inclined to question the authority of the Apostolic See.

By the 1370s, Wyclif had become a well-known figure in England through his service to the crown, working on a commission to investigate "papal provisions," namely fees and payments claimed by the papacy from the English throne. His support of royal prerogatives, including the right of the crown to tax church properties in times of need, helped to shield him from censure as he expanded his criticisms of the Roman Church, calling for a return to apostolic poverty, denying the papacy's fullness of power and rights to impose interdict, while insisting that popes renounce their claims to temporal dominion and goods. Wyclif also questioned core sacramental doctrines of the Roman faith, including transubstantiation. Over time, he developed the notion of an "invisible" and "visible" Church: the former represented the true community of believers, predestined to salvation; the latter, present-day ecclesiastical institutions, mired in corruption and greed.

In 1377, Pope Gregory XI condemned several of Wyclif's teachings and later imposed an ineffective ban of silence upon him. The university masters at Oxford also investigated him, as did a panel of churchmen at London in 1378. The English theologian escaped condemnation for heresy, although his opponents judged his ideas dangerous for the uneducated laity. The development of the Great Schism, however, only intensified Wyclif's criticisms of the Roman Church. In his tract *On the Power of the Pope*, he associated both the pontiffs at Avignon and Rome with the evil of Antichrist, comparing the proud and arrogant popes of the present unfavorably with the humble figure of Christ. In 1381, Wyclif took aim specifically at the misuse of crusading tithes by Urban VI to fight against Clement VII's supporters, declaring, "Any pope or prelate of the Church who diverges from the path of Christ is a manifest heretic, opposed to the law of Christ and the charity of the Church, and should therefore be shunned by the faithful as a disturber of the Church's peace."[19] A true pope, by contrast, would follow the life of Christ as closely as possible, living like a true shepherd for God's flock.

Exiled from Oxford and finally condemned by English authorities, Wyclif continued to write until his death in 1384. His teachings formed a source of inspiration for loose-knit communities of anti-clerical protesters, the so-called Lollards, who likewise believed in the priority of Scripture in matters of faith and the nature of Wyclif's "invisible Church," formed by the predestined elect. The Lollards generally questioned the special status of the priesthood in the Roman Church, denying the need for confession to a priest and clerical celibacy, along with a host of common devotional activities including pilgrimage and the veneration of relics. As revealed in various Lollard sermons, some of the English dissenters also associated the popes of Rome with the evils of Antichrist, although like many such apocalyptic critics of the papacy, they seemed to hope for the future reform and spiritual purification of the Roman Church rather than its outright abolition.

Farther afield, Wyclif's writings influenced the religious criticisms offered by Jan Hus, a theologian at the University of Prague. Starting in the 1390s, Hus began to denounce corruption in contemporary ecclesiastical institutions, identifying in particular Constantine's donation of wealth and property to the bishop of Rome as a disastrous turning point for the Church. Much like Wyclif, Hus prioritized Scripture as a source of religious authority and called for a more active involvement by the laity in their own salvation. Also similar to Wyclif, Hus benefited from royal protection, supported by Bohemian King Wenceslas IV. Hus became known for his fearless sermons, denouncing immorality among the clergy and praising many of Wyclif's ideas. Over time, he also began to question the validity of indulgences and crusading, insisting that the pope, if he acted contrary to the ways of Christ, represented Antichrist. Other Bohemian clerics, including some of Hus's own associates such as Jerome of Prague, likewise claimed that the pope embodied Antichrist's evil. Under pressure from Rome, ecclesiastical authorities in Prague began to take a harder line against Wyclif's teachings and Hus for his endorsement of them, but the outspoken Hus refused to back down.

The emergence of conciliarism

As the Great Schism persisted with no clear end in sight, the cardinals, university masters, and other churchmen searched for a resolution. Some supported the notion that both popes should resign, others insisted that the two popes should respect the decision of a tribunal appointed to settle the matter, and still others claimed that all the parties involved should withdraw their support from their respective popes. Increasingly, members of the clergy and Europe's rulers agreed that only a general council could truly resolve the disastrous schism.

This emphasis on conciliar authority raised a broader question about the true nature of governance within the Church, namely whether ultimate authority resided in a single figure, the pope, or the assembly of churchmen who invested the pope with his position of spiritual leadership. During the twelfth and thirteenth centuries, canon lawyers commenting on the *Decretum* and the *Decretals* had speculated in legal terms about the relative authority of the pope and general councils to speak in matters of consequences for the entire Church. Canon lawyers, even those sympathetic to a strong form of the papal office, generally conceded that Saint Peter's power to loosen and bind belonged in some respect to all apostles and by extension all bishops. They also postulated a difference between the Roman Church, denoting the entire body of the faithful, and the particular church in Rome. Although the former would not ever fail or err, the latter might, revealing the need for the general council as an alternative source of authority in the Church. The decretists (that is, commentators on the *Decretals*) sometimes asserted that the pope acting in concert with a general council possessed greater authority than the pope acting alone. The rising prominence of the cardinals likewise suggested that the corporate body of the clergy might possess some share of the Apostolic See's special powers and privileges, as evident when the cardinals effectively governed the Roman Church between papal elections.

As the Great Schism persisted, conciliarism seemed to promise the only way out of the current crisis. In 1409, a council assembled at Pisa, including twenty-four cardinals from both sides of the schism, eighty bishops, eighty-seven abbots, and several hundred delegates from others who could not attend. The cardinals dominated the scene. They had, so to speak, created the schism by reversing their decision to elect Urban VI in the first place, and now it was their responsibility to end it. After a series of heated debates and deliberations, the council decided upon the deposition of both popes, the current Roman one, Gregory XII (1406–15), and Benedict XIII at Avignon, electing a new pope, Alexander V. France and England both recognized his election, although a number of other kingdoms refused to acknowledge him. Regardless, Alexander soon died and the assembled clergy elected yet another pontiff, who took the name John XXIII. Since neither Gregory XII nor Benedict XIII recognized the outcome of the council, Christians now faced a choice between three – not two – claimants to the Apostolic See.[20]

The Council of Constance

Under pressure from German King Sigismund and the cardinals, John XXIII reluctantly arranged for another round of deliberations to begin at Constance in November 1414. The council identified three major areas of business: ending the persistent schism, pursuing clerical reform, and the condemnation of various heresies, including the teachings of John Wyclif and Jan Hus. Under the promise of safe conduct, Hus journeyed to the council to defend his position, fearlessly defending Wyclif's ideas about predestination. Despite John XXIII's guarantees of protection for the Bohemian theologian, the council's authorities arrested him and placed him on trial. Bundling together earlier condemnations of Wyclif, they condemned three hundred of the English cleric's statements – many taken out of context – including his doctrine of predestination, denial of transubstantiation, and rejection of papal primacy. Facing similar charges, Hus refused to recant and died at the stake in July 1415, executed for heresy. Jerome of Prague, also present in Constance, suffered the same fate the following year.[21]

Meanwhile, John XXIII faced his own problems. For the first time, the churchmen voted in national blocks (for example, as French, English, or German delegations), demonstrating the growing importance of such regional identities in the Roman Church. Voting in this way also countered John XXIII's attempt to manipulate the proceedings by approaching individual churchmen. It soon became clear that the council planned to wipe the slate clean by deposing all three of the current claimants to the papal office. In March 1415, after taking an oath that he would resign his position, John fled Constance with a number of sympathetic cardinals and threatened to dissolve the council. The assembly, in turn, declared him deposed. John was soon captured by the council's deputies and imprisoned, leaving King Sigismund effectively in charge of the proceedings, backed by the national delegations rather than the cardinals.

As the synod progressed, figures such as the University of Paris master Jean Gerson delivered sermons that legitimated the general council as the ultimate source of authority in the Church. Such a council, Gerson proclaimed, formed "an assembly called under lawful authority at any place, drawn from every hierarchical rank of the whole Catholic Church," excluding none of the faithful who desired to be heard, to discuss those things "which affect the proper regulation of the Church in faith and morals." In the decree *Haec sancta*, issued in April 1415, the synod explicitly challenged the dominant mode of monarchical papal governance, declaring that the general council held power "directly from Christ" and that "everyone of whatever estate or dignity he be, even papal" was obliged to obey the council's decisions. In practical terms, the churchmen maneuvered to secure the abdication of the remaining two popes. In 1415, Sigismund met with Benedict XIII in order to convince him to step down. Benedict had already been driven from Avignon by forces friendly to Alexander V during his brief time as a papal contender. He refused and took refuge in southern Spain, insisting that he remained pope but disregarded by virtually everyone. Under pressure, Gregory XII surrendered his own claim to the papal office.[22]

In order to prevent future divisions among the faithful, the assembled clergy issued the decree *Frequens* in October 1417, a mandate for future general councils: the first one to be held after a period of five years, another one seven years after that, followed by further meetings at regular intervals of every ten years. Additional safeguards against another schism were put in place, including a rule that a council would be automatically triggered in the event of another papal schism. As the synod proclaimed, "the frequent holding of general councils ... roots out the briars, thorns and thistles of heresies, errors and schisms, corrects excesses, reforms what is deformed, and brings a richly fertile crop to the Lord's vineyard." The neglect of councils, by contrast, "spreads and fosters the foregoing evils."[23] On November 11, 1417, the Council of Constance elected a new pope, Oddo Colonna, who took the name Martin V (1417–31), marking the end of the Great Schism. This moment represented a high point for the proponents of conciliarism, promising a new order for the governance of the Roman Church. Despite its apparent success, however, Constance equally revealed the fracturing of ecclesiastical loyalties along national lines. Many of the proposed reforms at the council were never enacted, while the burning of Jan Hus had left a bad taste in the mouths of many observers. When Martin V finally made ready to leave Constance and return to Rome in 1418, the future of the papacy must have seemed anything but settled.

Chapter 8: Rome at the Close
of the Middle Ages

In 1440, the Italian scholar Lorenzo Valla finished his work, *A Discourse on the Forgery of the Alleged Donation of Constantine*. At the time, he was serving in Naples as a secretary to King Alfonso V of Aragon, who laid claim to the kingdom of Sicily despite fervent opposition from the papacy. Writing to support his patron, Valla took aim at the long-standing assertion that Emperor Constantine had yielded his imperial power to the popes of Rome, granting them numerous lands and islands, some of which now rightfully belonged to Alfonso. As we have seen, Valla was hardly the first person to question or dispute the legitimacy of Constantine's supposed donation to Pope Sylvester and his successors. Valla, however, employing the linguistic skills of his age, cast doubt on the very language of the text. Comparing it with other documents from the fourth century, he highlighted anachronistic words and expressions that did not even exist in the Latin of Constantine's day, such as the Persian term "satrap" used to denote Roman officials. "Numskull, blockhead!," he wrote, "Whoever heard of satraps being mentioned in the councils of the Romans? I do not remember ever to have read of any Roman satrap being mentioned, or even of a satrap in any of the Roman provinces." Based on this sort of evidence, Valla concluded that the famous donation represented a forgery dating from centuries later.[1]

For modern observers, Valla's assault on the *Donation of Constantine* puts him among the critics who tore down the medieval papacy's pretensions to temporal power, symbolizing the innovative intellectual spirit of his age: the Renaissance, an era of cultural "rebirth" based on the study of the Greek and Roman classics, accompanied by new principles of humanism, an appreciation for the power of learning to transform the individual, cultivating the skills and morals needed for living well in the world. Like other Italian humanists, Valla generally disapproved of what he saw as the papacy's moral failings and worldly ambitions, above all its abusive behavior as the ruler of the Papal States. Such scathing critiques and questioning of received truths earned him his share of trouble. At one point, he faced questioning by inquisitors due to his claim that the Apostles' Creed did not actually originate in the era of the apostles. Yet the profession of humanistic values did not make Valla any less of a Christian. In some of his other works, he called for reform in religious life, expressing his sincere desire for the betterment of the Roman Church. Not to mention the fact that his opposition to the papacy remained quite selective. Earlier in his career, Valla had tried unsuccessfully to secure a position at the papal court, seeking a job that had formerly belonged to his deceased uncle. In 1448, after Alfonso of Aragon and Rome had patched up their differences, Valla finally landed the job that he had always wanted – at the papal curia. Apparently his new patrons were willing to let bygones be bygones, valuing the humanistic thinker's rhetorical skills over his former sharp words.

In the aftermath of the Great Schism, successive popes succeeded in restoring their position as the effective rulers of Rome and central Italy, securing their financial footing and protecting the political integrity of the Apostolic See. All the same, they faced greatly altered circumstances in their immediate orbit and the wider world. The shifting values and perspectives of humanistic thinkers such as Lorenzo Valla represented only one such historical change. Among other events and developments, the increasing power of late medieval states, the fall of Constantinople to the Ottoman Turks in 1453, the invention of the printing press around the same time, and the "discovery" of the Americas all contributed to profound shifts in Europe's political, social, and religious landscape. Eventually, the papacy confronted the Protestant Reformation, an open challenge to the authority, teachings, and sacraments of the Roman Church that fractured what remained of Christian unity. Like other schemes of periodization for history, the division between the medieval and modern eras represents an artificial line drawn in the chronological sand. Nevertheless, around the turn of the sixteenth century, one can identify the emergence of a European world – and a Roman Church – no longer recognizable as medieval.

The Papacy Restored

Weakened after the Great Schism and the rise of conciliarism, the popes in the mid- and late fifteenth century turned their attention to reasserting central authority over the ecclesiastical hierarchy of the Roman Church and the Papal States. Navigating the altered landscape after the Council of Constance, the papacy successfully contained the challenge posed by the conciliarists, struck new deals with Europe's national powers, and emerged in a stronger – although, in scope, far more restricted – position than it had enjoyed in generations.

Martin V and the Papal States

With the election of Martin V, Christian Europe had settled upon one pope, but the papal role in the governance of the Church remained an open question. After his election, hardly bargaining from a position of strength, Martin signed a number of concordats with various European powers, including the German, English, and French crowns, along with Castile, Aragon, and others. Through these agreements, the pope made various concessions, for example, limiting direct papal involvement in appointments to vacant offices, or agreeing to share the revenues from annates with local churches. The signing of these concordats signaled an ongoing trend in the fifteenth century, the slow but steady erosion of papal administrative control over churches around Europe, ceding these rights to monarchs and local clerical authorities. Generally speaking, many of the reforms called for at Constance with the support of Europe's secular powers involved imposing restraints on papal control over the curia and ecclesiastical finances. These moves also included efforts to regulate the sale of papal indulgences, the remission of penance owed in this life or the next from the Roman Church's "treasury of merit." The drive to implement such reforms would be ensured by the summoning of regular councils, as mandated by the conciliar decree *Frequens*. From this perspective, the pope remained the spiritual head of Christendom, but his effective reach into the management of the Church would be limited.

Martin spent his papacy trying to roll back these limitations and restore the condition of papal monarchy, and had considerable success. He quickly realized that reasserting control over the Papal States and their resources represented the key to establishing his papacy on a secure footing. During much of their stay at Avignon, popes had tried to restore some measure of stability to the Italian peninsula that might favor their eventual return to Rome, combating the political centrifuge caused by the collapse of Hohenstaufen dynasty, the failure of Angevin rule, and the papal move to Avignon. During the councils of Pisa and Constance, this challenge had continued for the various claimants to the Apostolic See. At that point, an Italian *condottiere* named Ladislas of Durazzo dominated Rome. Battling to assert their position as the "real" Roman pope, both John XXIII and Gregory XII tried to subdue Ladislas and regain control of the Papal States, which seemed to be on the verge of complete collapse. In 1412, John managed to cut a deal with Ladislas, offering him concessions and payments for his assistance against Gregory XII, but within two years Ladislas had died and the Council of Constance was gearing up to settle the Great Schism, spelling an end to John and Gregory's claims.

Before he could assume control over the Papal States, Martin faced his own strong competitor in the region, a warlord named Braccio da Montone. Over the course of his eighteen-month journey from Constance back to Rome starting in 1418, the new pope built alliances among various Italian city-states, stopping in Mantua and Florence among other places. Martin had little money at his disposal, but managed through negotiations, promises, and concessions to bring many of Italy's major and minor powers around to his side, including all-important Florence and Bologna. In 1419, he displayed his support for the Angevin cause in Italy, issuing a bull that recognized Louis of Anjou as the rightful successor to the kingdom of Naples after the current queen, Joanna, died. By 1420, Martin maneuvered Braccio da Montone into an uneasy peace, allowing the pope and reconstituted curia to return to Rome in September 1420.

Conflict continued over the following years, as Braccio da Montone and Alfonso V of Aragon, less than pleased by papal support for Louis of Anjou, fought together against papal and Angevin forces. Through a combination of shrewd tactics, armed force, and luck – Braccio fell in battle in 1424 – the pope managed to secure his grip on the city and then began the task of asserting his direct authority over the Papal States. With the Roman commune more or less defunct and no major warlord contesting papal rule over Rome, the papacy found itself in a stronger – although by no means entirely secure – position in the city than it had enjoyed for generations. Seeking to govern the region immediately and effectively after decades of disarray, Martin turned properties and resources over to his own Colonna family to help him manage papal territories and finances, contributing to his reputation for nepotism.

For the remainder of his papacy, Martin tried and managed to regain some of the rights that he had signed away at Constance. Many of the concordats he approved had five-year limits, opening the door to their renegotiation. At the same time, he attempted to minimize the role that future general councils would play in the governance of the Roman Church. Although he duly called a council to meet at Pavia (later moved to Siena) five years after Constance, as required, he did everything he could to keep the number of attendees small and quickly dissolved the assembly. Martin's attempts to stymie the conciliar movement worked together with his project to restore papal control over the Papal States. Increasingly deprived of European-wide revenues after the Council of Constance and the concordats that accompanied it, Martin decided that the papacy must secure its territorial integrity and immediate financial resources to ensure its independence from future general councils and European secular powers. To a remarkable extent, he succeeded in this policy. Seven years later, still following the letter of the law laid out in *Frequens*, the pope called for another general council to meet at Basle in 1431, but he died before it convened.

The Council of Basle-Ferrara-Florence

The next pope, Eugene IV (1431–47), generally followed in Martin V's footsteps, making moves to restore the papacy's "monarchical" rule over the Church, although he immediately set about rescinding many of the privileges and properties granted by his predecessor to the Colonna family. As a condition of his elevation to the Apostolic See, Eugene issued an election capitulation, agreeing to certain terms and conditions before becoming pope, such as re-delegating a portion of the Roman Church's incomes directly to the College of Cardinals (something first done by Pope Nicholas IV in 1289). As one more sign of the papacy's compromised position, this sort of capitulation became a standard part of subsequent papal elections. Eugene, however, also set the precedent of largely disregarding the agreement once he became pope. His position grew more and more uncomfortable, above all due to resentment from the dispossessed Colonna. On May 31, 1433, the pope crowned King Sigesmund emperor in Rome, but the German ruler quickly left the city. About a year later, riots broke out against the pope, forcing him to flee down the Tiber while crowds on the banks shot arrows and threw rocks at him.

Escaping unharmed, Eugene took refuge in Florence and turned his attention to another problem, the Council of Basle. After his election,

Eugene had quickly attempted to dissolve the assembly before it really started, claiming that insufficient numbers of churchmen had arrived to participate. The clergy already gathered at Basle refused to acknowledge the pope's decision and dug in their heels. In 1433, bowing to pressure, Eugene grudgingly recognized the council's ecumenical status. Over the following years, the clergy at Basle passed a number of reform measures, including the abolishment of annates in 1435, but Eugene never stopped trying to lessen or undo the council's moves to constrain papal prerogatives. At first, the council enjoyed considerable support from Europe's national powers, more than happy to see limits imposed on the papacy's ability to manage ecclesiastical offices and revenues inside their borders. Over time, however, support for the council began to erode due to the threat of another protracted division in Christian Europe. In a masterful stroke, Eugene also took advantage of ongoing negotiations between Rome and the Greek Church over the possibility of their ecclesiastical reunion. In 1437, the pope transferred the Council of Basle to the city of Ferrara in Italy, presented as a far better site to meet with Greek envoys coming to join the deliberations. Two years later, due in part to an outbreak of plague, the pope moved the assembly to Florence.

Although a portion of the clergy gathered at Basle had departed for Ferrara, others held their ground. In 1439, this "rump" council elected a new pope, Felix V, and declared Eugene's deposition. This maneuver, however, largely backfired. Few, even those eager to impose limitations on papal authority, were eager for another schism in the Roman Church. The papacy found a particularly effective, influential spokesperson in Nicholas of Cusa. Initially, Nicholas favored the argument that general councils could rightfully – but not rashly – place limits on papal authority. As he wrote in his 1433 *Catholic Concordance*, if "equal power was given to all by Christ, then it is clear that the pope received no more power than did the other bishops." Over time, however, disillusioned with the Baslean faction, Nicholas emerged as a champion for Pope Eugene IV and the primacy of the Apostolic See.[2]

Meanwhile, developments at Florence favored Eugene and his position. Unlike Constance, the assembled clergy did not vote in national blocs, but rather were organized into three "estates," similar to representative assemblies in France and England, the first consisting of cardinals, archbishops, and bishops; the second, of abbots and regular clergy; and the third, of university doctors and other dignitaries. For a measure to pass, all three estates had to agree with a two-thirds majority in each of them. Representatives from the Greek Church formed another delegation at the council. Responding to the growth of Ottoman power in the Eastern Mediterranean, Byzantine Emperor John VIII favored an accommodation with Rome as part of his effort to win European military assistance against his Islamic opponents. Eugene, seeking to discredit the churchmen at Basle, had his own reasons to push for reconciliation between the Latins and Greeks, seeking to resolve the now centuries-old dispute over *filioque*, debates over the nature of Purgatory, the issue of papal primacy, and other sources of controversy between them. On June 6, 1439, the Council of Florence issued the decree *Laetentur coeli*, which marked the formal reunion of the two churches under the authority of Rome. Among its declarations, the agreement stated:

> We define that the holy Apostolic See and the Roman pontiff hold the primacy in the whole world, and that the Roman pontiff is the successor of blessed Peter, prince of the Apostles, and the true Vicar of Christ, head of the whole Church, and stands out as the father and teacher of all Christians; and to him in blessed Peter has been delivered by our Lord, Jesus Christ, the full power of feeding, ruling, and governing the universal Church, as is also contained in the acts of the ecumenical councils and in the sacred canons.[3]

Much like the union achieved in 1274, the majority of Greek clergy back in Byzantium refused to recognize the outcome of the council of Florence. In the short term, however, the agreement between the Latin and Greek Churches provided a powerful boost to papal claims of primacy in the face of resistance from the clergy at Basle. Clearly, as Nicholas of Cusa pointed out, the Greeks gathered at Florence had recognized the pope's proper leadership over the Church, unlike the schismatic Basleans, who had lost their own authority when Eugene had transferred the gathering to Ferrara-Florence.[4]

From this point forward, those advocating for conciliarism stood on the losing side of this ongoing battle to determine the nature of authority in the Church. Repudiating Martin V's commitment to the Angevins, Eugene struck a bargain with Alfonso V that allowed him to return to Rome in 1443, where he spent the remainder of his years consolidating his position. In 1449, two years after Eugene's death, the anti-pope Felix V conceded his position to Eugene's successor, Nicholas V (1447–55), who formally brought the Council of Basle to an end. In 1460, Pope Pius II (1458–64) put the final nails in conciliarism's coffin, issuing the papal bull *Execrabilis* that unambiguously denounced any appeals to general councils in lieu of the pope.[5] Less than fifty years after the Council of Constance, the Roman papacy had managed to beat back conciliarism as a challenge to papal primacy and restore Rome's privileged position as the Apostolic See. The price for doing so, however, included an overall rejection of proposed major reforms for the administrative and religious life of the Roman Church, although figures such as Nicholas of Cusa never stopped calling for desperately needed changes in how the papal curia and College of Cardinals did business.

Rome and the powers of Europe

While Martin V and Eugene IV contained the challenge to papal authority posed by conciliarism, Europe's secular sovereigns continued to expand their influence and direct administrative control over ecclesiastical offices and properties as part of their rightful power, often at papal expense. Due to the Great Schism, the extent of royal influence over domestic churches had reached an unprecedented level. As seen at the Council of Constance, where the assembled clergy voted in national blocs, churchmen across Europe had begun to identify themselves as belonging first and foremost to their own regional churches – and largely voted according to those interests. By signing a number of concordats with those delegations as part of the terms for his election, Martin established a precedent for his successors, many of whom signed similar agreements before assuming office. He also signaled the restored papacy's willingness to engage in direct diplomatic relations with other European powers, securing pragmatic goals rather than pressing theoretical claims of universal primacy.

This trajectory of papal accommodation with sovereign rulers intensified as a consequence of the split between the papacy and the churchmen assembled at Basle, which opened the door to new pressures on Rome by European governments. In 1438, following deliberations by an assembly of French clergy, King Charles VII issued the Pragmatic Sanction of Bourges, a decree that limited the right of the Roman papacy to collect annates, appoint benefice holders, and hear appeals in the kingdom of France, restating several of the conciliar decrees recently issued at Basle. In effect, the Pragmatic Sanction made the administration of ecclesiastical properties and offices in France an internal French affair. At the same time, Charles never broke off relations with the papal curia and refused to recognize Basle's decision to depose Eugene IV and elect Felix V in 1439. By shrewdly playing the two parties against each other, the king pushed Eugene into making further concessions to the French crown.

Eugene's successors continued to carry out such negotiations with European rulers, responding to the push and pull of "international" politics much like the leaders of other European states. In 1448, dealing with the German ruler Frederick III, Nicholas V scored a success by signing the Concordat of Vienna, an agreement that guaranteed many of Rome's privileges in the regions under Frederick's control, including the right to collect annates and fill vacant offices. In 1452, the pope crowned King Fredrick emperor in Rome – the final imperial coronation ever held in the city. Four years after that, Nicholas next signed the Treaty of Lodi, creating an alliance between the emerging "superpowers" of the Italian peninsula, including the papacy, Milan, Florence, Venice, and Naples, united through the common goal of keeping peace in Italy and foreign powers out of the peninsula. After more than a century and a half of disorder and disruption, stability had reemerged on the Italian peninsula.

The papacy's willingness to make deals with individual European powers did not mean that Rome completely abandoned its claims to universal leadership over Christendom. Reacting to the growing Ottoman threat, a series of popes attempted to revive the crusading spirit, calling for united Christian action against the infidels. The Muslim conquest of Constantinople in 1453 brought a new urgency to such appeals, sending shock waves around Europe. As Aeneas Sylvius Piccolomini – the future pope Pius II – lamented in a letter shortly after the fall:

> What, however, the madness of the Turks will do to the royal city I do not know, but it is easy to guess. The people who hate our religion will leave nothing there holy, nothing clean … Either the noble city will be destroyed or it will be made the seat of the Turks, to the great detriment of the Christian people.[6]

Aeneas's latter guess was on the mark, as the Ottomans made Constantinople into the capital of their empire, renaming it Istanbul. The Byzantine Empire was no more. Apocalyptic sentiments once again filled the air, as Western clergy and Greek refugees proclaimed that the fall of the imperial capital represented a sign of the end times. In reaction to the loss of the city, Nicholas V called for a crusade, asking rulers from around Europe to donate funds for this purpose. The recently signed Peace of Lodi seemed to offer the ideal conditions of peace in Italy for launching a new expedition. Few seemed interested, however, many still recalling the misuse of crusading funds by previous popes for Rome's internal political struggles. As part of his election capitulation, Nicolas's successor, Callixtus III (1455–58), swore an oath to free Constantinople from the Turks and began gathering funds for this purpose. Again, nothing came of such plans.

Undeterred, after his election in 1458, Pius II likewise committed himself to a new crusade, instigating the last significant push for such a venture under Rome's initiative. In June 1459, the pope held a congress at Mantua to plan for the expedition, summoning the major European powers to attend. Harmony among Christians, he believed, like many popes before him, formed an essential precondition for a successful crusade. Indeed, his denunciation of conciliarism demonstrated his belief that the Church must stand united under papal leadership before undertaking the battle against the Ottomans. The assembly at Mantua, however, revealed the inability or unwillingness of secular rulers to commit themselves to this enterprise. The French crown refused to make any significant contributions to the crusade, punishing the papacy for backing the Aragonese claim to Naples. Venice, a source of critical naval support, likewise held back, more concerned with maintaining their commercial ties to the Ottomans than fighting against them. Pius, no doubt frustrated, persisted in his efforts. In 1461, he crafted a remarkable letter addressed to the Ottoman sultan Muhammad II, explaining the virtues of the Christian faith, offering refutations of the Qur'an, and calling for the Muslim ruler's conversion. It is not clear whether the pope ever sent this letter, intended perhaps as a source of inspiration for fellow Christian readers more than anything else.[7] Three years later, Pius called for an army to assemble at Ancona, where he would personally assume command of the crusade. In 1464, he died at the coastal city, still waiting in vain for his crusaders to arrive.

The final imperial coronation in Rome in 1452, the fall of Constantinople in 1453, the failed crusade and death of Pius II a decade later – this convergence of events did represent a sign of the times. Not the coming of the apocalypse, as some contemporaries might have believed, but rather deep-seated transformations in the historical conditions of Christian Europe, as universalizing concepts such as empire and crusade either lost their appeal or changed beyond recognition from their medieval forms. Still acting as monarchs, so to speak, popes ruled over the Papal States much like other European sovereigns. Concordats, not crusades, were the signs of success for the restored papacy of the fifteenth century.

Renaissance and New Worlds

As some doors closed for the popes of Rome, others opened. Close to home, Italian thinkers, authors, and artists contributed to an epoch famously known as the Renaissance, styled by them as a "rebirth" of classical values and learning in literature, art, philosophy, and architecture. A new kind of Renaissance pope resulted, creating a papal court of dazzling opulence. Farther afield, explorers pushed the boundaries of European geographical knowledge, resulting in the encounter with the Americas and sea routes around the southernmost point of Africa that allowed European ships to enter the Indian Ocean, promising a truly global Christian Church.

Rome, humanism, and the arts

Somewhat paradoxically, Renaissance humanism both challenged the fifteenth-century Roman papacy and inspired it to innovative cultural heights. On the one hand, so-called humanist values – an emphasis on the priority of human affairs and achievements, on the natural dignity of humankind, on the importance of the individual – stood at odds with the Roman Church, an institution oriented toward the divine, eternal order, the corporate guarantor of salvation for all through the sacraments and priestly authority. As described above, Lorenzo Valla's assault on the *Donation of Constantine* provides a well-known example of the dynamic challenge posed by humanism to venerable papal claims. By Valla's day, few viewed the *Donation of Constantine* as a meaningful mandate for Rome's universal authority or believed that popes stood as the arbiters of empire. Nevertheless, his philological deconstruction of the text marked an important moment in the history of papal primacy, revealing the power of humanistic studies to erode the long-standing traditions, time-honored beliefs, and apparent historical truths, while inaugurating new ways of looking at art, literature, and history. Indeed, based on a sense of critical distance from the past, Renaissance-era thinkers created the notion of the medieval era, envisioning a "middle age" that stood between their own modern times and the classical world.

Nevertheless, humanistic values did not invariably stand against Christian ideas and ideals, or even the papacy. Indeed, some of the Roman Church's most ardent critics comfortably operated within the orbit of papal power. Valla, famous for his attack on Rome's clerical privileges, was far from the only humanist thinker who ended up working at the curia. Immersed in Latin culture, skilled as writers and rhetoricians, intellectuals such as Valla represented a valuable asset to the papal court. Humanists read more than the classical literature of the ancient world. By learning Greek and even Hebrew, they returned to the original languages of the Bible, unsatisfied with the Latin Vulgate that had formed the standard version of Scripture since the days of Saint Jerome. By trying to better understand the origins of Christianity, not attacking that faith, humanists challenged contemporary ecclesiastical institutions and practices, asking hard questions about the history of the Church since the days of the apostles through their modern age.

Starting in the mid-fifteenth century, successive popes largely embraced this elite sense of rebirth and restoration that characterized the times, taking full advantage of humanist thinkers' eloquence, learning, and artistic inspiration to adorn their own power and personal life. By doing so, they inaugurated a new phase in Rome's urban history under direct papal management, a celebration of the city's triumphant past as the heart of empire and the Apostolic See. Nicholas V, for example, the first pope who made his permanent residence in the Vatican rather than the Lateran palace, made ambitious but unrealized plans for the renovation of Saint Peter's basilica, and restored a number of churches around Rome, building new roads, piazzas, and other structures. He sponsored numerous translations of classical and early Christian works from Greek into Latin, and collected rare manuscripts from around Europe, laying the foundations for the Vatican Library. In 1450, he also declared another Jubilee year, bringing thousands of pious pilgrims flooding into the holy city. These artistic and architectural boom times continued under Pius II, Paul II (1464–71), despite his overall distaste for humanism, and Sixtus IV (1471–84), who supported the restoration of churches around Rome and continued the project of creating a peerless library in the Vatican. Over the course of a few decades, as a result of papal initiative and patronage, Rome went from being a dilapidated cultural backwater to the preeminent center of Renaissance art, architecture, and learning.[8]

The papal court and administration

In terms of their personal lives, Renaissance popes comported themselves much like other royal dynasties around Europe, building an elaborate web of alliances and familial ties to sustain their governance of Rome and the Papal States. After the dominance of French interests in the fourteenth century, the fifteenth-century papacy, curia, and cardinalate became thoroughly Italianized, reflecting the restored papacy's scaled-down horizons. Not all of the popes were themselves Italian. One of the most famous – most would say infamous – families to dominate the papal office during this era, the Borgias, including Popes Callixtus III and Alexander VI (1492–1503), hailed from the crown of Aragon. Alexander VI, in particular, earned a reputation for awarding important ecclesiastical positions to his relatives, including his own children born from a number of illicit sexual relationships. Alexander's son, Cesare Borgia, had held several bishoprics by the age of eighteen and was later made a cardinal. Throughout his colorful and violent career, he pursued his family's interests without hesitation, fighting their foes and rewarding their friends, all the while benefiting from his father's support. Alexander VI's daughter, Lucretia, likewise pursed Borgia interests, marrying multiple times – her second husband was apparently murdered by Cesare's minions after his usefulness to the Borgias had passed – to align the Borgias with various aristocratic factions and foreign powers. In this regard, the papal court stood at the center of a tangled web of treaties, marriages, and dynastic alliances woven to secure the Borgias' position as a power on the Italian peninsula.

Associated with larger-than-life personalities and undisguised nepotism, this era has given papal history some of its more salacious episodes and an enduring reputation for particular decadence, featuring yet more "bad popes." Certainly, Alexander's dalliances with his mistresses, staging of elaborate parties complete with prostitutes at the Vatican, and the favors he showered on his family do not seem like the behavior of a proper pope. Beneath the eye-catching stories, however, the hum of mundane business at the papacy curia continued unabated, not all that different from other governments around Europe. In addition to being the head of the Church, the pope remained a temporal ruler in his own right, served by an ever-expanding bureaucracy centered on the cardinals and the consistory, including the papal chamberlain, treasurer, lawyers, notaries, and more. The sale of offices and church benefices, making them part of private patrimonies, mirrored common practice in other European courts, where governmental positions were bought and sold as a matter of course. Bankers from cities such as Florence and Venice played an expanded role in papal government and policy making, much as they did in other states, underwriting the papacy's restoration after the Great Schism and its cultivation of the arts. Considering Rome's disastrous condition when Martin V arrived in 1420, one can imagine why his successors viewed the growth and relative stability of papal government as a triumph rather than a betrayal of the Roman Church – although, as we will see, not everyone viewed the papacy's increasing worldliness in such a forgiving light.

The papacy and the globe

As the papacy constructed a majestic Renaissance court, dramatic changes were happening in the wider world for the state of Christianity as a global religion. After a contraction in their geographical horizons during the fourteenth century, caused by the plague, the destabilization of the Mongol Empire, and the growing Ottoman presence in the Mediterranean, Europeans began to explore in new directions, including a series of overseas expeditions by the Portuguese and Spanish crowns in the Atlantic Ocean. In some ways, this expansion into the Atlantic world built upon the preexisting crusading ideology and experiences of the Portuguese and Spanish, whose voyages promised to open new fronts in their military campaigns against the Islamic powers of northern Africa. This policy would also allow Europeans direct access to the gold mines and slave trade in sub-Saharan Africa. By sailing all the way around Africa or west across the ocean, Christian explorers hoped to reconnect with the fabled rulers of Asia – known from earlier travel accounts, including that of the Venetian merchant Marco Polo – and their fabulous wealth. Some even believed that they might locate the rumored lands of "Prester John," a priestly Christian king, who would join forces with the Christians of Europe in a grand alliance against the Muslim world. Through such voyages, Jerusalem would be restored, Islam defeated, and profit realized.

As early as 1419, Martin V had issued a bull supporting Portuguese expansion in Africa against Muslim territories. His successors offered similar privileges to the Portuguese and Spanish crowns. These papal authorizations included calls for Christian monarchs to spread and defend Christianity, convert pagans, and found churches in newly won lands. Popes also promised crusading indulgences to Christian conquerors and explorers, making their voyages into the spiritual equivalents of crusades. More than anything else, however, competition between the Portuguese and Spanish opened the door to papal involvement in the world of Atlantic exploration, as both sides appealed to Rome for the legitimation of their conquests.

The European arrival on the Canary Islands provides a case in point. Located off the coast of western Africa, the Canaries had been settled well over a thousand years earlier by the Guanches, a people of Berber descent. There had been little or no contact between the islanders and mainland Africa since. When the first Portuguese and Spanish ships arrived at the Canaries during the 1300s, they began to trade with the Guanches, but also enslaved some of them. Exposed to European diseases for the first time, large numbers of the native population died over the course of several generations. Hearing about the abuse of the Guanches by raiders and slavers, Pope Eugene IV tried to forbid further Portuguese expansion in the islands until measures could be taken to protect the native peoples from exploitation and ensure their conversion. By 1436, the pope decided to approve and support Portugal's presence in the islands, instead calling upon the Portuguese crown – as the lesser of evils – to rein in the slave trade and foster the missionary presence among the Guanches. He also called upon the Portuguese and Spanish crowns not to create a scandal by competing over the islands. To some extent, Eugene's struggle with the churchmen at Basle influenced his decision to intervene. A year earlier, the council had deliberated over the rival Portuguese and Spanish claims to the Canary Islands. The pope wanted to demonstrate his own leadership by settling the matter.[9]

In 1492, Christopher Columbus's westward voyage to the "Indies" opened a new arena for European expansion in the New World, pursuing the same combination of material and spiritual interests that drove the earlier Portuguese and Spanish activities in the Atlantic. Columbus, popularly seen as a modern man who intrepidly sailed into the unknown, in fact shared a common understanding among educated Europeans that the world was round and could be circumnavigated, reaching the East by sailing west. He also believed that his voyages of discovery might lead to the recovery of Jerusalem from Islam and the spread of Christianity around the world, fulfilling biblical prophecies. For Columbus, however, eager to celebrate the power and prestige of the patrons who sponsored his expedition, Ferdinand and Isabella of Spain, the key to his successful spread of Christendom lay with his royal backers rather than Rome. As Columbus addressed the king and queen in his ship's logbook,

> Your Highnesses decided to send me, Christopher Columbus, to see these parts of India and the princes and peoples of those lands and consider the best means for their conversion. For, by the neglect of the popes to send instructors, many nations had fallen to idolatry and adopted doctrines of perdition, and your Highnesses as Catholic princes and devoted propagators of the holy Christian faith have always been enemies of the sect of Mahomet and of all idolatries and heresies.[10]

Whether accurate or not, Columbus's critique of the Roman papacy captured a sense that the heirs of Saint Peter had ceded their place to Europe's secular powers as the chief opponent of Islam and drivers of Christian mission, a far cry from the days when popes had inspired actual crusades and dispatched their envoys to far-off lands.

In 1493, the papacy intervened once more between Portuguese and Spanish interests when Pope Alexander VI issued *Inter caetera* and several accompanying bulls that divided the world into separate spheres of conquest and colonization for the two Iberian powers, an arrangement later confirmed by the Treaty of Tordesillas. This apparent act of papal mastery on a world-wide scale, justified in part by reference to the *Donation of Constantine*, represented a convenient fiction. Even if it wanted to take action, the papacy had little means to shape the colonial policies or the often devastating realities of European settlement in places such as the Canaries or the Americas. Ironically, Alexander's successful settlement between Portugal and Spain effectively ended their disputes, giving them free rein to pursue their political and commercial interests without further appeal to Rome. For the time being, as Christianity began truly to become a global religion, the Apostolic See more or less sat on the sidelines.

Toward the Reformation

In the realm of religious piety, the closure of the Middle Ages experienced equally momentous changes. However disillusioned they may have been with the present-day ecclesiastical institutions, men and women grew more – not less – committed to taking an active hand in their own salvation. Eagerly seeking indulgences, reading the Bible in vernacular languages, immersing themselves in religious confraternities, celebrating direct and mystical bonds between the believer and God, some Europeans found creative outlets for their faith, while others leveled new and devastating critiques at the Roman Church. On the edge of the modern era, the religious unity of Christian Europe – the medieval papacy's ongoing and to some extent successful project – stood on the knife's edge of dissolution.

Piety, print, and anti-clericalism

As seen generations earlier with the Franciscans and Dominicans, innovative expressions of lay religiosity did not necessarily lead to outright rejection of papal authority. Gert Groote, for example, who taught ideas and practices known as the Modern Devotion in the Low Countries during the mid- to late fourteenth century, inspired men and women to live with their goods in common and dedicate their lives to a program of prayer, spiritual contemplation, and the reading of Scripture. Although he criticized the clergy for their evident failings, he did not overtly question the priesthood or papal authority. Indeed, he received support from powerful churchmen, including Pope Martin V. Later followers of Groote's teachings, the Brothers and Sisters of the Common Life, lived much like the earlier Beguines, reading the Bible in the vernacular, living together without formal vows, placing an emphasis on personal study and contemplation of God. Cautiously critical of the clergy, the Brethren of the Common Life attracted praise from highly placed members of the ecclesiastical hierarchy, who pointed to the group as source of spiritual renewal in the Roman Church.

The fifteenth-century papacy, which generally resisted calls for administrative or clerical reform, did not always reject or condemn such creative expressions of religious piety. The print revolution, inaugurated by Johannes Gutenberg's printing of the Latin Bible around 1454, served rapidly to accelerate lay reading of Scripture, as printing presses established in Germany, Italy, and elsewhere began to publish vernacular Bibles, sermon collections, saints' lives, and other Christian literature. Even a relatively conservative pope, Paul II, supported the establishment of the first printing presses in the Papal States. Linked to this new technology, the Roman Church experienced a preaching revival during the later fifteenth century, as clerics drawing upon printed sermons spoke to eager crowds about the sacraments and doctrines of the catholic faith. At the same time, numerous Christians continued to make pilgrimages to Rome, as seen during the Jubilee Years of 1450 and 1500, which brought throngs of visitors seeking forgiveness of their sins. Indulgences, criticized by some, remained incredibly popular, one sign of how much average Christians continued to believe in the Apostolic See's spiritual capital.[11]

This outpouring of devotional activity in the religious life of the laity, however, also had the potential to generate severe criticism of the papacy, if not the entire Roman Church. As described in the previous chapter, the Lollards in England, drawing in part upon the writings of John Wyclif, turned their own forms of religious expression into a vehement attack on common devotional practices and core Church doctrines, among them pilgrimage, the veneration of saints and relics, and the transubstantiation of the Eucharist.

With encouragement and support from Rome, the English clergy actively began to suppress the Lollards, banning the possession of vernacular Bibles, burning convicted heretics at the stake, and driving the loose-knit movement into a state of hiding. Following the execution of Jan Hus at the Council of Constance, his followers in Bohemia – called Hussites – started a full-blown revolution against the Bohemian crown and clerical authorities, plunging the region into civil war. In 1420, Pope Martin V had declared the first of several crusades against the Hussites. Eventually forced to the bargaining table, the Hussites shrewdly negotiated with Rome for recognition and concessions, taking advantage of the papacy's vulnerability during its struggle against the Council of Basle.

The printing press – a source of Bibles, sermons, and other catholic literature – also served to print and disseminate tracts on "suspect" forms of Christian devotion, including diatribes against clerical corruption and critiques of papal power by thinkers such as John Wyclif and Jan Hus. With the coming of print, the genie of religious protest was fully out of the bottle. For some critics of Rome, their rejection of papal authority took on fiery apocalyptic significance. From 1494 to 1498, the Florentine preacher, prophet, and radical reformer Savonarola offered visions of the future that directly challenged the contemporary Roman Church. Even though he insisted on his loyalty to Rome, Savonarola railed against abuses by the clergy and the pope, while promising a better tomorrow after a period of tribulation. Picking up on the notion of the "angelic pope," Savonarola imagined the transfer of the Church's primary seat to the Holy Land: "The present Rome," he declared, "that is, the wicked of Rome, will be reproved and snuffed out, while the flower of Christians will be in the region of Jerusalem ... under one pope, Jerusalem will flourish in good Christian living."[12] For several years, this prophetic rabble-rouser found eager listeners in Florence after forces of the French King Charles VIII pushed the ruling Medici family from power in the city. In 1497, Alexander VI excommunicated Savonarola; the following year, tired of his growing influence over the city, the Florentines arrested him and burned him at the stake. Such criticisms of Rome, however, did not die with him.

The "Fearsome Pope"

The restored Roman papacy, successful at containing the challenge of conciliarism, securing its political integrity through diplomacy and armed force, did not face these changes in the religious arena with nearly as much effectiveness. For the most part, the popes of Rome continued to pour their energies into maintaining the precarious web of alliances and military strength that protected the Papal States and Italian peninsula from foreign interference. Charles VIII's invasion of Italy in 1494, pressing his claim to the kingdom of Naples, had once again set the papacy at odds with the French crown. After the death of Alexander VI and the brief papacy of Pius III (September–October 1503), Julius II (1503–13) literally took up arms to protect papal holdings and subdue Rome's belligerent neighbors. As the sixteenth-century Italian historian Francesco Guicciardini described him, Julius "had nothing of the priest except the dress and the name." According to another contemporary story, Julius, sometimes called the "Fearsome Pope," did not even have the dress of a priest. After he died, it was said, when he approached the gates of Heaven, Saint Peter rebuked him for wearing priestly garb over his "blood-stained" armor.

Julius also ordered the construction of a monumental basilica at the site of Saint Peter's church, completely leveling the Constantinian edifice that had stood there since the fourth century. The audacious, impressive design of the new building – which took decades to complete and still stands today – represented an architectural triumph, although it cost staggering amounts of money. Julius spared no expense. He also commissioned the Italian artist Michelangelo to paint his famous scene of the Last Judgment and other biblical episodes in the Sistine Chapel, viewed as an unrivaled masterpiece of Renaissance art. Measured as a warrior, statesman, diplomat, and patron, Julius II numbers among the greatest popes of the early modern era. For those contemporaries who wished to look to Rome for spiritual guidance and pastoral leadership, however, he fell far short of the qualities they sought. After Julius died in 1513, his Medici successor Pope Leo X (1513–21) continued in a similar vein, supposedly saying, "now that God has given us the papacy, let us enjoy it."

The last medieval council

During the years 1512 to 1517, Julius II and Leo X oversaw the Fifth Lateran Council, which one scholar has called the "conciliar swan song of the medieval papacy."[13] In keeping with the reduced scope of papal influence, the assembly consisted mostly of Italian bishops. Julius had first called for the council because of pressure from a rival council held at Pisa, summoned by mostly French cardinals and the French King Louis XII. Although Pius II had managed to secure the revocation of the Pragmatic Sanction of Bourges in 1461, many of the changes it made to ecclesiastical administration in France had remained in effect. Charles VII's successors, Louis XI and Charles VII, had continued to hold the Pragmatic Sanction over the papacy's head, a thinly veiled threat that they would reinstate its full conditions if Rome proved unwilling to support French aims. Louis XII eventually took this course of action and called for the pope's deposition. Coming to terms with Louis's successor, Francis I, Leo X secured the final revocation of the Pragmatic Sanction, but signed a new agreement with the French king, the "Concordat of Bologna," which allowed the French kings the right to appoint bishops and other clergy in France, while conceding similar rights over the filling of benefices. In this way, the papacy finally recognized the reality of church governance in France – that the king and French clergy, not the pope, controlled ecclesiastical offices and properties.

Judging by the proceedings of the council, the Roman papacy had little sense that it stood on the edge of a precipice. The clergy passed some modest reform measures. Tellingly, they paid virtually no attention to missionary work being undertaken in Africa and the Americas, although the attendees did celebrate when they heard news about the Portuguese discovery of Madagascar, conquest of Ceylon, and naval victory over Ottoman forces at Calicut. Some of the participants did foresee problems and promises on the horizon. At the beginning of the council, Giles of Viterbo gave an address that predicted imminent trials for the followers of Rome, including schism, conquests by Muslims, wars, and other challenges for the faithful. Present signs of danger were everywhere, manifesting God's desire for renewal and reform before the end times, when Christians would defeat Islam, recover Jerusalem, and spread the Gospel around the world. The churchmen at the Fifth Lateran Council, he intimated, would begin that process of reforming the Church. Developing this same theme, Thomas Cajetan described the Roman Church in his opening address to the council as the "New Jerusalem," and the "perfect city of the Apocalypse." Unlike the radical predictions offered by Savonarola years earlier, these apocalyptic speculations seemed designed to comfort rather than provoke their listeners, assuring them that Rome was more than up to such challenges and tasks.[14]

Little did Cajetan know that in 1518, after the close of the council, he would be sent by Leo X to confront the German theologian Martin Luther, whose teachings would help to shatter any lingering illusions about the status of the Roman Church as that New Jerusalem. Starting years earlier at the University of Wittenberg with some rather unremarkable works of biblical commentary, Luther's teachings emphasized the priority of God's grace and justification by faith for salvation. Over time, he began openly to question common devotional practices of his day, including pilgrimage, the cult of relics, and, above all, the issuing of indulgences, going so far as to deny the status of penance as a sacrament. In 1517, he posted his "Ninety-Five Theses" at Wittenberg cathedral, opening a frontal assault on the papal authority to remit sins. Reacting to the sale of indulgences to pay for the renovation of Saint Peter's basilica, Luther wondered: Why did the pope not entirely empty Purgatory out of love and the need of souls, rather than hawking indulgences to pay for the building? Since the pope was so wealthy, why did he not simply pay for the new basilica, rather than taking money from poor believers? Although he did not entirely deny the merits of papal intercession, Luther insisted that repentant Christians could receive God's forgiveness without letters of indulgence from the bishop of Rome. In such ways, Luther challenged the papacy's claims to absolve sinners in exchange for payment, part of wider critiques leveled at the Roman Church and its sacramental system.

Protected by the prince of Saxony, Luther continued to defy Rome, even after Pope Leo X excommunicated him in 1521. Over the following years, his support grew, opening the door to further sixteenth-century critics of Rome, including Huldrych Zwingli, Philipp Melanchthon, and John Calvin. Under the leadership of German princes, portions of the Holy Roman Empire formally broke away from Rome, creating their own Christian churches along the lines envisioned by Luther and others. The German Bible, translated by Luther himself, displaced the Latin Vulgate. The Protestant Reformation, as it became known, soon spread to England and other parts of Europe. The gap between Christendom as imagined by the medieval Roman Church and the realities of early modern Europe had opened up so wide that even the most fervid of imaginations, apocalyptic or otherwise, would never again be able to close it.

Epilogue

In February 2013, Pope Benedict XVI (2005–13) announced that he would retire from the Apostolic See. As the media frequently pointed out, this decision made him the first pontiff to do so since Gregory XII resigned under pressure in 1415, and the first to abdicate voluntarily since Celestine V in 1294. Suddenly, the medieval papacy had surfaced in discussions of the modern one. The news grabbed headlines and attention from every corner of the globe, not just among the world's Roman Catholic Christians, numbering well over a billion. Crowds gathered in the main square before the Basilica of Saint Peter in Rome when the papal conclave began its deliberations to elect a successor. After two days, on March 13, 2013, the announcement was made from the church's main balcony overlooking the square, "Habemus papam," that is, "We have a pope," the traditional declaration of a successful election since the fifteenth century. The new pope, Argentinian cardinal priest Jorge Mario Bergoglio, took the name Francis (2013–) after the thirteenth-century saint famed for his commitment to poverty, symbolizing Bergoglio's own concern for the poor in the era of globalization.

For an historian of the papacy, the centuries after the Middle Ages continue to provide meaningful episodes of Rome's involvement in issues of European, if not global significance. One need only recall the Council of Trent (1545–63), which inaugurated the so-called Counter-Reformation or Catholic Reformation, to see how the revitalized papacy of the early modern era continued to make its presence felt. One can easily find high-profile examples of the Roman Church's ongoing intervention in religious and political life, such as the papal sponsorship of Jesuit missions that spread around the globe, or the papacy's condemnation of Galileo, accused of heresy

195

for his claim that the earth rotated around the sun and not the other way around. Nevertheless, considering the major events and trends that shaped modern European history, one is forced to conclude that the popes of Rome played a negligible or non-existent role in determining their course. With the formation of the Italian nation-state in 1870, the papacy effectively ceased to exist as a political entity, losing what remained of the Papal States and confining direct papal authority to the modest confines of the Vatican City.

As secular values and scientific ideas came to dominate the modern world during the nineteenth and twentieth centuries, the bishop of Rome seemed a more and more marginal figure. Reduced in their stature and influence, conservative-minded popes continued to offer leadership for Roman Catholic Christians, or, according to their critics, failed to offer such leadership when needed most. Indeed, the papacy sometimes seemed like an idea and an institution still inhabiting the Middle Ages or somehow frozen in history. One reason for the rapt attention paid to recent papal elections, including that of Francis, seems to be the mystery and pageantry associated with them, signs of days gone by – the conclave, the different-colored puffs of smoke sent up from the Sistine Chapel to indicate whether a pope has been chosen or not, the procession of the Swiss Guard with their halberds into Saint Peter's square. This is not to say that the Roman Church remained entirely oblivious to the challenges and problems it faced in the rapidly changing modern era. At the Second Vatican Council from 1962 to 1965, when Popes John XXIII (1958–63) and Paul VI (1963–78) oversaw a number of far-reaching reforms, the papacy seemed to declare a truce with modernity, opening the door to a new round of reconciliation between venerable Catholic traditions and the realities of twentieth-century living.

Or perhaps not. Over the last several decades, above all in the wake of the Cold War, the once confident narrative of Western secularization has faced numerous challenges, including the open reemergence of religious convictions as a source of guidance for moral decisions and political action. This phenomenon, of course, is not limited to the followers of the Roman Catholic tradition, but involves various branches of Christianity, not to mention Judaism and Islam. Under these circumstances, the Roman papacy reemerged with particular prominence as an influential voice. Among other matters, Paul VI's 1968 encyclical *Humanae vitae* set the stage for the sexual and reproductive politics that continue to dominate Roman Catholic attitudes toward everything ranging from contraception to AIDS, cloning to abortion. More than any other recent pope, John Paul II (1978–2005) brought the papacy back into the media limelight through his opposition to communism in Soviet-dominated Europe and his tireless globe-trotting that attracted throngs of believers wherever he went. Although most would agree that Benedict XVI lacked John Paul's charisma, the elderly pope continued to make his presence felt in the international arena, whether calling for peace between Muslims and Christians or condemning the dangers of secularism for religious believers.

Pope Francis's pontificate is still taking shape, although his choice of a papal name after Francis of Assisi quickly captured the imagination of many Catholics, promising yet another moment of renewal and reinvention for the Roman papacy. In a recent sermon, he even suggested that atheists might go to Heaven. Meanwhile, the Vatican continues to confront an ongoing sexual abuse scandal among the clergy. In July 2013, the United Nations declared its intention to investigate charges of sexual assault against children by Roman Catholic clergy, the first such move by an international organization. On still another front, some Catholics push for the ordination of women and allowing priests to marry, trying to undo the legacy of the eleventh-century Gregorian reform. In US politics, the presence of six out of nine Supreme Court Justices who profess the Catholic faith has further elevated Catholicism's profile in America. To be sure, the modern papacy might seem inconsequential compared to the days when medieval popes set crusading armies in motion, excommunicated emperors, and claimed primacy over the entire world. Nevertheless, now more than at any other time in living memory, the bishops of Rome demand our attention as both spiritual and political players on the global scene, reminding us that the Apostolic See of Saint Peter continues to view its earthly mission as encompassing far more than the shepherding of souls toward their eternal salvation.

Notes

Introduction

1. *Select Historical Documents of the Middle Ages*, trans. E. F. Henderson (London, 1892), 319–29; revised in *Carolingian Civilization: A Reader*, ed. P. Dutton, 2nd ed. (Toronto, 2004), 14–22.
2. On the growing restriction of the title "pope," see J. Moorhead, "*Papa* as Bishop of Rome," *Journal of Ecclesiastical History* 36 (1985): 337–50.
3. See, among many classic examples, D. Hay, *Europe: The Emergence of an Idea* (Edinburgh, 1957); and C. Dawson, *The Formation of Christendom* (New York, 1967).
4. M. Gabriele, *An Empire of Memory: The Legend of Charlemagne, the Franks, and Jerusalem before the First Crusade* (Oxford, 2011), 6.

1   The Memory of Saint Peter

1. *The Didache*, trans. J. A. Kleist, Ancient Christian Writers, vol. 6 (New York, 1948), 15–25.
2. *The Epistles of St. Clement of Rome and St. Ignatius of Antioch*, ed. and trans. J. A. Kleist, Ancient Christian Writers, vol. 1 (New York, 1946), 32, 73.
3. *A New Eusebius: Documents Illustrative of the History of the Church to A.D. 337*, ed. J. Stevenson (1958; London, 1968), 1.
4. *Epistles of St. Clement*, 82.
5. *A New Eusebius*, 2–3.
6. *Epistles of St. Clement*, 83.
7. *The Apocryphal New Testament: A Collection of Apocryphal Christian Literature in an English Translation*, ed. J. K. Elliott (Oxford, 1993), 385–7, 399–426; for the combined acts, see the *Ante-Nicene Fathers*, ed. A. Roberts and J. Donaldson, vol. 8 (1885–96; Grand Rapids, Mich., 1971–85), 477–85.

8. *Apocryphal New Testament*, 387, 425.

9. Eusebius of Caesarea, *The History of the Church from Christ to Constantine*, trans. G. A. Williamson (New York, 1984), 88, 97.

10. Eusebius, *History of the Church*, 105; Lactantius, *The Minor Works*, trans. M. F. McDonald, The Fathers of the Church, vol. 54 (Washington, DC, 1965), 139.

11. Eusebius, *History of the Church*, 105.

12. *Epistles of St. Clement*, 35–36.

13. Irenaeus of Lyons, *Against the Heresies* (Book Three), trans. D. J. Unger, Ancient Christian Writers, vol. 64 (New York, 2012), 32–3.

14. Tertullian, *The Prescription against the Heretics*, in *Early Latin Theology*, ed. and trans. S. L. Greenslade, Library of Christian Classics, vol. 5 (Philadelphia, 1956), 52, 57.

15. Eusebius, *History of the Church*, 229–34.

16. Cyprian, *The Lapsed and the Unity of the Church*, trans. M. Bevenot, Ancient Christian Writers, vol. 25 (New York, 1956), 46–7; *The Letters of St. Cyprian of Carthage*, trans. G. W. Clark, Ancient Christian Writers, vol. 46 (New York, 1986), 91.

17. *The Letters of St. Cyprian of Carthage*, trans. G. W. Clark, Ancient Christian Writers, vol. 47 (New York, 1989), 50, 88–9. See also J. P. Burns, "On Rebaptism: Social Organization in the Third-Century Church," *Journal of Early Christian Studies* 1 (1993): 367–403.

18. Eusebius, *History of the Church*, 282.

19. *Church and State Throughout the Centuries: A Collection of Historical Documents with Commentaries*, ed. and trans. S. Z. Ehler and J. B. Morrall (Westminster, Md., 1954), 5–6.

20. *A New Eusebius*, 172, 296.

21. C. J. Hefele, *A History of the Christian Councils after Original Documents*, trans. W. R. Clark, 2nd ed., vol. 1 (Edinburgh, 1894), 389. On the ecumenical councils of the early Church, see N. P. Tanner, *The Councils of the Church: a Short History* (New York, 2001), 13–45.

22. Hefele, *A History of the Christian Councils*, vol. 2, 112–29.

23. Athanasius, *History of the Arians*, quoted in K. Baus, H.-G. Beck, E. Ewig, and H. J. Vogt, *The Imperial Church from Constantine to the Early Middle Ages*, trans. A. Biggs, Handbook of Church History, vol. 2 (New York, 1980), 83.

24. B. Croke and J. Harries, *Religious Conflict in Fourth-Century Rome: A Documentary Study* (Sydney, 1982), 7–8. See also D. Trout, "Damasus and the Invention of Early Christian Rome," *Journal of Medieval and Early Modern Studies* 33 (2003): 517–36.

25. Hefele, *A History of the Christian Councils*, vol. 2, 357–9.

26. *Documents Illustrating Papal Authority A.D. 96–454*, ed. E. Giles (London, 1952), 130–1 (translation slightly modified).

27. *Decretales Pseudo-Isidorianae et capitula Angilramni*, ed. P. Hinschius (1863; reprint, Leipzig, 1963), 31.

2 Empire and Christendom

1. E. Gibbon, *The History of the Decline and Fall of the Roman Empire*, ed. D. Womersley, 4 vols. (1776–89; London, 1994).

2. Saint Jerome, Letter no. 127, *Nicene and Post-Nicene Fathers*, ed. P. Schaff and H. Wace, second series, vol. 6 (1885–96; Grand Rapids, Mich., 1971–85), 257; Augustine of Hippo, *City of God*, trans. H. Bettenson (London, 2003).

3. *Patrologia cursus completus: series Latina* (hereafter *PL*), ed. J. P. Migne (Paris, 1841–64), vol. 13, cols. 1133, 1164, 1188.

4. *PL*, vol. 20, col. 470.

5. Leo the Great, *Sermons*, trans. J. P. Freeland and A. J. Conway, The Fathers of the Church, vol. 93 (Washington, DC, 1996), 18–23. In addition to W. Ulmann, "Leo I and the Theme of Papal Primacy," *Journal of Theological Studies* N.S. 11 (1960): 25–51, see K. Uhalde, "Pope Leo I on Power and Failure," *The Catholic Historical Review* 95 (2009): 671–88.

6. Leo the Great, *Letters*, trans. E. Hunt, The Fathers of the Church, vol. 34 (New York, 1957), 39.

7. Leo the Great, *Letters*, 96.

8. Leo the Great, *Letters*, 89.

9. *Readings in European History*, trans. J. H. Robinson (Boston, 1905), 72–3.

10. *Epistolae Romanorum pontificium et quae ad eos scriptae sunt a s. Clemente usque ad Innocentium III*, ed. P. Coustant (Paris, 1721; reprint, Farnborough, UK, 1967), appendix, 52. See also J. Hillner, "Families, Patronage, and the Titular Churches of Rome, c. 300–600," in *Religion, Dynasty, and Patronage in Early Christian Rome, 300–900*, ed. K. Cooper and J. Hillner (Cambridge, UK, 2010), 225–61.

11. *The Book of Popes (Liber Pontificalis)*, ed. and trans. L. R. Loomis, Records of Civilization: Sources and Studies (New York, 1916), covers the period until Pope Pelagius II (579–90). See also R. McKitterick, "Roman Texts and Roman History in the Early Middle Ages," in *Rome Across Time and Space: Cultural Transmission and the Exchange of Ideas c. 500–1000*, ed. C. Bolgia, R. McKitterick, and J. Osborne (Cambridge, UK, 2011), 19–34.

12. See P. Brown, *The Rise of Western Christendom: Triumph and Diversity A.D. 200–1000*, 2nd ed. (Malden, Mass., 2003), 13–17; and the response from P. Delogu, "The Papacy, Rome and the Wider World in the Seventh and Eighth Centuries," in *Early Medieval Rome and the Christian West*, ed. J. Smith (Leiden, 2000), 197–220.

13. *The Letters of Gregory the Great*, trans. J. R. C. Martyn, vol. 1 (Toronto, 2004), 121.

14. *Morals on the Book of Job*, trans. J. H. Parker, Library of the Fathers of the Holy Catholic Church, vols. 18, 21, 23, 31 (Oxford, 1844–50); *Saint Gregory the Great, Dialogues*, trans. O. J. Zimmerman, The Fathers of the Church, vol. 39 (New York, 1959); and *Pastoral Care*, ed. and trans. H. Davis, Ancient Christian Writers, vol. 11 (New York, 1978).

15. *Dialogues*, 186–7. On Gregory's sense of mission and the apocalypse, see B. McGinn, "The End of the World and the Beginning of Christendom," in *Apocalypse Theory and the Ends of the World*, ed. M. Bull (Oxford, 1995), 58–89.

16. *Letters of Gregory the Great*, vol. 1, 154, 171, 304–5.

17. See R. Sullivan, "The Papacy and Missionary Activity in the Early Middle Ages," *Mediaeval Studies* 17 (1955): 46–106.

18. *Letters of Gregory the Great*, vol. 3, 802–3.

19. *Letters of Gregory the Great*, vol. 2, 532–45; vol. 3, 779–82.

20. *Bede's Ecclesiastical History of the English People*, trans. B. Colgrave and R. A. B. Mynors (Oxford, 1969), 154–9.

21. Gregory of Tours, *History of the Franks*, trans. L. Thorpe (Harmondsworth, UK, 1974), 335.

22. *Bede's Ecclesiastical History*, 249–52.

23. *The Letters of Saint Boniface*, trans. E. Emerton (New York, 2000), 10–11.

24. *The Lives of the Eighth-Century Popes (Liber Pontificalis)*, trans. R. Davis, Translated Texts for Historians, vol. 13 (Liverpool, 1992), 4; *Letters of Saint Boniface*, 51.

25. *Letters of Saint Boniface*, 34; *Lives of the Eighth-Century Popes*, 8–9.

26. See H. Pirenne, *Mohammed and Charlemagne* (1939; London, 1958); and R. Hodges and D. Whitehouse, *Mohammad, Charlemagne, and the Origins of Europe: Archeology and the Pirenne Thesis* (Ithaca, 1983).

27. *Bede's Ecclesiastical History*, 170–3.

28. See L. Brubaker and J. Haldon, *Byzantium in the Iconoclast Era c. 680–850: A History* (Cambridge, 2011), especially 69–155; and L. Brubaker, *Inventing Byzantine Iconoclasm* (London, 2012).

29. *Lives of the Eighth-Century Popes*, 11, 20.

30. *Source Book for Mediaeval History*, ed. O. Thatcher and E. H. McNeal (New York, 1905), 97.

31. H. Rahner, *Church and State in Early Christianity*, trans. L. D. Davis (San Francisco, 1992), 276–84 (quotation, 280). Rahner apparently accepted these letters as genuine.

3   The Reordering of the West

1. For two contemporary accounts of Charlemagne's coronation, see *The Lives of the Eighth-Century Popes (Liber Pontificalis)*, trans. R. Davis, Translated Texts for Historians, vol. 13 (Liverpool, 1992), 187–8; and Charlemagne's biographer Einhard, in *Two Lives of Charlemagne*, trans. D. Ganz (London, 2008), 38.

2. *Source Book for Mediaeval History*, ed. O. J. Thatcher and E. H. McNeal (New York, 1905), 101–2; *Carolingian Chronicles: Royal Frankish Annals and Nithard's Histories*, trans. B. W. Scholz with B. Rogers (Ann Arbor, 1970), 39.

3. *Lives of the Eighth-Century Popes*, 71.

4. *Lives of the Eighth-Century Popes*, 136.
5. *Christianity Through the Thirteenth Century*, ed. M. W. Baldwin (New York, 1970), 115–19.
6. See R. McKitterick, "Unity and Diversity in the Carolingian Church," in *Unity and Diversity in the Church*, ed. R. N. Sawnson, Studies in Church History, vol. 32 (Oxford, 1996), 59–82; and Y. Hen, "The Romanization of the Frankish Liturgy: Ideal, Reality, and the Rhetoric of Reform," in *Rome Across Time and Space: Cultural Transmission and the Exchange of Ideas c. 500–1000*, ed. C. Bolgia, R. McKitterick, and J. Osborne (Cambridge, UK, 2011), 111–23.
7. Stephen II to Pippin, no. 10, ed. W. Gundlach, *Monumenta Germaniae Historica* (hereafter *MGH*): *Epistulae Karolini Aevi*, vol. 3 (Hanover, 1892), 501.
8. *Carolingian Civilization: A Reader*, ed. P. Dutton, 2nd ed. (Peterborough, Ont., 2004), 14–22.
9. On these mosaics, see T. F. X. Noble, *The Republic of Saint Peter: The Birth of the Papal State, 680–825* (Philadelphia, 1984), 323–4.
10. For a dated, but still invaluable discussion of the cardinalate, see S. Kuttner, "Cardinalis: The History of Canonical Concept," *Traditio* 3 (1945): 129–214.
11. See T. F. X. Noble, "Topography, Celebration, and Power: The Making of a Papal Rome in the Seventh and Eighth Centuries," in *Topographies of Power in the Early Middle Ages*, ed. M. de Jong, F. Theuws with C. van Rhijn (Leiden, 2001), 45–92.
12. *Pauli continuatio Romana*, ed. G. H. Pertz and G. Waitz, *MGH: Scriptores rerum Langobardorum* (Hanover, 1878), 203.
13. *Carolingian Chronicles*, 117.
14. *Le liber pontificalis*, ed. L. Duchesne, vol. 2 (Paris, 1955), 87–8.
15. *De expeditione contra Sarracenos facienda*, ed. A. Boretius and V. Krause, *MGH: Leges*, vol. 2 (Hanover, 1897), 65–8.
16. *Le liber pontificalis*, 123–5.
17. Leo IV, no. 28, ed. K. Hampe, *MGH: Epistulae*, vol. 5 (Berlin, 1899), 601.
18. Nicholas I, no. 99, ed. E. Perels, *MGH: Epistulae*, vol. 6 (Berlin, 1912), 568–600.
19. *The Annals of St-Bertin*, trans. J. Nelson (Manchester, 1991), 141.
20. *De imperatorial potestate in urbe Roma libellus*, ed. G. H. Pertz, *MGH: Scriptores*, vol. 3 (Hanover, 1839), 722.
21. Liudprand of Cremona, *The Complete Works of Liudprand of Cremona*, trans. P. Squatriti (Washington, DC, 2007), 219.
22. *Works of Liudprand of Cremona*, 222.
23. E. R. Chamberlain, *The Bad Popes* (New York, 1969), 40–61.
24. K. Cushing, *Reform and Papacy in the Eleventh Century: Spirituality and Social Change* (Manchester, 2005), 20.
25. Quoted from W. Ulmann, *The Growth of Papal Government in the Middle Ages: A Study in the Ideological Relation of Clerical to Lay Power*, 2nd ed. (London, 1965), 241.

4 Reform and Crusade

1. *The Papal Reform of the Eleventh Century: Lives of Leo IX and Gregory VII*, trans. I. Robinson (Manchester, 2004).
2. G. Tellenbach, *Church, State and Christian Society at the Time of the Investiture Contest*, trans. R. F. Bennett (1936; Oxford, 1948), 1.
3. See G. Ladner, "Terms and Ideas of Renewal," in *Renaissance and Renewal in the Twelfth Century*, ed. R. L. Benson and G. Constable (Cambridge, Mass., 1982), 1–33.
4. B. Tierney, *The Crisis of Church and State 1050–1300* (Englewood Cliffs, NJ, 1964), 28–9.
5. Rodulfus Glaber, *Historiarum libri quinque (The Five Books of the Histories)*, ed. and trans. J. France (Oxford, 1989), 173–7, 281–2.
6. *De ordinando pontifice auctor Gallicus*, ed. E. Sackur, *MGH: Libelli Ldl* 1 (Hanover, 1891), 8–14.
7. *History of the Dedication of Saint Remy at Reims*, PL, vol. 142, col. 1432.
8. *De sancta Romana ecclesia*, ed. P. Schramm, *Kaiser, Rom und Renovatio*, vol. 2 (Berlin, 1929), 129.
9. *The Collection in Seventy-Four Titles: A Canon Law Manual of the Gregorian Reform*, trans. J. Gilchrist, Medieval Sources in Translation, vol. 22 (Toronto, 1980); Peter Damian, *Letters*, trans. O. J. Blum, vol. 3 (Washington, DC, 1989), 24–39.
10. Tierney, *Crisis of Church and State*, 44.
11. Tierney, *Crisis of Church and State*, 42–3.
12. M. Miller, *Power and the Holy in the Age of the Investiture Controversy: A Brief History with Documents* (Boston, 2005), 81–3.
13. Miller, *Power and the Holy*, 83–90.
14. Quoted in C. Morris, *The Papal Monarchy: The Western Church from 1050–1250* (Oxford, 1989), 109.
15. Miller, *Power and the Holy*, 104–12.
16. Suger of Saint Denis, *The Deeds of Louis the Fat*, trans. R. Cusimano and J. Moorhead (Washington, DC, 1992), 46–54; Tierney, *Crisis of Church and State*, 89–90.
17. Tierney, *Crisis of Church and State*, 82–3.
18. Tierney, *Crisis of Church and State*, 91–2.
19. Glaber, *The Five Books of the Histories*, 195–7.
20. See J. Y. Malegam, *The Sleep of Behemoth: Disputing Peace and Violence in Medieval Europe, 1000–1200* (Ithaca, 2013), 55–75.
21. A. Gieysztor, "The Genesis of the Crusades: The Encyclical of Sergius IV (1009–1012)," *Medievalia et Humanistica* 6 (1950): 3–34; see also the first part of his analysis, *Medievalia et Humanistica* 5 (1948): 3–23.
22. *The First Crusade: The Chronicle of Fulcher of Chartres and Other Source Materials*, ed. E. Peters (1971; Philadelphia, 1998), 1–15.
23. *Letters from the East: Crusaders, Pilgrims, and Settlers in the 12th and 13th Centuries*, trans. M. Barber and K. Bate (Farnham, UK, 2010), 30–3.
24. *The First Crusade*, 32–4.

5 Papal Monarchy

1. Bernard of Clairvaux, *Five Books On Consideration: Advice to a Pope*, trans. J. D. Andersen and E. T. Kennan, Cistercian Fathers Series, vol. 13 (Kalamazoo, Mich., 1976), 31, 36, 57–7, 67–8, 117.

2. For the full text of the *Decretum*, see the *Corpus Iuris Canonici*, ed. A. Friedberg, 2 vols. (Graz, 1955); portions are translated in *The Treatise on Laws*, trans. A. Thompson and J. Gordley (Washington, DC, 2003).

3. See J. Van Engen, "The Crisis of Cenobitism Reconsidered: Benedictine Monasticism," *Speculum* 61 (1982): 269–304; and G. Constable, *The Reformation of the Twelfth-Century* (Cambridge, UK, 1996).

4. *Liber censuum Romanae ecclesiae*, ed. P. Fabre and L. Duchesne, 3 vols. (Paris, 1889–1910).

5. *The* Historia Pontificalis *of John of Salisbury*, ed. and trans. M. Chibnall (Oxford, 1986), 75–7.

6. Quoted by I. Robinson, *The Papacy 1073–1198: Continuity and Innovation* (Cambridge, UK, 1990), 138.

7. Otto of Freising, *The Deeds of Frederick Barbarossa*, trans. C. C. Mierow (New York, 1953), 143–4.

8. *The* Historia Pontificalis *of John of Salisbury*, 65.

9. *The Crusades: A Reader*, ed. E. Amt and S. J. Allen (Toronto, 2003), 184–5.

10. G. Constable, "The Second Crusade as Seen by Contemporaries," *Traditio* 9 (1953): 213–79.

11. Bernard of Clairvaux, *On Consideration*, 57–8. See also G. A. Loud, "Some Reflections on the Failure of the Second Crusade," *Crusades* 4 (2004): 1–14.

12. Bernard of Clairvaux, *On Consideration*, 117–18.

13. John of Salisbury, *Policraticus: On the Frivolity of Courtiers and the Footprints of Philosophers*, ed. and trans. C. J. Nederman (Cambridge, UK, 1990), 32.

14. B. Tierney, *The Crisis of Church and State 1050–1350* (Englewood Cliffs, NJ, 1964), 64–5.

15. Otto of Freising, *The Deeds of Frederick Barbarossa*, 180–6, 190–4.

16. Quoted by Robinson, *The Papacy*, 141.

17. Tierney, *Crisis of Church and State*, 113.

18. See W. L. Wakefield and A. P. Evans, *Heresies of the High Middle Ages: Selected Sources Translated and Annotated* (New York, 1969).

19. E. Peters, *Heresy and Authority in Medieval Europe: Documents in Translation* (Philadelphia, 1980), 170–4.

6 The Whole World to Govern

1. See J. C. Moore, *Pope Innocent III (1160/61–1216): To Root Up and Plant* (Leiden, 2003), 25–30; and *The Deeds of Pope Innocent III by an Anonymous Author*, trans. J. Powell (Washington, DC, 2004), 56.

2. Relevant sources are collected in *Regestum Innocentii III papae super negotio Romani imperii*, ed. F. Kempf, Miscellanea Historia Pontificae, vol. 12 (Rome, 1947).

3. D. Waley, *The Papal State in the Thirteenth Century* (London, 1961), 60.

4. *Select Letters of Pope Innocent III Concerning England*, ed. and trans. C. R. Cheney and W. H. Semple (London, 1953), 177.

5. A. J. Andrea, *Contemporary Sources for the Fourth Crusade* (Leiden, 2000), 11.

6. Andrea, *Contemporary Sources for the Fourth Crusade*, 116–17. See also B. Whalen, "Joachim of Fiore and the Division of Christendom," *Viator* 34 (2003): 89–108.

7. Moore, *Pope Innocent III: To Root Up and Plant*, 208.

8. *Disciplinary Decrees of the General Councils: Text, Translation, and Commentary* (St. Louis, 1937), 236–96.

9. *Francis of Assisi: Early Documents*, ed. and trans. R. J. Armstrong, J. W. Hellmann, and W. J. Short (New York, 1999), 570.

10. D. Abulafia, *Frederick II: A Medieval Emperor* (London, 1988), 342–3.

11. This correspondence is collected in *Die Beziehungen der Päpste zu islamischen und mongolischen Herrschern im 13. Jahrhundert anhand ihres Briefwechsels*, ed. K.-E. Lupprian, Studi e Testi, vol. 291 (Vatican City, 1981).

12. *Matthew Paris's English History*, trans. J. A. Giles, vol. 2 (London, 1853), 312.

13. C. Dawson, *Mission to Asia* (1955; Toronto, 1980), 74; B. Tierney, *The Crisis of Church and State 1050–1350* (Englewood Cliffs, NJ, 1964), 155–6.

14. Alexander von Roes, *Alexander von Roes Schriften*, ed. H. Grundmann and H. Heimpel (Stuttgart, 1958), 149–71.

7   The Papacy in Crisis

1. See B. Whalen, *Dominion of God: Christendom and Apocalypse in the Middle Ages* (Cambridge, Mass., 2009), 221–6.

2. See G. Dickson, "The Crowd at the Feet of Pope Boniface VIII: Pilgrimage, Crusade, and the First Roman Jubilee," *Journal of Medieval History* 25 (1999): 279–307.

3. B. Tierney, *The Crisis of Church and State 1050–1350* (Englewood Cliffs, NJ, 1964), 175–6.

4. Tierney, *Crisis of Church and State*, 178–9, 185–7.

5. Tierney, *Crisis of Church and State*, 188–9.

6. *Giles of Rome's On Ecclesiastical Power: A Medieval Theory of World Government*, ed. and trans. R. W. Dyson (New York, 2004), 23; James of Viterbo, *On Christian Government (De regimine Christiano)*, ed. and trans. R. W. Dyson (Woodbridge, UK, 1995), 86.

7. John of Paris, *On Royal and Papal Government*, trans. A. P. Monahan (New York, 1974), 20.

8. John of Paris, *On Royal and Papal Government*, 114.

9. Dante, *Monarchy*, ed. and trans. P. Shaw (Cambridge, UK, 1996), 66–7, 80–3. See also G. Holmes, "*Monarchia* and Dante's Attitude to the Popes," in *Dante and Governance*, ed. J. Woodhouse (Oxford, 1997), 46–57.

10. *Babylon on the Rhone: A Translation of Letters by Dante, Petrarch, and Catherine of Siena on the Avignon Papacy*, trans. R. Coogan (Potomac, Md., 1983), 76, 80.

11. Pierre Dubois, *The Recovery of the Holy Land*, trans. W. Brandt (New York, 1956), 90, 100.

12. *Documents on the Later Crusades*, ed. and trans. N. Housely (New York, 1996), 64.

13. Marsilius of Padua, *The Defender of the Peace, Volume II: The* Defensor pacis, trans. A. Gewirth (New York, 1956), 12, 113, 309–13.

14. Marsilius of Padua, *Defender of the Peace*, 313–20, 331–44.

15. *Medieval Political Theory: A Reader (The Quest for the Body Politic, 1100–1400)*, ed. C. J. Nederman and K. L. Forhan (London, 1993), 208–20.

16. See B. Tierney, *Origins of Papal Infallibility 1150–1350: A Study on the Concepts of Infallibility, Sovereignty, and Tradition in the Middle Ages* (Leiden, 1988).

17. *Babylon on the Rhone*, 106–7, 114.

18. *Babylon on the Rhone*, 119.

19. *Documents on the Later Crusades*, 98–100.

20. J. Gill, "The Representation of the *universitats fidelium* in the Councils of the Conciliar Period," in *Councils and Assemblies*, ed. G. J. Cuming and D. Baker, Studies in Church History, vol. 7 (Cambridge, 1971), 177–95 (quotation, 178).

21. E. C. Tatnall, "The Condemnation of John Wyclif at the Council of Constance," in *Councils and Assemblies*, 209–18.

22. *Unity, Heresy, and Reform: The Conciliar Response to the Great Schism*, ed. C. M. D Crowder (New York, 1977), 81–3.

23. *Unity, Heresy, and Reform*, 128–9.

8   Rome at the Close of the Middle Ages

1. *The Treatise of Lorenzo Valla on the Donation of Constantine: Text and Translation into English*, ed. and trans. C. B. Coleman (New Haven, 1922), 83–7.

2. Nicholas of Cusa, *Writings on Church and Reform*, trans. T. M. Izbicki (Cambridge, Mass., 2008) 105, 113.

3. *Unity, Heresy, and Reform: The Conciliar Response to the Great Schism*, ed. C. M. D. Crowder (New York, 1977), 171.

4. See J. Gill, *The Council of Florence* (Cambridge, UK, 1959).

5. *Unity, Heresy, and Reform*, 179–81.

6. *Reject Aeneas, Accept Pius: Selected Letters of Aeneas Sylvius Piccolomini (Pope Pius II)*, trans. T. M. Izbicki, G. Christianson, and P. Krey (Washington, DC, 2006), 310.

7. *Epistola ad Mahometam II (Epistle to Muhammad II)*, trans. A. R. Baca (New York, 1989).

8. See C. L. Stinger, *The Renaissance in Rome* (Bloomington, Ind., 1998), 14–82.

9. See J. Muldoon, "*Auctoritas, Potestas* and World Order," in *Plenitude of Power – The Doctrines and Exercises of Authority in the Middle Ages: Essays in Memory of Robert Louis Benton*, ed. R. C. Figueira (Aldershot, UK, 2006), 125–39.

10. *The Four Voyages of Christopher Columbus*, ed. and trans. J. M. Cohen (London, 1969), 37. See also P. M. Watts, "Prophecy and Discovery: On the Spiritual Origins of Christopher Columbus's 'Enterprise of the Indies'," *The American Historical Review* 90 (1985): 73–102.

11. See D. L. d'Avray, "Papal Authority and Religious Sentiment in the Late Middle Ages," in *The Church and Sovereignty c. 590–1918*, ed. D. Wood, Studies in Church History, vol. 9 (Oxford, 1991), 393–408.

12. *Select Writings of Girolamo Savonarola: Religion and Politics, 1490–1498*, ed. and trans. A. Borelli and M. P. Passaro (New Haven, 2006), 287.

13. W. Ulmann, *A Short History of the Papacy in the Middle Ages*, 2nd ed. (1974; London, 2003), 326.

14. See N. H. Minnich, "Prophecy and the Fifth Lateran Council (1512–1517)," in *Prophetic Rome in the High Renaissance*, ed. M. Reeves (Oxford, 1992), 63–87.

Suggestions for Further Reading

Because the Roman papacy touched upon so many aspects of medieval European history, the scope for research relating to the popes of Rome is almost limitless. A comprehensive bibliography of the subject would represent a massive project, including works in Italian, French, German, and other languages. The following suggestions for further reading are highly selective, mainly limited to secondary literature in English and prioritizing studies that were particularly helpful during the writing of this present volume. To avoid redundancy, the citations for primary sources in translation included in the notes are not repeated here.

Certain resources for the study of the medieval Church, including the papacy, are available online. The *Catholic Encyclopedia* (http://www.newadvent.org/cathen/) forms a valuable point of reference, although users should be aware that the online version is now a century old and unabashedly biased. The *Internet Medieval Sourcebook* (http://www.fordham.edu/halsall/sbook.asp) includes primary source selections (often from older translations no longer under copyright) covering antiquity and the medieval era on a variety of topics, including sections on the papacy and church history. The *Labyrinth* (http://labyrinth.georgetown.edu/) is another valuable website for medieval studies, with sources in translation, bibliographies, dictionary entries, and links to additional online resources. For translations of primary sources from the early Church, see the *Christian Classics Ethereal Library* (http://www.ccel.org/) and *Fourth-Century Christianity* (http://www.fourthcentury.com/). Those looking for additional primary sources in English should take advantage of the *Online Medieval Sources Bibliography* (http://medievalsourcesbibliography.org/), a search engine for sources in translation. For those who read Latin, the *Documenta Catholica Omnia* (http://

www.documentacatholicaomnia.eu/) represents a massive, if unwieldy database of documents relating to the history of the Catholic Church. The *Medieval Canon Law Virtual Library* (http://web.colby.edu/canon-law/) includes electronic versions of key Latin sources for the study of canon law.

General Reference and Surveys

As a starting point for ecclesiastical history, one can still turn to the first four volumes of the *Handbook of Church History*, ed. H. Jedin and J. Dolan, 7 vols. (New York, 1965), covering the period from the Bible until the Protestant Reformation. For more recent perspectives, consult the first four volumes of *The Cambridge History of Christianity*, ed. M. M. Mitchell et al. (Cambridge, 2006). For a survey of the Western Church during the Middle Ages, see R. Southern, *Western Society and the Church in the Middle Ages* (Harmondsworth, UK, 1970), and B. Hamilton, *Religion in the Medieval West*, 2nd ed. (London, 2003). For two masterful works concentrating on the later Roman Empire and Early Middle Ages with considerable attention to ecclesiastical history, see J. Herrin, *The Formation of Christendom*, 2nd ed. (London, 2001), and P. Brown, *The Rise of Western Christendom: Triumph and Diversity A.D. 200–1000*, 2nd ed. (Malden, Mass., 2003). C. Morris, *The Papal Monarchy: The Western Church from 1050–1250* (Oxford, 1989), admirably covers the Roman Church during the High Middle Ages. For the Late Middle Ages, see F. Oakley, *The Western Church in the Later Middle Ages* (Ithaca, 1979). H. Chadwick, *East and West: The Making of a Rift in the Church from Apostolic Times until the Council of Florence* (Oxford, 2003), surveys Church history with a particular eye toward relations between the Western and Eastern Churches.

For the history of the Roman papacy specifically, J. N. D. Kelly, *The Oxford Dictionary of Popes* (1996; Oxford, 2010), provides a valuable source of essential information. Manageable and responsible surveys of papal history, some limited to the Middle Ages, others covering its entirety, include W. Ulmann, *A Short History of the Papacy in the Middle Ages* (1972; London, 2003); G. Barraclough, *The Medieval Papacy* (New York, 1968); B. Schimmelpfennig, *The Papacy*, trans. J. Sievert (New York, 1992), compromised somewhat by its flawed translation; E. Duffy, *Saints and Sinners: History of the Popes* (1997; New Haven, 2001); and R. Collins, *Keepers of the Keys of Heaven:*

A History of the Papacy (New York, 2009). On ideas behind papal governance, see also W. Ulmann, *Medieval Papalism: The Political Theories of the Medieval Canonists* (London, 1949), and *The Growth of Papal Government in the Middle Ages: A Study in the Ideological Relation of Clerical to Lay Power,* 2nd ed. (London, 1965). Readers should be aware, however, of a long-standing academic debate over Ulmann's work: See, among others, F. Oakley, "Celestial Hierarchies Revisited: Walter Ulmann's Vision of Medieval Politics," *Past and Present* (1973): 3–48. See also P. Partner, *The Lands of St Peter: The Papal State in the Middle Ages and the Early Renaissance* (Berkeley, 1972), who focuses on the administrative history of papal territories in central Italy.

The Memory of Saint Peter

For developments in the early Christian Church, including Rome, see W. H. C. Frend, *The Rise of Christianity* (Philadelphia, 1984); R. Markus, *The End of Ancient Christianity* (Cambridge, 1990); and H. Chadwick, *The Church in Ancient Society: From Galilee to Gregory the Great* (Oxford, 2001). J. S. Jeffers, *Conflict at Rome: Social Order and Hierarchy in Early Christianity* (Minneapolis, 1991), and B. Green, *Christianity in Ancient Rome: The First Three Centuries* (London, 2010), concentrate on the early church at Rome, including the development of the city's "monarchical" bishop. H. Rahner, *Church and State in Early Christianity,* trans. L. D. Davis (1943; San Francisco, 1992), contextualizes ecclesiastical relations with secular powers, providing selections from primary sources. On the third-century disputes over rebaptism, see J. P. Burns, "On Rebaptism: Social Organization in the Third-Century Church," *Journal of Early Christian Studies* 1 (1993): 367–403. Constantine's conversion and its aftermath has been the subject of countless studies. Among them, see C. M. Odahl, *Constantine and the Christian Empire* (London, 2004), and T. Barnes, *Constantine: Dynasty, Religion, and Power in the Later Roman Empire* (Malden, Mass., 2011). J. R. Curran, *Pagan City and Christian Capital: Rome in the Fourth Century* (Oxford, 1999), and D. Trout, "Damasus and the Invention of Early Christian Rome," *Journal of Medieval and Early Modern Studies* 33 (2003): 517–36, examine the transformation of Rome's landscape after Constantine. Unfortunately, I have not yet had a chance to examine the new, promising work by G. Demacopoulos, *The Invention of Peter: Apostolic Discourse and Papal Authority in Late Antiquity* (Philadelphia, 2013).

Empire and Christendom

Herrin, *Formation of Christendom*, and Brown, *Rise of Western Christendom*, provide wide-ranging context for the history of the late imperial and early medieval Church, including the papacy. On the development of papal decretals, see D. Jaspar and H. Fuhrmann, *Papal Letters in the Early Middle Ages* (Washington, DC, 2001). On the papacy of Leo I, see S. Wessel, *Leo the Great and the Spiritual Rebuilding of Universal Rome* (Leiden, 2008), and the insightful study by K. Uhalde, "Pope Leo I on Power and Failure," *The Catholic Historical Review* 95 (2009): 671–88. F. Marazzi, "Rome in Transition: Economic and Political Change in the Fourth and Fifth Centuries," in *Early Medieval Rome and the Christian West*, ed. J. M. H. Smith (Leiden, 2000), 21–42, examines the ongoing changes in Rome's social fabric and landscape. On the period of the Laurentian Schism, see J. Hillner, "Families, Patronage, and the Titular Churches of Rome, c. 300–600," in *Religion, Dynasty, and Patronage in Early Christian Rome, 300–900*, ed. K. Cooper and J. Hillner (Cambridge, 2010), 225–61, and R. McKitterick, "Roman Texts and Roman History in the Early Middle Ages," in *Rome Across Time and Space: Cultural Transmission and the Exchange of Ideas c. 500–1000*, ed. C. Bolgia, R. McKitterick, and J. Osborne (Cambridge, 2011), 19–34. Among the numerous studies of Pope Gregory I, see R. A. Markus, *Gregory the Great and His World* (Cambridge, 1998), and C. Straw, *Gregory the Great: Perfection in Imperfection* (Berkeley, 1988). There has been a recent outpouring of scholarship on iconoclasm, including T. F. X. Noble, *Images, Iconoclasm, and the Carolingians* (Philadelphia, 2009), and L. Brubaker and J. Haldon, *Byzantium in the Iconoclast Era* c. *680–850: A History* (Cambridge, 2011).

The Reordering of the West

For a look at the Carolingian Church, including its relations with Rome, see R. McKitterick, *The Frankish Church and the Carolingian Reforms, 789–895* (London, 1977). See also R. McKitterick, "Unity and Diversity in the Carolingian Church," in *Unity and Diversity in the Church*, ed. R. N. Sawnson, Studies in Church History, vol. 32 (Oxford, 1996), 59–82, and Y. Hen, "The Romanization of the Frankish Liturgy: Ideal, Reality, and the Rhetoric of Reform," in *Rome Across Time and Space: Cultural Transmission and the Exchange of Ideas c. 500–1000*, ed. C. Bolgia, R. McKitterick, and J. Osborne (Cambridge, 2011), 111–23. T. F. X. Noble, *The Republic of*

Saint Peter: The Birth of the Papal State, 680–825 (Philadelphia, 1984), provides an invaluable investigation of the "Franco-papal alliance" and its role in the development of papal claims to political sovereignty in Italy. See also T. F. X. Noble, "Topography, Celebration, and Power: The Making of a Papal Rome in the Seventh and Eighth Centuries," in *Topographies of Power in the Early Middle Ages*, ed. M. de Jong, F. Theuws with C. van Rhijn (Leiden, 2001), 45–92, for a discussion of changes in the city's architectural landscape. Although focused on the Carolingians not the papacy, K. F. Morrison, *The Two Kingdoms: Ecclesiology in Carolingian Political Thought* (Princeton, 1964), discusses Frankish attitudes toward Rome across the ninth century. On Nicholas I and contemporary events, see J. C. Bishop, *Pope Nicholas I and the First Age of Papal Independence* (Columbia University, 1980); J. Herrin, "The Pentarchy: Theory and Reality in the Ninth Century," in *Cristianità d'occidente e Cristianità d'oriente (secoli VI–XI)* (Spoleto, 2004), 591–626; and L. Simeonova, *Diplomacy of the Letter and the Cross: Photios, Bulgaria and the Papacy, 860s–880s* (Amsterdam, 1998).

Reform and Crusade

There is a vast bibliography on the papacy and the eleventh-century reform. For starters, see the classic work by G. Tellenbach, *Church, State and Christian Society at the Time of the Investiture Contest*, trans. R. F. Bennett (Oxford, 1948), and G. Tellenbach, *The Church in Western Europe from the Tenth to the Early Twelfth Century*, trans. T. Reuter (Cambridge, 1993). See also U.-R. Blumenthal, *The Investiture Controversy: Church and Monarchy from the Ninth to the Twelfth Century*, 2nd ed. (Philadelphia, 1992), and K. Cushing, *Reform and the Papacy in the Eleventh Century: Spirituality and Social Change* (Manchester, 2005). On the College of Cardinals, dated but still invaluable, see S. Kuttner, "Cardinalis: The History of Canonical Concept," *Traditio* 3 (1945): 129–214. H. E. J. Cowdrey, "Eleventh-Century Reformers' Views of Constantine," in *Conformity and Non-Conformity in Byzantium*, ed. L. Garland (Amsterdam, 1997), 63–91, offers a fascinating look at representations of the first Christian emperor in reform-era circles. On the views of history and theology framing reform, see B. McGinn, "Apocalypticism and Church Reform: 1100–1500," in *The Encyclopedia of Apocalypticism: Apocalypticism in Western History and Culture*, ed. B. McGinn (New York, 1998), 74–109, and J. Y. Malegam, *The Sleep of Behemoth: Disputing Peace and Violence in*

Medieval Europe, 1000–1200 (Ithaca, 2013). For Latin–Greek relations, see S. Runciman, *The Eastern Schism: A Study of the Papacy and the Eastern Churches during the XI and XII Centuries* (Oxford, 1955), and (from the Byzantine perspective) T. Kolbaba, *The Byzantine Lists: Errors of the Latins* (Chicago, 2000). H. E. J. Cowdrey, "The Papacy, the Patarenes, and the Church of Milan," *Transactions of the Royal Historical Society* 18 (1968): 25–48, remains an excellent starting point on the Pataria. On the Investiture Conflict, in addition to Tellenbach and Blumenthal, see H. E. J. Cowdrey, *Gregory VII, 1073–1085* (Oxford, 1998). The bibliography of the First Crusade and other crusades is also extensive. For starters, see J. Riley-Smith, *What Were the Crusades?*, 3rd ed. (New York, 2002). On connections between church reform and crusade, see the highly influential work by C. Erdmann, *The Origin of the Idea of the Crusade*, trans. M. W. Baldwin and W. Goffart (Princeton, 1977). See also H. E. J. Cowdrey, "The Gregorian Papacy, Byzantium and the First Crusade," *Byzantinische Forschungen* 13 (1988): 145–69, and "Pope Urban II's Preaching of the First Crusade," *History* (1970): 178–88. J. Rubenstein, *Armies of Heaven: The First Crusade and the Quest for Apocalypse* (New York, 2011), has recently highlighted the apocalyptic dimensions of the crusade.

Papal Monarchy

For an overall sense of this dynamic period, one can start with the essays collected in *Renaissance and Renewal in the Twelfth Century*, ed. R. L. Benson and G. Constable (Oxford, 1982). On the papacy specifically, in addition to Morris, *Papal Monarchy*, see I. S. Robinson, *The Papacy 1073–1198: Continuity and Innovation* (Cambridge, 1990), especially valuable for his close look at the mechanism of papal governance. On the controversial changes in religious life during this era, see G. Constable, *The Reformation of the Twelfth-Century* (Cambridge, 1996). For the Second Crusade, in addition to J. Phillips, *The Second Crusade: Extending the Frontiers of Christendom* (New Haven, 2010), see R. Hiestand, "The Papacy and the Second Crusade," in *The Second Crusade: Scope and Consequences*, ed. J. Phillips and M. Hoch (Manchester, 2001), 32–53. For a discussion of the "two powers" and canon law, see S. Chodorow, *Christian Political Theory and Church Politics in the Twelfth Century* (Berkeley, 1972). Studies of twelfth-century popes include the essays in *Adrian IV: The English Pope, 1154–1159*, ed. B. Bolton and A. J. Duggan (Aldershot, UK, 2003); and M. W. Baldwin,

Alexander III and the Twelfth Century (New Jersey, 1968). Generally, on the problem of heresy in the High Middle Ages, see R. I. Moore, *The Origins of European Dissent* (Harmondsworth, UK, 1977), and his influential *Formation of a Persecuting Society: Authority and Deviance in Western Europe*, 2nd ed. (Malden, Mass., 2007), although Moore does not focus much on the papal involvement in targeting heresy. On the apocalyptic dimensions of papal monarchy, see B. Whalen, *Dominion of God: Christendom and Apocalypse in the Middle Ages* (Cambridge, Mass., 2009).

The Whole World to Govern

Among the numerous studies on Innocent III, see J. Sayers, *Innocent III: Leader of Europe, 1998–1216* (London, 1994), and J. C. Moore, *Pope Innocent III (1160/61–1216): To Root Up and Plant* (Leiden, 2003). See also J. A. Watt, "The Theory of Papal Monarchy in the Thirteenth Century," *Traditio* 20 (1964): 179–314; D. Waley, *The Papal State in the Thirteenth Century* (London, 1961); and K. Pennington, *Pope and Bishops: The Papal Monarchy in the Twelfth and Thirteenth Centuries* (Philadelphia, 1984). For the events of the Fourth Crusade, see D. Queller and T. Madden, *The Fourth Crusade: The Conquest of Constantinople*, 2nd ed. (Philadelphia, 1997). Works in English on Innocent's immediate successors, Gregory IX and Innocent IV, are lacking. See, however, D. Abulafia, *Frederick II: A Medieval Emperor* (London, 1988), who looks at the clash between church and empire from the imperial perspective. Thirteenth-century crusades are examined by M. Purcell, *Papal Crusading Policy, 1244–1291* (Leiden, 1975), and R. Rist, *The Papacy and Crusading in Europe, 1198–1245* (London, 2009). On the development of inquisitorial procedures and institutions, see B. Hamilton, *The Medieval Inquisition* (London, 1981), and E. Peters, *Inquisition* (New York, 1988). On canon law, including the *Decretals*, see the essays in *The History of Medieval Canon Law in the Classical Period, 1140–1234*, ed. W. Hartmann and K. Pennington (Washington, DC, 2008). For Christian relations with the wider world during Europe's medieval expansion, see K. M. Setton, *The Papacy and the Levant (1204–1571)*, 4 vols. (Philadelphia, 1976); J. Muldoon, *Popes, Lawyers and Infidels: The Church and the Non-Christian World, 1250–1550* (Philadelphia, 1979); and B. Whalen, "Corresponding with Infidels: Rome, the Almohads, and the Christians of Thirteenth-Century Morocco," *The Journal of Medieval and Early Modern Studies* 41 (2011): 487–513.

The Papacy in Crisis

On the charged atmosphere surrounding Pope Boniface VIII and contemporary events, see B. McGinn, "Angel Pope and Papal Antichrist," *Church History* 47 (1978): 155–73, and G. Dickson, "The Crowd at the Feet of Pope Boniface VIII: Pilgrimage, Crusade, and the First Roman Jubilee (1300)," *Journal of Medieval History* 25 (1999): 279–307. For the period of the Avignon papacy, see Y. Renouard, *The Avignon Papacy 1305–1403*, trans. D. Bethell (Hamden, Conn., 1970); K. Plöger, *England and the Avignon Popes: The Practice of Diplomacy in Late Medieval Europe* (London, 2005); and S. Menache, *Clement V* (Cambridge, 1998), who offers a close study of the pope who started the Avignon era. N. Housely, *The Italian Crusades: the Papal–Angevin Alliance and the Crusades against Christian Lay Powers, 1254–1343* (Oxford, 1982), and *The Avignon Papacy and the Crusades, 1305–1378* (Oxford, 1986), looks at the Avignon popes' military and crusading policies. On the Great Schism and its aftermath, see W. Ulmann, *The Origins of the Great Schism: A Study in Fourteenth-Century Ecclesiastical History* (1938; Hamden, Conn., 1972); R. N. Swanson, *Universities, Academics and the Great Schism* (Cambridge, 1979); and the essays in *A Companion to the Great Western Schism (1378–1417)*, ed. J. Rollo-Koster and T. M. Izbicki, Brill's Companions to the Christian Tradition, vol. 17 (Leiden, 2009). See also B. Tierney, *Foundations of the Conciliar Theory: The Contributions of the Medieval Canonists from Gratian to the Great Schism* (Cambridge, 1955), and *Origins of Papal Infallibility, 1150–1350* (Leiden, 1988).

Rome at the Close of the Middle Ages

On the religious circumstances faced by Rome during the Late Middle Ages, see D. L. d'Avray, "Papal Authority and Religious Sentiment in the Late Middle Ages," in *The Church and Sovereignty c. 590–1918*, ed. D. Wood, Studies in Church History, vol. 9 (Oxford, 1991), 393–408, and M. Harvey, "Unity and Diversity: Perceptions of the Papacy in the Later Middle Ages," in *Unity and Diversity in the Church*, ed. R. N. Swanson, Studies in Church History, vol. 32 (Oxford, 1996), 145–70. For the "restored" papacy, see P. Partner, *The Papal State under Martin V: The Administration and Government of the Temporal Power in the Early Fifteenth Century* (Rome, 1958). On the Council of Basle-Florence and related events, see J. Gill, *The Council of Florence* (Cambridge, 1959), and M. Watanabe, "Pope Eugene IV, the Conciliar Movement, and the Primacy of Rome," in *The Church, the Councils, and Reform: The Legacy of the Fifteenth Century*, ed. G. Christianson, T. M. Izbicki, and C. M. Bellito (Washington, DC, 2008), 177–93. C. L. Stinger, *The Renaissance in Rome* (Bloomington, Ind., 1985), explores the impact of the Renaissance on the papacy and Rome's architectural landscape, while P. Partner, *The Pope's Men: The Papal Civil Service in the Renaissance* (Oxford, 1990), examines the state of ecclesiastical governance during the period. On the later crusades, see M. Meserve, "Italian Humanists and the Problem of the Crusade," in *Crusading in the Fifteenth Century: Message and Impact*, ed. N. Housely (New York, 2004), 13–38, and N. Bisaha, "Pope Pius II and the Crusade," *Crusading in the Fifteenth Century*, 39–52. For the apocalyptic sentiments at the Fifth Lateran Council, see N. H. Minnich, "Prophecy and the Fifth Lateran Council (1512–1517)," in *Prophetic Rome in the High Renaissance Period*, ed. M. Reeves (Oxford, 1972), 63–87.

Index

Printed and bound in the United States of America